General Motors: Life Inside The Factory

One Blue-Collar Worker's Journey

Richard Thomas Gall

authorHOUSE®

AuthorHouse™
1663 Liberty Drive
Bloomington, IN 47403
www.authorhouse.com
Phone: 1-800-839-8640

First published by AuthorHouse   12/30/2010

ISBN: 978-1-4567-1672-1 (sc)
ISBN: 978-1-4567-1673-8 (e)
ISBN: 978-1-4567-1674-5 (hc)

LIbrary of Congress Control Number: 2010919009

Printed in the United States of America

Dedication

This book is dedicated to my fellow blue collar workers , to all of the men and women who have worked on the factory floor. I admire you and consider myself lucky to be among your numbers.

Introduction

This is the story of my working life. It begins the day I hired into General Motors as an hourly employee. It is not flashy. There is not much drama in it. However, I felt the need to document the way things were in General Motors and Flint, Michigan, back in the 1970s. It was probably the heyday of both.

In writing my story, I hope to accomplish four things. First is the honest telling of what I experienced and witnessed in the factory. I hope others like me will read this story and reminisce about what they themselves went through. I would consider it a huge compliment if this book sparked lively discussions and recollections of the "Here's what I went through" kind.

Second, I hope it depicts what life was like for me growing up in Flint, Michigan. Flint was a typical factory town, and I enjoyed growing up there. The book also highlights some of what the community endured from being solely reliant on General Motors alone. As GM struggled, so did Flint. A common saying around here is "If GM catches a cold, Flint catches pneumonia."

Third, I hope this book provides a valuable reading experience for the reader. I am humbled that someone would read my story—the story of a typical factory worker in a typical factory town.

When I started to write this book, I was leaning heavily toward what the factory was all about. I was focusing more on the nuts and bolts of how the factory produced its products. I soon found that there wasn't much rich reading material there. My writing then evolved to telling the stories of the people who touched my life while I was at work—some in a good way, and some in a bad way.

As the story unfolded and I was at the point of attempting to make permanent supervisor, I began to realize the profound effect that my enlistment in the marines had on me. I had never given it much thought before I started the book. As I wrote my story, I found that time and time again, my experiences and training in the marines prepared me for my leadership role in the factory and in life in general. It provided a foundation of self-confidence, commitment, and courage—the courage to stick to my beliefs when times got tough.

I wish the executive leadership of General Motors could go through the Marine Corps boot camp to learn firsthand the marines' fundamentals on respecting people. Don't get me wrong; the marine experience was no picnic. It was the toughest and most demanding organizational experience I have ever had. Yet, if you followed your training and went along with the program, you could excel in their system. The marines continue to excel today with their basic "respect for people" philosophy.

Lastly, I found writing this book to be a type of therapy for me. I was reaching back thirty-five to forty-five years into my past. I had the opportunity to not only recall events in my life but to document them as well. As I worked my way through these events, I realized I knew and understood myself a little better. It felt good to get them out into the open.

I learned a little about my writing style as well. I found myself going chronologically through my life experiences and then arriving at a point at which I felt the need to go way back in my history to gain a clearer understanding of the thoughts that I presently held. I am calling these flashbacks. There are several of them in the book. The reader will find himself or herself moving along in the book when suddenly the chronological order of things changes. This might be confusing. . I went back and attempted to bridge the material so the sudden change of pace has a smooth transition. Some of these I simply labeled "Flashback" to alert the reader that I was going back in time to talk about my past.

1
The First Ninety Days

New Hire

It all started in September 1973. I had recently been discharged from the United States Marine Corps after completing a three-year hitch. I went home and started school at the local community college, but three weeks later, I realized I wasn't ready for school. I had a very poor academic record from high school, and at that time, college was too big of a step for me. I dropped out of college after this very short beginning. I felt confused and alone. I found myself longing for the routine and certainty of the Marine Corps.

So not knowing what to do, I went to the unemployment office in Flint, Michigan, and signed up for work. A couple of days later, I received an offer to hire into General Motors as an hourly employee. With nothing else seemingly available, I accepted the offer and thus began my thirty-five-year auto-industry career. I hired into Chevrolet Flint Frame and Stamping. Flint Stamping is located in a complex of three large General Motors plants. In addition to Flint Stamping, the Flint Truck Assembly and the Flint Engine plants are located at the corners of Bristol Road and Van Slyke, at the very southern edge of the city of Flint.

My first morning on the job is a blur for me. I attended some sort of new-hire orientation that lasted for a couple of hours. Then we were walked out onto the factory floor—or I should say, down to the factory floor, as we were on the mezzanine level of the plant and took the down escalator to the floor.

What a shock I received as I rode down that escalator to the shop floor for the first time! I couldn't believe my eyes. The first thing I heard was the deafening roar of the line presses stamping out the sheet metal parts. In the orientation, they had warned us about the high decibel level of noise in the plant and told us we would be subject to discipline if we didn't wear the earplugs the company provided for us. I was thankful for the earplugs I was now wearing.

I could also feel the tremendous heat generated by all of the industrial equipment operating as far as my eyes could see. It seemed like an endless sea of men and machinery. There were miles of monorails from one end of the plant to the other. Never in my wildest imaginings would I have pictured the shop to look like this. As we reached the floor level, there was a guy who looked at us, laughed, and said, "You'll be so-o-r-r-y!" Somehow, we were handed off to our foreman to be given our first job assignments. My first supervisor was a guy named Joe.

My first job assignment was to operate a small spot welder. This is a stand-alone machine that assembles and prepares subassemblies for further use later on. My training consisted of the following: "Take this bracket out of the gondola and place it in the welder. Place the second piece of metal over the first, and then put your hands up here, one on each of the two palm buttons. Continue holding the palm buttons until the machine has completed its entire cycle. Remove the welded assembly out of the machine, and place it in the finished-parts gondola." The foreman left after I ran a couple of pieces correctly and after warning me about poor quality and not running fast enough—so much for my training on the floor!

Left alone, I began to run as many parts as I could as fast as I could. I really needed this job. A short time later, another hourly employee came up to me and told me to slow down; there was a set amount that could be run in one hour's time, and I was in danger of violating the agreed-upon standards. I continued to run as instructed by my supervisor while I eyed this guy and sized him up. He was fairly tall but had a rotund stomach and looked to be very out of shape. Remember, I was just six weeks out of the Marine Corps infantry and was highly trained not to take any crap from anybody. This included navy swabbies, army doggies, and out-of-shape production employees. I thought about how I could take this guy down: first, a swift kick to the groin area to start things out and then a couple of quick punches to the head and then maybe a knee to the face as he faltered. This was how I had been trained and what I had been brainwashed into thinking over the past three years. It all came back to me very quickly, in an instant. I was reacting, not thinking. However, in our orientation (which I think was one of the first of its kind in the plant), labor relations went over the "shop rules," one of which was no fighting allowed. So I thanked the gentleman and slowed way down, praying that my foreman would understand when he came back.

When the foreman showed up again, he wasn't interested in the parts I had run. We had an emergency, and he needed me to fill in on the press line. He told me that because I had short hair, he was going to give me a "good" job. I was placed on the press line that stamped out tie bars for the 1974 Chevrolet Impala. A tie bar is a piece of sheet metal that goes on the front end of a vehicle. It used to go between the hood and the grille. Nowadays, this part is incorporated into the hood itself.

My job turned out to be painting die goop all around the perimeter of the part as it came out of what I think was the trim die. So I had a bucket of goop and a long-handled brush, and I painted this gooey substance around the perimeter of the entire part. Poor Joe, though, because if he could have seen how I anticipated having my hair long in about six months, he wouldn't have given me the "good" job. I hated my Marine Corps haircut; it was high and tight in an era of long hair. When I was home on leave in 1972, I was mildly harassed in a local bar because of my short hair, and I was determined to grow it long enough to have a ponytail. I wanted to fit back into society.

I don't remember how my first day ended, but for the start of my second day, I knew I had to "punch in" my time card to start my shift. The words I remember my foreman saying at the end of the shift were, "Don't be late. It's a violation of the shop rules." I became very nervous, thinking that I might not be able to find my way to my department in the morning. Then a brilliant idea hit me. I noticed there was a set of train tracks right near the time clock. Feeling good about my discovery, I left the two-million-square-foot facility for the first time. I thought it would be a snap to return quickly to my department time clock location first thing in the morning.

When I got to my car in the parking lot, I realized I hadn't anticipated the shift-change activity. The second shifters were still coming in, and the first shifters were leaving. There were well over four thousand hourly employees working at the plant, round the clock on three shifts. We had full employment at the time. The parking lot was a nightmare, and I learned that when the hourly employees left the plant, you'd better get out of the way because all hell broke loose. There was the revving of engines, the squealing of tires, the curses, and the shouts to move in a quagmire of gridlock. After being under lock and key all day, the animals had been let free. That first day, I sat in my car and waited for the parking lot to clear before I ventured safely out. Later, I was no different in revving my engine and squealing my tires. I was finally free, and this animal was in control of his life again.

The next morning, I arrived at the plant forty-five minutes early. That left me plenty of time to walk to the time clock and get punched in. I followed the train tracks for what seemed like forever, but I couldn't locate my department. I was starting to feel uncomfortable, but I still had twenty minutes or so left to get to my time clock. Then I discovered another set of train tracks in the plant. Now things were looking up; I could find my way. Maybe this was the right way to go. I followed this set of tracks for what seemed like an eternity, but I still couldn't locate my department. There was now less than three minutes to go before punch in. Just great, my second day in the shop, and I'm going to be late. *Holy Crap!*, I thought. I had been a sergeant in the Marine Corps. I was always the responsible one. I was always in charge, and I took care of everything. We always said in the marines, "Don't be a worthless piece of shit," and that was how I felt at that moment. I was a "shit bird," just like all of the other guys who couldn't get themselves squared away in the Marine Corps! We marines never desired to be a shit bird.

Another employee must have seen the panic on my face because he asked if he could help me. I told him I was looking for the time clock for my department and it was located by the train well. He told me there were three main train wells and a couple of smaller ones located throughout the plant. He said that you had to go by the column locations. I had no idea what he was talking about. He told me to look up and see the markings on each of the lamb's-wool green (that's the General Motors paint color) column posts. I looked up, and sure enough, a letter from the alphabet and a number marked each one. He asked me which department I was assigned to. I told him department 176. He was kind enough to walk me to my department and to the time clock. Waiting there for me was the foreman, and he wasn't very happy. The kind soul explained the situation to the foreman, and the foreman told me he'd let me go this time but never to be late again. Thank you, kind soul, who helped me so long ago.

Wages and Benefits

I hired into General Motors on a Friday morning. I worked ten hours that day and ten hours on Saturday. For Friday, I received two hours of overtime pay. At General Motors, for every hour of overtime I worked, I was paid one and one half hours. So, for the two hours of overtime I worked on Friday, I was paid for a total of three hours. I worked ten hours on Saturday and received time and one half all day. I was paid for fifteen hours for Saturday. My first week, I was paid for a total of twenty-seven hours for two days of work.

Now at this point, my older brother was looking down his nose at me for working in the shop. He reminded me of one of my father's favorite sayings while we were growing up, which was, "Is that all you want to be, a sweeper in the shop?" And there I was, an hourly production worker—a sweeper if you will—and he was letting me know of his disapproval. When I brought home my first paycheck, we compared them ours. I made way more per hour than he did, and for two days of work in the shop, my paycheck was larger than his for a full forty hours' worth of work. He was working in downtown Flint for a company that backed up hospital records on a computer during the night. Later, my older brother hired into the plant, but he never got his ninety days in and was never called back. In addition to my hourly wages, which I think were around five dollars and thirty-two cents an hour, I received full medical benefits after thirty days. In those days, we didn't pay a penny for any health-care services. Prescription drugs were covered in full. I started accumulating pension and vacation credits as well. So all in all, it was not too bad of a start for me financially.

Shop Rat

Sometime in the fall of 1973, I went to a friend of a friend's new house in Flushing, Michigan. It was a beautiful three-bedroom, tri-level home his grandmother helped him purchase. He and his wife were throwing a housewarming party. They didn't have much furniture because they bought as much house as they could afford, and they were going to let inflation pay the mortgage. Inflation was on the rise in 1973, and it was a very popular act to purchase as much house as you could.

I was having a pretty good time at the party, and I began talking to the owner's wife. She was some sort of medical technician, and he was a new-car salesman. She asked me where I was working, and I told her at Chevrolet Flint Stamping. Well, the cold look of disgust that came across her face startled me. It seemed as if everyone and everything at the party went into super-slow motion. All noise stopped, and you could hear a pin drop. She stared at me coldly and said loud enough so everyone could hear, "You are a shop rat!" I could have crawled into the closest hole I could find, but there was nothing available. I was extremely embarrassed and nodded my head weakly. I left the party shortly thereafter with a severe blow to my morale. It seemed everybody in Genesee County was down on us shop rats.

I soon realized that I liked the shop. I liked what I was doing, and I liked the comforts my job provided. Now granted, I wanted and desired to better myself, but for the time being, I was in a good place. Yes, I admit it. I was a Flint, General Motors, purebred, *shop rat*, 100 percent certified!

Working the Press Line

A short while later, I was transferred to the press line that produced the right-hand fender outer panel for the 1974 Chevrolet pickup truck. I must've been assigned to the third or fourth press into the line. A typical press line consists of several pieces of complex machinery. All the machines are located in a straight line. There are many operations. The largest machines are called stamping presses. These machines house the tooling and provide the motion that performs the work of making a stamped production part. A stamping press completes one cycle in which the ram of the press travels down to the bottom of its stroke and then returns back up to the top of its stroke. Presses come in all shapes and sizes. On my fender line, the first press was the draw. It is the largest press in the line and can produce the greatest tonnage. The larger the tonnage, the greater work the press is rated to perform. As the draw press hits bottom and the die does its work, the floor shakes and vibrates on the massive hitting action required to draw the sheet metal into shape. The next press in line is the trim press. It also has a high tonnage capacity. After a blank receives its initial form from the draw operation, it is called a panel. The trim operation removes the excess steel no longer required from the panel. After the trim operation, there are three or four additional operations that complete the panel. The results of these operations fold (called a flange) and pierce holes in the panel.

The tools that perform the work are called dies. The dies are mounted in the presses. As a press cycles, the dies complete their work. Dies are complicated tools that need a great deal of attention, especially with outer panels, such as hoods and fenders.

When a panel has cycled through a press, an "iron hand" removes it. This mechanical device is an air cylinder mounted in the back of the press. It has a jaw attached to the cylinder. As the cylinder is driven forward by air pressure, the jaw clamps down on the panel and holds it tightly. The cylinder is then moved backward and takes the panel with it. At the precise moment the air is released from the cylinder, the jaw drops the panel onto a conveyor belt. Between each press, there is a conveyor with some type of moving belt on it. The conveyor belt transfers the panel up to the next press in the line. The operator then manually loads the panel in the press and holds down the two palm buttons, which cause the press to cycle or turn over. This is repeated until a panel works its way through the entire press line. (At Flint Stamping in 1973, this was the typical line setup. In the stamping arena, there are many variations of line setups.)

The stamping presses I ran at Chevrolet Flint Frame and Stamping were 1950s vintage. They were about twenty years old when I hired into the plant. They had not been maintained very well. Every hour, it seemed as if something wasn't working right. The line foreman kept a constant vigil on the equipment as we were running production. At the first sign of trouble, he was to alert the various skilled tradesmen to come and take a look at the problem. The tradesmen were hardly ever provided the proper time to make repairs. They were always making quick fixes to get the press line running again; even on weekends, they didn't have time to make things right. They were not allowed to come back after hours to make a proper repair as this was considered too costly to the plant. Most of the tradesmen who babysat the lines became expert at "patch jobs." Rather than install a new hose, we'd just patch the old one. Rather than install a new oil pump, we'd just turn the pressure switch down so the press would continue to run but with improper oil pressure. Rather than repair an oil leak, we'd make an oil catch pan and hose it back to the oil tank. When I got to Flint Stamping in the fall of 1973, the plant consisted of a lot of junk machines that were very unreliable.

We always seemed to have quality issues or machine breakdowns. For quality, we desired a pristine part every time we made one. Reality, however, was quite different. In the first place, no one ever solicited assistance or advice from the "hourly people." Second, we were never allowed to shut the line down for any reason. To protect our production numbers, we would run ahead blanks through the draw and trim operations and place them on wheeled carts in case either of these two operations failed. We could still feed the rest of the line with the banks of parts we had stored up by the thousands. Needless to say, this led to many a quality issue, which supposedly was the number-one goal. But we always did a good job making our daily numbers.

On my first few days running the line, I was uncertain as to what to do. My job amounted to following the part down a chain conveyor, lifting it up and off the conveyor, and then sliding it into the die. Now this may sound easy, but there were many caveats. As always, our hands were tied. We had to wear thickly padded gloves that seemed like oversized mittens with leather padding. The edges of these parts after the trim press were as sharp as razor blades. After a while, the gloves were all slit up from the continuous barrage of lifting and sliding the parts into the die. I also learned how to be a contortionist to achieve the goal of sliding and locating the part correctly into the die. Well, how the hell do you place a part in the die with no hands, as yours have hockey-goalie-like gloves on them? Each part came coated with die goop, so it was as slippery as a bar of soap. Talk about making an easy job difficult! Holy shit. And oh, by the way, if the part wasn't located correctly, the die coming together would destroy the panel, and the iron hand set up to remove it probably couldn't get it out. Then all hell would break loose. And yes, you guessed it: it was a violation of the shop rules to run poor-quality parts and to sabotage the machinery. (That's one thing that stands out in my mind about my early GM days. Those stinking shop rules.)

I have a vague memory of running parts all day long ten hours a day, six days a week. One time, early on, we had a "big breakdown." I believe a press wouldn't cycle properly. Here, I learned what we hourly morons were supposed to do. The person running a press near me came over and asked me to sit down with him on the work platform. He offered me a cigarette, but I told him I had quit smoking just before leaving the marines. While we were sitting there, the supervisor ran by directing the maintenance employees to the problem. I asked my partner what was going on. He said that we had to have the parts, but there was a problem with a press not turning over properly. I asked him if it was bad, and he thought it was. Turns out, if we didn't get 365 parts per hour off the line, the supervisor could lose his job, as he had no union protection. The frenzied supervisor ran past us again, and this time, I had to wipe my eyes, because I couldn't believe what I was seeing. I saw the personification of the expression "He was running around like a chicken with its head cut off." I daydreamed of what a great movie opening scene this could one day make. I took that cigarette from my partner and watched the show. A short time later, we were moved to another press line. There, we ran parts we didn't need, but we were seen as being productive.

Supervisor's Worst Nightmare

Supervisor and *foreman* are used as interchangeable terms here. In the beginning, the first-tier manager was likened to a working boss and was called a foreman. To improve the image, the name was changed to supervisor, which was seen as an upgrade. Back when I hired in, the older senior hourly employees referred to their boss as a foreman. In those days, supervisors were rated on their efficient use of hourly manpower. They had a formula they used to show each hour's production efficiency and their total shift efficiency. It didn't take long to figure out that we hourly workers were there for our brawn not for our brains. We couldn't and didn't contribute to the running of the business. A good hourly employee was seen as one who came into work every day, didn't violate the shop rules, and didn't give the supervisor a hard time. We just did exactly as we were told to do. (Let me tell you, it tore at my self-respect and dignity on a daily basis.) I always felt I was a good hourly employee. During my eleven years as an hourly employee, I was never "written up" for violations of the shop rules. I probably deserved it a couple of times, but I always got by.

What I learned as time went on was that a line breakdown was a supervisor's worst nightmare. He immediately loses efficiency. A good supervisor who is efficiency driven runs around like a chicken with its head cut off to either get the line running again or move the hourly employees to another line so his hourly production numbers don't go negative. Frequently, there were no other lines available to go to because all of the other production lines in the plant were breaking down as well. Other supervisors had already moved their employees to empty lines to avoid cuts in their efficiency ratings. We hourly were simply like cattle driven back and forth wherever we were told to go. Looking back on it, General Motors never really utilized the resources they always had available. There was the educated class—mainly General Motors Institute graduates, who ran the plants—and there were the hourly employees, who did as they were told. At the time, General Motors was the largest and most successful company the world had ever known. Who knew what was about to happen in the fall of 1973?

I believe the efficiency numbers were calculated from a formula. This formula was the number of people used with the number of parts run per productive hour. If the supervisor used less people, his efficiency went up as the hourly count number was achieved. Sometimes, a supervisor could show more parts run in an hour, and his efficiency rate would go up. Supervisors would store parts up for a rainy day. I was never a production supervisor, so I am not an expert on this system. What I did learn then was there was a high degree of pressure placed on a supervisor to get his production numbers every hour by whatever means necessary. Numbers were king. Numbers were way more important than quality or taking proper care of the machinery or the people who ran them.

Back to the line breakdown ...

Once the skilled tradesmen figured out what was wrong with the machinery, they devised a work-around plan. It was determined that the press that was broken would be down a long time. Maintenance tinsmiths worked through the night, and when we came in the next morning, there was a long chute we had to use to push fender skins about fifty feet over to the next press line. They had an empty press that the die from our broken press was set up in as a temporary bypass operation. After we ran the part through the temporary setup, we had to push it back to the home press line to complete the process of making the outer skin.

The fender inner was run in a parallel line with the outer. The inner was then run through a zinc-coating process that had a very peculiar odor. Standing by the zinc house for long would get you a headache. After the zinc was applied, the inner and outer skins came together, and the inner panel was inserted into the outer skin. This was called the marriage station. From there, the fender was run through the welder, and at the end, there emerged a completed truck fender. This setup occurred for both the right-hand and left-hand units.

Product Handler

After a short time of running a press, I got bumped to the end of the production line where I removed the fenders from the exit conveyor and hung them on the monorail, which carried them down to the shipping department. I got bumped because I was classified as a product handler not a press operator. There existed hundreds of very specific job titles in the plant. It was a violation of the United Automobile Workers' (UAW) contract for one classification of worker to perform the work of another classification. This I learned was called "scab labor." These hundreds of classifications were seen as resulting in many good-paying jobs. This was a hard-earned victory won by the UAW, and they protected this right with a vengeance. Two years before I hired in, the UAW had gone out on strike against the company. This was during national contract negotiations. The UAW failed to get the contract terms they desired, and they shut the company down for about one hundred days in the fall of 1971 or so. Many of the hourly employees I met were still bitter about the strike. While they were off work, they received very little money from the UAW. It was just enough to purchase a few groceries to feed their families. Most of the strikers were not financially prepared to weather the storm that the duration of the strike forced them into. As a remnant of the strike, the hourly employees held sacred their hard-won rights.

I soon learned that if it wasn't my job classification's work to do, I was to sit and wait until the foreman could find a person in the right classification to do the work. I don't remember anyone specifically telling me this; it was just something I picked up along the way. There were no training programs in place for new production employees. If you attempted to do another job classification's work, the other hourly people would come heavily down on you with peer pressure. Sometimes, it got physical as well. In this case, a higher seniority press operator complained about my running a press, so I was moved to accommodate his seniority privileges.

This was the first time I can recall being involved with the complicated work rules that had evolved in the plant with the union contract. At some point, my committeeman introduced himself to me and let me know he was very anxious to represent me after I got my ninety days in at the plant. Until that time, I was not "represented" and management could discharge me at any time for no reason at all. Well, it would seem like management could do whatever they wanted, but their hands were tied. As I hired in through the Michigan unemployment office, so did many others. In fact, I believe I was a part of the very last wave of large employment hirings in the Flint area. But as far as management having total control, I'm not sure, as I hired in with convicts on work-release programs. There was a government-sponsored program going on to rehabilitate convicts, so when they were released back into society, they would become citizens in good standing. I believe a high percentage of convicts quickly returned to prison after their release back into society. These people were forced onto employers' rolls at this time. There were government rules that protected these new hires. If they were protected, then by default, so was I. Scary, huh? I walked in with and worked with convicted felons. I really don't recall any problems with these employees that were different from the ones with the rest of us. And by the way, I received preferential hiring because I was a veteran. But before we got our ninety days in, we really had to watch ourselves and stay out of the foreman's way. I remember one guy had to bring in two lunches every day because his foreman always ate his first one. This went on for most of the first ninety days, and then after gaining seniority, he called his committeeman who put a quick stop to that problem.

My next assignment was to remove a completed truck fender off of the final conveyor, lift it up in the air, and place it on a moving hook of the monorail. Oh my God! Did I say each fender weighed around thirty pounds! Keep in mind, I didn't have seniority as of yet, so if I couldn't keep up with the line, I could be terminated. I needed this job. I was a third-generation autoworker. My grandfather was a tool grinder from the Buick complex, and my father was a die engineer. I couldn't let these people down; after all, they had made it in the factory, and so must I. But can you imagine how hard it was to lift 365 parts per hour and place them on a moving hook? Every so often, people would come by and tap the hook of the monorail, which made the hook sway back and forth. I would miss it and have to lift the fender all over again. After a few hours at this, I felt I couldn't lift anymore. My arms felt like rubber. I commanded them to move, but they wouldn't. I felt as if I was in big trouble. I wasn't going to make it to the end of the shift.

The employees who worked in the nearby area were complaining and making a big fuss about something. Turns out, they were all complaining about me. My supervisor wasn't living up to the union contract by keeping me on the job for four hours straight. To my surprise, I discovered that the job had been negotiated for one half hour on and one half hour off to rest. So really, the people were not complaining *about* me; they were complaining *for* me. I was not sure if the people were so concerned about me personally or probably more about the contract violation, but I needed a break to rest my arms. Shortly thereafter, the committeeman showed up and another person took my place. I had the rest of the shift off to make up for the four hours straight that I worked. I'm proud to report that after a couple of weeks, I could do this job all day long standing on my head. I could now hit the moving hook of the monorail even if it was swaying after being tapped by someone walking by! I did take off every thirty minutes to hang around the guys working in the repair booth, read the paper, or get some sleep, as there was nothing else to do. I also built up some very nice arm muscles as well.

Like I said before, in those days, the hourly production count was king. At the end of the line was a chalkboard where the line supervisor would write in each hour's production count. Every once in a while, the department superintendent would come by and observe our production counts. On many occasions, he would say, in his big, booming voice loud enough so we all could hear, "I don't give a shit about anything else, but I better see three hundred and sixty-five parts every hour on this board." I know General Motors has always bragged about its product quality. We all remember the GM "mark of excellence" commercials on television. But it was a different story in the 1970s. At one point, we were running very poor numbers off the line and every part coming down the final conveyor was marked for repair. The conveyor itself was about fifty feet long. Many people could evaluate our panels as they rode down the conveyor. Stationed at the beginning of the conveyor was the inspector lady. Her job was to observe each panel as it passed by. If she saw any defects, she would circle them with her inspection marker, which signaled to those of us removing the panels to place them on the repair monorail and not on the regular shipping one. These parts didn't count toward the hourly production number. They didn't get to the end of the line at the shipping dock. Often, the supervisor would stand after the inspector lady to observe what she was marking as defects. On this day, the inspector lady marked up every panel that passed by her as she saw defects of one kind or another. The supervisor took a spot along the conveyor after the inspector. In a panic, he wiped off the markings, and we had to place the fenders on the monorail that went to shipping. The inspector lady was pissed off. The supervisor felt his hourly numbers were more important than the quality of the panel. Later, I heard a supervisor was fired for this very thing. But in 1973, this was a commonly occurring event.

If you remember earlier, I talked about banks of parts from the press line that we used in situations where the draw or trim operation broke down. When these stored panels were used, they were found to be misformed from sitting in a stack or scratched or dinged in some way that was considered a quality defect. When these panels were painted at the assembly plant, these marks were highlighted and stuck out like a sore thumb. Prospective customers tend to judge the quality of the vehicle by observing the sheet metal first.

The foreman of the press line didn't care, because he got his numbers, but the end-of-line foreman was stuck with all of the bad product and he had to handle all of the repairs. The department superintendent didn't care, because all he wanted was his numbers. In fact, I believe we had about six months' worth of completed fenders stored up in case we broke down and didn't make our numbers. We were like squirrels storing nuts for the coming winter. Everywhere you looked, you saw inventory stored in case an emergency happened. Inventory piled up was viewed as "money" in the General Motors business accounting system. If we ever had a going-out-of-business sale, we could sell our parts inventory for cash. I never quite understood who would buy these incomplete parts, but that question was never asked.

There's no telling what type of defects lay in all those parts stored. Usually, we ran into white-rust problems. As our stored panels sat in their racks waiting for shipment to the assembly plants, they would begin to rust. This rust had to be removed by hand. Many panels had to be scrapped out because they were beyond repair. In any event, most of these panels were shipped to the assembly plants to be used on vehicles. My product was a fender for the pickup truck; if one of the assembly plants was fussy and wouldn't use our parts, another one of the five truck assembly plants would. I had heard of cases in which we had received a quality failure from one assembly plant and turned around and sent the entire shipment to another plant where they were used without question.

During the rest of my time as a "product handler," things were fairly routine.

The Know-It-Alls

Not having any mentors in the plant, I became friends with a lot of the product repairmen. These guys made the various repairs required to the finished fenders so they could be shipped to the assembly plants. If they weren't repaired, they had to be scrapped out, which was viewed as very costly. These guys worked at product repairs full-time. They each had their own repair booth, complete with a set of personal tools. They were all high-seniority employees; they had been around a long time. They seemed to know everything about the shop. They had seen it all, and they weren't shy about schooling me about the ways of the plant or about life in general.

The end-of-the-line supervisor was an okay guy, but every once in a while, he got cranky. One day, he was getting pretty ornery, so the repairmen decided to brighten up his day. One of them called him over to the repair booth to inspect damaged fenders. Another employee snuck over to the supervisor's desk and took die bluing ink and coated the receiver of his telephone with it. In those days, there were no cell phones. Die bluing ink is a thick, sticky substance die makers use as they work on perfecting their dies. Die bluing ink hardly ever dries. If you got this ink on you, it was very hard to get off. People were always pulling tricks on each other with this ink. When the supervisor returned to his workstation, his phone started ringing. When he answered the phone, he placed the receiver to his ear and mouth. The entire right side of his jaw and ear were smothered in die blue. The supervisor realized he had been pranked. When he looked up, the entire department was laughing at him. That was a good laugh.

Then came the big yearly push to sign up for either the United Way campaign or government bonds. It was a big deal to the supervisors, as somehow, they were graded on their employee participation. The supervisor came by and solicited my contribution. I wasn't sure what to do. So I asked around and was schooled by my shop buddies. Here's the deal they told me about. They advised me not to sign up for anything until the last sign-up day. They told me the supervisor would panic and would begin to provide incentives for signing up. They told me that the previous year, he had even given away a couple bottles of wine. Our supervisor had obtained 100 percent participation that year. They also counseled me that after you signed up for the contributions, the next week, you could go to personnel and cancel your yearly pledge. This seemed to be a standing joke amongst the department employees. It was a yearly ritual. Sure enough, on the last day, I received five dollars from my supervisor to sign up. My supervisor obtained 100 percent participation for the year once again. The following Monday, most of us went to personnel and canceled our pledges. Apparently, we were done with this exercise until next year.

Deer Hunting

Another incident came in mid-November. In Michigan, opening day of firearm deer season is a big event. Many General Motors employees took time off of work to go up north and get into the woods to hunt deer—both the two-legged kind and the four-legged kind. I also had the itch to hunt. I had just bought a brand-new thirty-odd-six (30.06) rifle from the Cougar and Hunter sporting goods store in Flushing, Michigan. There was one problem though. I didn't have seniority, and I had no vacation time coming. I was explaining my problem to the grand poo-bahs of the line. These were my buddies who worked in the repair booth. They knew everything. They had seen it all. It was they who taught me how to bypass the system. They gave me clear instructions on what I must do to accomplish my goal. They told me to tell the supervisor that I didn't feel well and I needed to go to medical. Then they told me on the way to medical to drink a cup of the hottest coffee I could find. On my way to medical, I was to stop by the men's restroom and put soap on the heels of my feet, as this would elevate my body temperature. If you had an elevated body temperature, the nurse would send you home. If the nurse sent you home, there was nothing the supervisor could do. If the nurse thought you were contagious, she had to send you home to prevent you from spreading your virus to other employees.

Now, I was thinking to myself, *These guys are crazy. They're just pulling my leg.* That thought must have been showing on my face because they reassured me it would work. So I did what they said. I asked to go to medical. I drank the hot coffee, and I put the damn powdered soap in my socks right under my heels. I reported to medical and told the nurse I was not feeling very well. I told her I was aching all over and felt hot. The nurse took my temperature. It must have been higher than normal. She dismissed me not only for the balance of that day, which was Wednesday, but for Thursday and Friday as well. This was great. Now I had Thursday, Friday, and the entire weekend to hunt for deer. I was told to leave the plant immediately in case I was contagious. As I grabbed my things, the grand poo-bahs of repair smiled and waved good-bye.

As soon as I got home, I packed for deer camp. My father had left a day earlier and had set up camp in a trailer in Gladwin, Michigan. Gladwin is about one hundred miles north of Flint. It is located in the upper part of Michigan's Lower Peninsula. It took me about two hours to get to the deer camp. Traffic was very heavy on I-75; the headlines in the newspapers always read, "The Red Army Moves North." I arrived just in time to unpack my things and prepare to have dinner at the Wooden Shoe bar in town. The Wooden Shoe bar hosted the "Deer Hunters' Ball" each year. I was excited to get my first look at this festive event.

I was stunned by what I observed upon our arrival. There was every type of off-road vehicle you could imagine in the parking lot. The parking lot itself was crammed full of vehicles. We were lucky to find one of the last remaining parking spots. As we walked inside the bar, I found myself in a very large room. It was packed with a sea of red hunting outfits. Red was the traditional color hunters wore in those days. The idea was to wear red for safety. By wearing red into the woods, you made yourself easily recognizable to other hunters so they could determine you were not a deer or other hunted animal. (This sometimes failed though, and usually one or two hunters died from gunshot wounds.)

These guys and girls had weapons strapped all over them. Most guys had large hunting knives attached to their belts. A few wore pistols around their waists. My father and I wore our street clothes. I was grateful that we didn't wear our hunting outfits to the ball. We ordered dinner and waited for the dance to begin. Shortly thereafter, the musicians arrived. I was quite disappointed in the band. It was an eighty-year-old man and his wife. He played a small organ, and his wife sang. They opened the dance with the song "Funny Face," which was popular at that time. Every one got up and danced. Now this was in the seventies, and it was deer-hunting time. This was a man's time. The couples were all male and female. It wasn't acceptable back then for someone to come out of the closet. If there were any alternative lifestyle people in the bar that night, they didn't reveal it. Even though there didn't seem to be many women in the bar, the dance floor was full. In a short time, a couple of fights broke out over the few women at the ball. It seems like alcohol, women, and men in deer-hunting outfits just don't mix very well. These fights were short-lived, and the ball continued. There was an electric charge in the air though, because first thing in the morning, firearm deer season opened up!

Later that night, my dad's friends arrived at the Wooden Shoe. There were about five or six of them. They were sharing the trailer with us during deer camp. All of them began drinking heavily. In fact, everyone in the bar began drinking heavily except for one guy. This guy was a recovering alcoholic named Mike. He ordered a martini and sniffed it all night long. He never drank a drop. I watched him go over to the pool table and get in on a game of pool. Soon, a large, violent fight erupted at the table. Guys were hitting each other with pool sticks. Here came Mike back to our table with a huge smile on his face. I asked him what had happened. He said he told one guy his opponent was cheating him in the game. He also told the opponent that the other guy was cheating as well. They must have believed him—it probably didn't take much prodding—and all hell broke loose. This fight was more difficult to break up than the earlier ones. People were getting more psyched up for tomorrow's hunt, and they were getting drunker by the minute. Now it occurred to me that in a few short hours, all of those drunken hunters would be out in the woods with fully loaded firearms. This was kind of unnerving to me given all of the safety training I had received with weapons in the Marine Corps. Shortly thereafter, I left the bar to get ready for the following day's hunt. I went back to the trailer and fell asleep.

Around three o'clock in the morning, the rest of the campers showed up at the trailer. They had a small problem. In their drunken stupor, they had veered off the road and hit a tree with their pickup truck. The cab of the pickup was bent, and one of the front wheels had the brake caliper locked up. The brake hub was cherry red. The truck couldn't be driven.

My dad got out of bed and attempted to call a tow truck, but no one would come out at that time of the night. We tried to drive the truck, but it was no use; it wouldn't move with the brake locked up.

My dad and I got in his car and headed into town after the rest of the guys went to bed. We found an all-night diner that was open, went in, and had breakfast. We still had to find someone who would come get the truck. I was beginning to feel a little down on my luck. Here it was the first morning of my deer-hunting experience and I had to take care of some other guy's car wreck because he got drunk.

Around five in the morning, we finally found a gas station that had opened up. We talked with the owner about the pickup truck. He agreed to get it as soon as daylight broke. He knew where our deer camp was located. Now things started looking up. My dad and I prepared to enter the woods.

I was excited to get into the woods. I was familiar with finding my way around in a woods-type environment from my Marine Corps training. I had been in the infantry, and we were well trained with the use of a compass in the field. We would hold periodic compass marches and became quite skilled at arriving at our destinations. Now this would be of some value out here in the Michigan deer woods.

We drove to the spot where my dad had been hunting the previous few years. We parked the car and got ready to hunt. It was about a half hour until daybreak. We took out our flashlights and walked into the woods. We didn't travel too far. This was our plan. At daybreak, we would move deeper into the woods, but for now, we moved a couple hundred yards off of the main trail. We then split up and sat down looking for the first sight of a deer.

Daylight soon appeared. I could see for a few yards. Then I could see much further. I couldn't believe my eyes. There must have been at least fifty hunters strung out along the main trail. We were located in a horseshoe-shaped arrangement. My first thought was that if a deer wandered into this field of fire, it would be cut up into tiny pieces. There would be nothing left of it. Hell, if any animal, even a mouse, showed its face, it would be annihilated. Then the thought of the previous night's Deer Hunters' Ball came to my mind. *My God,* I thought, *how many of these hunters are still drunk?* If these guys started firing their weapons, one half of the horseshoe formation would wipe out the other half. I quickly got up and walked deeper into the woods.

I kept walking until I found what appeared to be a highway of deer tracks. Deer appeared to come from every which way into the crossing. This felt like a good location to stay at for a while. I had walked for about a half an hour and knew I was safely away from the trailside hunters. Their bullets couldn't reach me here. I turned to face the wind. I had read that deer could smell hunters from miles away and to be a successful hunter, you had to sit facing the wind. I positioned myself into the wind and where I could observe anything coming down the highway of deer tracks. I sat down against a tree stump. I watched the trail long and hard. I kept moving my eyes back and forth just as I had been taught. Then all the events from the previous twenty-four hours started catching up with me. Also, breakfast was weighing heavily on my stomach. I promptly fell asleep. I hope I didn't snore.

When I woke up, I was startled to see a deer standing in the crossing in front of me. It was about thirty-five yards away. It had horns! I fired my 30.06 rifle. Blam! Then I realized my rifle was pointed at the sky. I had a case of buck fever! My heart was pounding in my chest. I thought it was going to explode. My arms were shaking. My Marine Corps training once again kicked in. I ejected the spent round of ammunition and loaded another round. I instantaneously moved into a kneeling position. I aimed my rifle at the deer. I could see its head straining to look at me. I moved my gun sights to its shoulder area. I squeezed off a second round. The deer fell immediately. I had shot it through the heart. It was dead. I waited for what seemed like an eternity and then walked over to it. There it was, my first deer. I counted eight points on its antlers. I had bagged an eight-point buck!

Now I had to drag the deer back to the car. That was at least a forty-minute walk. I didn't know what to do. I grabbed the deer by the horns and attempted to walk and drag the deer carcass. The deer didn't move. It must have weighed at least 130 pounds. Now what? I knew I had to gut the deer to remove as much weight as I could. I had never been around anything like that in my life. I wasn't sure what to do. So I pulled out my hunting knife and began cutting. It really wasn't that bad. Most of the guts fell out on their own once I opened the deer up. Some of the stuff though, I had to cut out. What a mess I made out there in that field. Shortly thereafter, I completed the process.

I once again picked the deer up by its horns and started to drag it out of the woods. It was one of the most difficult tasks I had ever taken on. It didn't want to move. Every dam twig, stick, rock, and mound presented problems. I had gone only a short distance, and I was worn out. How the hell was I going to last for the entire trip back to the main trail? I dragged the deer maybe twenty feet at a time and then rested for about an hour. I hadn't gotten too far. A guy showed up in a Volkswagen Beetle from out of nowhere. He stopped to help me out. We tied the deer to his rear bumper, and he drove me to our car. Man, was I glad for that assist. My dad showed up shortly after that. We placed the deer on our car and headed back to camp. When we arrived, our drinkers hadn't gotten out of bed yet. It was somewhere around nine in the morning. We tied the deer to the deer post at the camp. My dad completed the gutting process, showing me what to do. He then coated the heart and liver in flour and fried them. It sounded very gross to me. I tried it at his urging, and it may have been the best-tasting meat that I had ever had.

When Mike, the guy who'd sniffed his drink all night and successfully started several fights without having to throw any punches, woke up, he was really pissed at me for shooting a deer—I mean really pissed. How could he explain to his wife that on my first hunting trip I had bagged a deer whereas he had never shot one in his many years of hunting? He told me I had ruined everything, and he was serious. Man, I didn't see that one coming. Another guy, who was the designated cook of the camp, told me he had never shot a deer either. I had been watching him. He would leave camp, walk about two minutes, sit down for about a half an hour, and then go back to camp. I realized that not many deer hung around the deer camps waiting to be butchered!

Not having anything else to do, I loaded the deer onto the roof of my car and headed for home. I sure was proud of that deer. I felt as though everybody in town was staring at my deer. I drove the long way home. The successful hunter returns. Along the way, I stopped at a rest area on I-75. The state had set up a deer-checking station to monitor the health of the herd. I received a successful deer hunter's patch for 1973 for my troubles. When I reached the Flint city limits, I drove all around town. I wanted everyone to see my prize. A couple of days later, I took the deer to the meat processor's and had it cut up into sausage. I had the head mounted as my trophy.

I hunted for the next four years. During that last season, I shot another deer. This time, when I walked up to the deer and touched it, I felt as if I had just shot my dog! I put my hunting stuff away and never went back. I guess the hardness of the Marine Corps had worn off.

One additional thought about deer hunting: I always enjoyed the peace and tranquility that came over me as I walked into the woods while hunting. I could always find clearness of thought, enjoyment of the simple things in life, and the wonderful feeling that everything was just A-OK. I've never been quite able to recapture that feeling unless I find myself in northern Michigan in the woods. A lot of people buy property up north and drive up every weekend, and I believe a good part of that is finding that peace and tranquility. It is a great escape from the daily rat race of life in the city.

October 1973 Oil Embargo

My biggest concern at that time was to get my ninety days in, gain seniority, and fall under the union contractual protection. In October, Egypt and Israel went to war. The Arab nations, through OPEC (Organization of Petroleum Exporting Countries), withheld oil shipments to our country because of our support for Israel. The United States' economy started to slow down as we had our first oil embargo. Things didn't look so good for employment. Somehow, I made it through to Christmas break 1973, allowing me to obtain my ninety days and gain union seniority. I now fell under the protection of the UAW. I thought this was quite ironic because just a few short weeks earlier, I would have been placed on ready alert at Camp Lejeune, North Carolina, in case the marines were called into the Middle East conflict. During my year and a half at Camp Lejeune, we had been placed on alert periodically due to the Middle East situation. Now having left the marines, this unrest was continuing to follow me. The use of fossil fuels in vehicles would follow my thirty-five-year career as well. This also opened the door for the Japanese car manufacturers in the United States. They specialized in small, fuel-efficient vehicles. When everyone panicked in October 1973, thinking that the era of cheap gasoline was over, they turned toward the smaller vehicles. They discovered great cars, better customer service, and more reliable vehicles. This marked the beginning of the end of the big three domestic automakers, as we had come to know them.

Having gotten my ninety days in, I qualified for all the benefits GM offered. I was paid for my first Christmas holiday break while employed at General Motors. This was the first of many to come. General Motors has been good to me. I liked the shop; I liked most everything about it. We returned from the Christmas holiday to more gloomy economic news. I believe we were in a full-blown economic recession, which, according to the wise shop workers, was just the new governmental word for a depression.

2
1974–1976 The Production Years

National Highway Transportation Act

When I returned to work after the Christmas holiday in January 1974, President Richard Nixon had signed into law a national transportation act. Part of that package was a speed limit of fifty-five miles per hour on all federal highways. Prior to the oil embargo, the speed limit for all the highways I traveled was seventy miles per hour. In the mountains on my way home from North Carolina, the posted speed was seventy-five miles per hour. There was common talk that the posted expressway speed in Michigan was going to be raised to seventy-five miles per hour.

Couple that thinking with the types of cars that were popular when I was in high school. This was the era of the Detroit muscle cars. Many of my friends had very souped-up, high-speed automobiles. Speed was a given fact of life. There was a lot of drag racing and occasionally a traffic fatality. Gasoline in those days was twenty-five cents a gallon and as plentiful as the ocean. How I longed for a mean, street-racing machine. My favorite car was a 1969 Chevrolet Z28 Camaro. Man, I wished I could have afforded one of those machines.

I don't precisely remember the exact day that the new law went into effect, limiting the expressway speed to fifty-five miles per hour. I do remember getting on the expressway at I-75 and Pierson Road and accelerating right up to seventy-five or eighty miles per hour, just like I had done for my entire driving career. That morning was different though. Now I was passing every vehicle in front of me. A couple of them blinked their lights at me to slow down. Now I believe part of the pitch to drive fifty-five was to be patriotic and save gas. We needed to help wean America off of her Middle Eastern oil dependency. But don't call me unpatriotic! I had just finished serving three years in the service of my country. I was very patriotic. Tell that story to all of those who didn't serve or left for Canada to avoid being drafted. Of my high school graduation class, several of us went into military service and some left for Canada to avoid the lower draft numbers. Those were the days of a draft lottery. The government drew days of the year and listed them from 1 to 365. The lower your number was, the higher your chances were of getting drafted.

Anyway, after a few short miles, the argument had played out in my head and I complied with the new law. I didn't like driving fifty-five miles per hour. It seemed like it wasn't very long before everybody was back to driving the normal speed, which was seventy miles per hour. Later, Sammy Hagar would sing a popular song titled "I Can't Drive Fifty-Five"; neither could I.

First Layoff

On Friday of the first week back, I received a pink layoff slip officially notifying me that as of the end of the shift, I was being laid off. According to my foreman, he had never in his career seen anything like this economic mess we were in, and he suggested I find another job, as he didn't think I'd ever be called back to the plant.

During my first week of layoff, I was required to go to the Michigan unemployment office that was located somewhere in downtown Flint to sign up for unemployment compensation. I think there was a specific day of the week designated for you to report by your Social Security number or your last name. On my assigned day, I got up early to report in and get signed up. When I found the building and parked my car, I saw a line of people waiting. It was a long one. It started on the inside of the building and wrapped around three-quarters of the outside perimeter. It was January in Michigan, and it was dark and cold. I believe those of us at the end of the line waited three to four hours just to get inside the building. It seemed that later that day, the line extended completely around the entire outside of the building. I got lucky by reporting early. Inside the building, it seemed to be utter chaos. There were several additional lines, very few signs, and very irate, rude, and demeaning people behind the counters. It took all day to get signed up. What a mess. I remember I came out of there feeling hopeless and helpless. I personally wasn't in a bad spot. I still lived at my parents' house and only had a car payment. I shudder to think about all of my fellow shop rats who had families and bills to pay. I remember watching the ABC nightly news with Harry Reasoner was who reporting about something called "stagflation." I believe this was a new term, and it was used to explain that the American economy was not only in a recession but was also experiencing a high degree of inflation at the same time.

For the first time, America was experiencing gasoline shortages. There were long lines at the gas stations, and the news showed people running out of gas while waiting in line. What a hopeless mess this appeared to be. The Middle East oil exporters had declared an oil embargo on the United States, and we were in a panic. Years later, the wise old shop employees told me it was all a big hoax and there was plenty of oil available. Ships full of oil were waiting offshore to be unloaded. Anyway, it appeared to me that my future with General Motors didn't look good and maybe my supervisor was right and I should move on. I wasn't sure what I wanted to do.

Somehow, I decided I wanted to become a tool and die maker like my father or a tool grinder like my grandfather. I looked up all of the tool and die shops listed in the yellow pages and began sending résumés to all of them. I may have driven to submit applications, as was the custom in those days. In any case, I landed a job at a small tool and die shop on Saginaw Street in Burton, Michigan. I was promised that if I worked out, I would start an apprenticeship in about six months. I agreed to this and started work the next day. The assignment I remember receiving was operating a radial arm drill press. This was a rather large drilling machine the likes of which I had never seen before. Like on my first day at General Motors, I received some basic instruction, but it was pretty much a learn-on-your-own situation. There was one very nice lady there who helped me very much. Soon, I received my first paycheck, and I was stunned. It was for about half of what I had earned at General Motors for harder work and longer hours. It seemed like the next day, the straw boss grabbed me by the arm and told me I walked too slowly through his shop. So from then on, as I went to the tool crib to get different drill sets, I half ran, half walked through the shop. There was no committeeman at this place. The kind lady told me the straw boss talked to everybody that way at first.

Shortly thereafter, I received a call from General Motors to come back to work. The man on the other end of the phone line told me he had openings for arc welders and asked if I was interested. I said I was and asked when I could start. He said the following Monday would be fine, but I insisted I start the very next day, and he agreed. What a relief it was to tell the manager of the job shop I was returning to General Motors. When I got back to the plant, the man who had hired me back in told me how lucky I was getting rehired. He said they only had a few openings for production welders, and many other employees with much higher seniority than I were all refusing to come over to the frame plant and change their classification to arc welder. He said some of these laid-off workers had twenty-plus years in at General Motors. He said the work was harder, and it was much dirtier in the frame plant than in the stamping plant. I really didn't care; I just wanted to get back to work with the high pay and the generous benefits.

Frame Plant

When I finally got to my new department, I found out I would be an arc welder on the 1974 Chevrolet X-body stub frame. This frame was used on the Chevy Nova. I had driven one of these cars for about two years while I was in Camp Lejeune, North Carolina. The production system consisted of two assembly fixtures where the frames were tac welded together and then placed on a conveyor that went to the merry-go-round. The merry-go-round was an oval-shaped track that had trunnions attached overhead and moved in a circular motion. Someone had mounted horses' heads and tails on each of the trunnions for visual effect. It seemed like there were ten or twelve trunnions on the merry-go-round. An operator would pull a frame off the feeder conveyor and load it into the next available trunnion. The frame would then make its way slowly around the merry-go-round track. At the end, the operator unloaded the frame, and it moved down the final assembly conveyor. From there, it was placed on a monorail that sent the frame into a large industrial washer. After that, it was painted, loaded, and shipped off to the assembly plant. It was much darker in this area of the plant, and it was very smoky from all the welding operations being performed.

I met my supervisor. He was named Joe and turned out to be a really good guy. He seemed to be able to get good performance out of the line workers and still have the respect and authority he needed to run the place. I believe he made superintendent later in his career, after it was okay to utilize the employees as resources rather than as muscle only.

I had to get sized up for my welding gear. I received a welding helmet, hammer, goggles, a long-sleeved welding coat, a welder's cap, and leather spats that were placed over my bootlaces to stop them from burning from the welding sparks. Someone took me to the back area to teach me how to weld. I had never been around welding or seen anything like it in my life. I must have practiced on scrap pieces of metal for a while, but I wasn't getting the hang of it. I was frustrated and scared because I felt pressure to be able to do the work or lose my job. I really didn't want to go back to the tool and die shop. But I kept blowing holes. This happens when you leave the welding rod in one place for too long. Too long would be about a millisecond, and yet if you moved too fast, no weld would take place at all. Oh boy! I must've pissed the first guy off because I vaguely remember somebody else trying to teach me. This wasn't going very well, and I really needed to get my butt on the merry-go-round and take my place on the production line.

Part of my problem was I couldn't see. I don't know how many of you have ever welded, but it has more caveats than trying to load slippery sheet metal panels into a die. Once again, my hands were tied. You see, I wore glasses back then. I had worn them since the fourth grade when I discovered I couldn't see.

***

Flashback: How I Discovered I Needed Glasses

One fall day, my father took us to a Flint Northern High School football game at Atwood Stadium. Feeling generous, he was going to teach my older brother and me how to read the scoreboard. He was doing a great job describing what all the different lights on the board meant and what to look for. When it was my turn to read back from the scoreboard, I couldn't do it. Well, let me tell you, this didn't go over very big. It seemed like I was ungrateful and pretty dumb. I remember I really tried, but I just couldn't get it. Finally, out of much frustration, my dad told me to put my brother's glasses on. When I did, a whole new world opened up for me. I could see! I remember shouting to my dad that I could see the players on the field, the scoreboard, and just about everything else. You see, I was as blind as a bat. The next day, I was at the optometrist's office where I got my first pair of glasses. The frames were gun-smoke gray. These were the same ones that my older brother wore. What a whole new world it was.

***

So now, here I was in a dark environment, wearing glasses as thick as Coke bottle bottoms, the triple-dark welding goggles that went over my glasses taking away all sense of depth perception and then having to flip the

27

welding helmet down, which also had a triple-dark welding lens attached to it. Every time I put the helmet down, I couldn't see anything. This was the second time in my life that I experienced total blindness. It reminded me of my jungle training days down in the Panama Canal. In that triple canopy jungle, after the sun went down, you couldn't see your hand in front of your face even as it touched your nose. I know I tried it.

***

Flashback: Jungle Training

We were on nighttime field maneuvers just outside of the Gatun Locks. I was part of a forward observation post, and the three of us were scared as hell. After the sun went down, it became the darkest I had ever seen. We heard all kinds of noises that kept getting closer to us. We radioed in to headquarters and asked for permission to open fire on whatever was in front of us, be it man or beast. Our request was denied. But we opened fire anyway! Nothing was going to get us. What dumbasses we were though, because all we had were blanks. Some marines we were! The lieutenant was pissed off at us, but what the hell; we made it through the night.

***

So now, under pressure to be able to weld, I'd flip that helmet down, go blind, and try to strike the welding rod to the metal so I could lay a really good bead of weld. Once the welding activity began, I could clearly see the metal pieces through the eerie green light given off by the flash from the welding rod. Finally, after a couple of days of practice and a few threats, I was ready to hit the merry-go-round and earn my pay. Production on the merry-go-round was 120 parts per hour. In the frame plant, we were allowed to "run ahead." Typically, if we ran faster than 120 parts an hour, we might finish our production forty-five minutes to one hour early each day. This was quite an incentive that we all enjoyed.

Being able to run ahead seemed to motivate all of the production line employees and the supervisors. The deal in those days was that the production line ran parts ahead at its own peril. If for some reason we went down, we started losing our "banked" parts minute by minute. For every minute we were down, we lost two parts that we had built ahead. It was like a game of roulette. We were always betting against the house. The house held all of the advantages. I remember that mostly, we came out ahead, and on really good days, we earned forty-five minutes off early by running ahead. After completing production, we were free to do whatever we wanted except leave the plant. Most of us went upstairs to the cafeteria. There were many games of euchre, checkers, and chess that were played up there. I was not much of a card player, but I got pretty good at euchre. I could hang with the best of them.

In time though, the local union struck a deal with management. The new agreement stated that if we chose to run ahead and the line went down, we didn't risk our banked parts. I feel that after this, the run ahead only favored the employees and the company got the short end of the stick. It seemed like it was never the same after that. The line slowed down, and we never seemed to get ahead. Later, it was negotiated between the parties for a fair day's work. In other words, there were no set standards. You would come in and run as many parts as you could and then go home. Needless to say, we never ran as many parts per hour as we did back in the day. Part of the new philosophy was from the Japanese just-in-time concepts that were beginning to make their way into the manufacturing process.

Being the lowest seniority employee, I was assigned the worst job on the merry-go-round. This consisted of hammering the spring seat reinforcement down and into position on the rail and then welding it in place. Now all this had to take place while the merry-go-round was *moving*! Holy shit! Have you ever tried this? The reinforcement bracket took about three or four good hits with a three-pound hammer to get it into a position so there wasn't much gap between the reinforcement and the rail. Any gap made it that much harder to weld. Here I was blind and just learning to weld and now this. Well, I started but didn't fare too well. I had all I could do just to get the damn reinforcement down into position, let alone try to weld it before the trunnion had fully passed by me. I think for a while, people took turns hammering away at the reinforcement bracket so all I had to do was weld. Then I got relieved off the line to see the supervisor. Joe wasn't very happy with all of the repairs I had been running. I was "blowing holes" in every rail I welded. He pointed to a large pile of frames that had been pulled off of the conveyor for repair. These repairs were from the spring seat area. Either the seat wasn't all the way down, not completely welded, or there were large holes that had been blown into the metal. The online repairman couldn't keep up with my errors. Downhearted, I dribbled back to the line and took my place. I tried and tried, and then finally, it seemed like I was starting to get it. But, oh my God, was my arm sore from all the hammering! I could hardly lift it up. I think I had to lift up my right arm with my left hand and then simply let my right arm fall down to hammer the bracket into position. I did this to make it through the shift. Somehow, even in these tough economic times, we were working ten hours a day five days a week. After a while, I got to where I could do this job, but it was the worst assignment I would ever have at General Motors.

The merry-go-round was a very rough-and-tumble place to work. It never shut off because of the pressure from the foreman to get his numbers and from the line workers to get done early. There are a couple of things I remember about this job assignment. After work, I couldn't move my right hand. It was stuck in a three-quarter-closed position. This was from the welding "stinger" that holds the welding rod. It had a lot of electricity that flowed through it from the welding cables, and as the insulation in the stinger wore down, it got very hot. I would go home after a ten-hour shift and work with my fingers to get them to move properly. Most nights, I had to soak my hand in warm water to get it to function correctly. This scared the hell out of me, and I couldn't imagine doing this for thirty or more years. What would my hands be like at the end of that time?

The other incident happened one day as we were routinely welding our hearts out. Someone fell down and passed out. From what I remember, the merry-go-round didn't miss a beat, and someone stepped up and did the down man's job as he lay there on the floor beneath it. Finally, the plant ambulance came and took the employee away. He had to have some type of surgery. He returned to the line in a couple of months. Back then, hospital stays were long and recovery times longer. Nowadays, it's all about outpatient surgery and back to work the next day.

After a few weeks passed, I received my prescription welding glasses. Now I didn't have to wear those godforsaken goggles. It greatly enhanced my ability to weld. I gained back my depth perception by removing the welding goggles I was required to wear. This was a good step in the right direction. I could now weld with the best of them.

Another skill you had to learn to survive being a welder was to be able to tell if it was your clothes that were on fire or someone else's. Rarely an hour went by in which no someone one would stop welding, cuss, and reach down to slap out a fire that had started on an article of clothing. The first few times this happens to you, you get very nervous. After a while, you learn to smell in advance the beginning of the burning process and stop right there to snuff it out. You also learned to listen to others if they suggested it might be you on fire. Many of my clothes were ruined from welding sparks. My Marine Corps utility shirts worked well as welding jackets.

At some point, I was asked if I wanted to work on the assembly fixtures. This was a very physical job, and most people would have no part of it. It didn't look all that bad to me, so I gave it a try on a fill-in basis. There were two assembly fixtures per merry-go-round, so the hourly output was sixty frames per hour per fixture. The work consisted of loading the fixture with two rails, a cross frame, and control arm brackets and mounting the transmission bracket on the back end. Two people were in the front, and they did all the welding. The third person was in the back. He loaded four bolts, two on each side, and then when the fixture was locked in place, positioned the transmission bracket over the bolts, placed lock washers and nuts over the bracket, and then tightened the nuts with an overhead air wrench. Then it was prepared for the next assembly.

I really liked this job. The job rotation made the time go by much faster. The three fixture operators kind of became a team and buddies. Shortly after this, I was bumped to second shift. Upon reporting to second shift, or afternoon shift, as some people called it, I was permanently assigned to the assembly fixtures. Let the good times roll.

Second Shift

I must have started second shift in the spring of 1974. I became friends with the other two guys in my crew, Steve and Dave. For a while, I was happy and content to be a production welder. I was young, free, and making very good money with very few expenses. I was living at home, and my parents never charged me for rent or food. In return, I did most of the yard work in the summer and shoveled the snow in the winter. It was the least I could do. At work, I could buy a good-size hamburger for one dollar and drink water for lunch. Water was free in those days. It came out of a water fountain. All I had was my car payment. Over the next few years, I saved up a sizable amount of money.

Around this time, I started to see the plant as it really was. The newness was wearing off. Also, I discovered I had been pretty brainwashed while I was in the military. I started realizing more and more how oriented I had become toward entering combat on a moment's notice. I believe this had to be for the sake of the military, so I am not complaining. I fully accepted being a marine and everything about it. I am proud of it. But about six months down the road, I was coming out of the military way of life. I'm not sure if I'm explaining this properly, but I was a little more tolerant of civilian living. I feel it took me about one year to fully readjust to civilian life from the ways of the military life.

As I was working on the assembly fixture, I started to notice other employees who were sitting down an awful lot. Inquiring about them, I was told they were die makers. *Hmm, they're sitting down most of the night, and I'm working.* Looking at other employees, I noticed electricians and welder repairmen—all skilled trades personnel. It didn't take long for me to figure out that that was what I wanted to do. They made more money per hour and were not tied to the production line all day. This sounded good to me.

Somehow, I was put in touch with the UAW apprentice coordinator as I inquired about becoming a skilled tradesman. He let me know there was a process in place to apply for and eventually start an apprenticeship. He also told me things didn't look good for now, because we had apprentices currently on layoff. He basically brushed me off. Little did he know my determination when I had set a goal.

I discovered that the process to receive an apprenticeship had three main parts scored on a point system and management and the union jointly administered it. Points were awarded for prior schooling, a score received on an apprenticeship aptitude test, and from a formal interview conducted by the plant apprentice coordinators. I saw on my high school academic transcripts that a request was made by the plant in February 1974 for my grades. The memory is fuzzy right now, but I was getting the urge to move forward in my life.

I had graduated from Flint Northwestern High School in June 1970. I graduated 363rd out of 623 students. Later, I would learn from a wonderful English teacher at Mott Community College that my high school diploma wasn't worth the paper it was printed on. Unfortunately, I was in agreement with that perception; she was right. My high school education wasn't very valuable to me.

Upon the advice of the apprentice coordinator, I enrolled at Mott adult high school to prep for taking the GED test. This is the test students take for a high school equivalency diploma. I took the test over a two-day period in July of 1974 and received an average standard score of fifty-six. I don't know if this was good or bad, but it started me on my way toward receiving a formal education. It also added some points to my score toward becoming an apprentice.

I also took the apprenticeship test administered by the plant. I believe there were a total of twenty-one points that could be earned through your test score. On my first go-round, I don't think I received more than five points, and that might be a stretch. I'm not sure how long afterward I took the test for the second time, but I failed miserably again. As I remember it, I scored very poorly. It was apparent I didn't have any natural mechanical aptitude. I remember being mentally crushed by this event. I remember my mother trying to cheer me up. I felt terrible. It appeared to me that I was never going to be able to better my life's standing.

Around this time, my fellow line workers were telling me that the union was holding training classes for the apprenticeship aptitude test at the local union hall. I talked to the committeeman about this, and he denied any such thing. He passed me on to the apprentice coordinator who also denied any such doings. Later, I verified with other apprentices who were lucky enough to be let into this training that it in fact did take place. What was made available was a running duplicate of the test with all the answers provided. As you memorized the answers to this test, you would master the answers for the authentic test. As you came out of these classes, you could easily score a 100 percent or gain twenty-one points toward an apprenticeship. The twenty-one points gave you quite an advantage over others who were trying to qualify for an apprenticeship. No wonder my poor scores were so out of whack with the rest of the applicants! They had quite an advantage over those of us who were not allowed to take the preparatory classes.

This was the first time I encountered EEO (Equal Employment Opportunity) activities in the plant by the UAW toward dues-paying members. To this day, I believe they'll deny doing any such thing to a union brother! So I began my quest toward earning a formal education in the summer of 1974 by humbly going back to take the GED exam. This was done to increase my prior academic scores from high school. Whether my GED test score was good or not good didn't matter to me. It earned me more points toward a possible apprenticeship.

Working on the Welding Fixtures

I started working with my new crew, and the three of us became a strong team. I did enjoy this job and the rotation it provided. Every hour, we rotated positions. First, I would do the right front rail job, and then we would switch the second hour and I would do the left rail job. For the third hour, I would go to the back of the fixture and work on the transmission bracket job. This provided a nice relief from welding all of the time. Soon,

I became bored with this job assignment, and then I became very bored. I just couldn't envision myself doing this for thirty more years and then retiring. One hour on the job could seem like an entire day. The production process was so repetitive. Load the fixture, clamp the fixture, tac weld the frame, unload the frame—time after repetitive time. Now I started getting antsy as to what to do with my life. I realized I wasn't moving forward. At home or somewhere, I kept reading that to go anywhere in life, you had to have a strong and wide-ranging vocabulary. So I started bringing in new vocabulary words to work. During the work shift, I would memorize them and give my mind something to do. I had gotten to the word *vegetating* when my friends caught up to me. They asked me what I was doing, and they about had a coronary laughing so hard when I explained it to them. To this day, I'll bet they'll laugh about my self-improvement process when I was memorizing the word *vegetating.*

Vegetating is to exist in a state of physical or mental inability or insensibility.

I was beginning to vegetate on this job. However, there were many things off the job to keep one occupied. Second shift was a whole different animal than first shift. For starters, there weren't as many "white shirts." This is the term used for upper management. The shift was made up of lower seniority employees. These tended to be younger and more carefree people who were full of piss and vinegar. Again, the wisest and most knowledgeable production workers were the repair employees. They were located behind our assembly fixtures. The repairmen were also the rough-and-tumble enforcers of the area. They forced their will on the entire production line. They could shut it down, and they could turn a poor productive night into a good one through their repair work. I began to keep my eye on the repairmen.

I noticed that they were always a bit rowdier after lunch. I didn't know how or why, but they were more animated and noisier after lunch. Then we discovered that they would race out of the plant for lunch—we had thirty minutes of unpaid time—and down a six-pack of tall boys. Tall boys were sixteen-ounce cans of beer. This happened every single night! They became our heroes. A few nights, they would get violent. A few fistfights broke out. They would generally restrain themselves, and management would either ignore them or not see them. One night, we watched in awe as they were throwing control arm brackets at each other. A control arm is a small metal bracket weighing around two pounds. Some guys were getting pelted pretty hard with them. Then they shook hands when it was all over. Amazing! Well, it didn't take long before the three of us had the bright idea to buy six-packs and down them at lunch. We could be kings like the repairmen. We made our plan, and one day, we raced out of the plant, purchased our beer, and began to down them. I looked at my watch, and from the time the lunch whistle blew, getting to the party store and back to the parking lot took fifteen minutes. The walk from the parking lot to our assembly fixture was a good five minutes. That left ten minutes to drink six beers. Seeing that this was our first time, we only bought twelve-ouncers not the tall boys, which the repairmen drained. So I started chugging my beer, all the beer I could. Finally, I finished my first one, but it was time to go. I left the other five cans in the car. How disappointed I was! *What a wussy I am!* I thought. I could only chug down one beer in ten minutes. I don't think Steve and Dave did much better. We got back to our workstation just as the end-of-lunch whistle blew.

I felt euphoric. I felt a free. I felt like a man! Yes, sirree, I was one of the guys. I could drink at lunch. There's no telling where I could go from there. In retrospect, I got buzzed on one can of beer. How pathetic is that? Well, the euphoria lasted for about forty-five minutes. Then I started to calm down. God, what a terrible feeling. It seemed like the welding helmet weighed one hundred pounds. I started to get all sweaty, and each movement became pure torture. What the hell? No one told me it would be like this. This feeling lasted the rest of the shift. After production, we didn't go upstairs; we just sat down by the time clock waiting to go home. Never again did I try drinking at lunchtime while I worked in the shop. I don't know how those repairman did it every night for all those years. It had to take its toll on them.

I did get drunk one time in the shop. I think it was around the Christmas holidays while I was still working production. We completed our production numbers early and went upstairs. Someone had brought in some hard liquor, and we started drinking in celebration of the holidays. Now I have to tell you, I don't drink hard liquor very well. It seems every time I drink hard liquor, I throw up. But for some reason, I drank it that night. At the end of the shift, I couldn't get to the time clock to punch out. Someone punched me out while someone else walked me to my car. I don't remember getting home. After that night, I never drank in the shop again.

Another time, I remember it seemed like every employee in the entire department used chewing tobacco. Everybody but a couple of guys working with me on the assembly fixture was doing it. One night, another guy and

I had the bright idea we were going to go out at lunch and buy us some Red Man chewing tobacco so we would be like everyone else. Even the committeeman, Chester, chewed. None of us liked it because when you talked with Chester, he either filled up a cup or a bottle with his excess saliva generated by the chewing tobacco.

So this other guy and I went out at lunch and bought some chew. I think my buddy Steve was already a chewer, and Dave wasn't interested. When we got back to the job after lunch, we decided the other guy would go first. He put a large wad of tobacco in his mouth and started chewing. The plan was after he got going, it would be my turn. It didn't take very long. It was only a couple of minutes later that my friend was gone from the assembly fixture. I found him at the fifty-five-gallon drum trash container. His head was buried in it, and he was puking his guts out. I immediately threw my Red Man chewing tobacco away. I haven't tried it to this day. No one told us you were not supposed to swallow it! We didn't know any better.

One night after work, our committeeman invited us to the union hall to a thank-you party. He wanted to thank us for reelecting him for another term. I believe they invited the entire second shift, which at the time was quite large. There were somewhere around four thousand hourly employees at the plant, so there had to be well over fifteen hundred people on second shift. We went over to the union hall after the shift ended. Fewer than twenty people had shown up for the party. The committeeman rolled out several kegs of beer. Another committeeman started rolling marijuana cigarettes—only they were more like large Cuban cigars than little tiny cigarettes. The committeeman with the beer started by giving everyone seated in the circle his or her own pitcher of beer—not a glass or a cup, but a full pitcher of beer. Then they gave everybody who wanted one a Cuban-cigar-size freshly rolled giant joint. I passed. Then the party began. About an hour later, the newly reelected committeeman in all earnestness stood up and asked what our problems in the plant were. Hell, by that time, I couldn't remember what plant we worked at, where we were, or how to spell my name. That man felt like a king that night because he had taken care of all the problems in his district! No one could come up with any complaints. That was the last union meeting I attended for a long time.

***

Flashback: Drugs

Arriving at this point in my work life, where drugs were introduced to me, took me back to when I first encountered them and how I had formed my views about them. Thank goodness the military had helped me to gain self-confidence and the ability to say no.

I am thankful that drugs were not available to me when I was in high school. During this time, before my military service, I believe I would have freely tried them. To my recollection, there were no drugs around high school right up to my graduation in late June 1970. I entered military service on August 3, 1970, so there wasn't a lot of time from when I graduated until I went into the service to get in much trouble. I had had my tonsils removed just before I graduated, and I wasn't feeling the greatest either. I was in boot camp and basic training for around seven months and came home on leave in February 1971. What a different world I came home to! It seemed everyone was using marijuana and LSD. I remember feeling isolated and distanced from my friends of a few short months earlier. I was preparing to go off to potential war as I had orders to travel overseas, and these guys were experimenting with drugs. I can't easily recall anyone who was not. I'm sure they were there, but they were not vocal about it. I thank my lucky stars that drugs didn't come around until after I had left for the service. That was a good break for me; otherwise, I'm sure I'd have been right in the middle of it.

I have to admit to experimenting with drugs. After my military leave of February 1971, I was sent overseas for my first permanent military assignment. The way my orders were written, I could have gone to Vietnam to fight for my country. I was ready, willing, and able. Our chartered airplane landed in Okinawa, a Japanese island three hundred or so miles south of Japan. It was the site of one of the last battles in the Pacific theater during World War II. There must have been two hundred or more marines who landed with me that day. We were lined up in formation somewhere at the airfield where we had just landed. Someone in charge called out the names of four people who were to go with him. My name was called out. I was not going to Vietnam. I had been selected for special duty at Camp Courtney, which was the headquarters for the U.S. Marines on Okinawa. Cheated! I felt cheated! All of my life I had been prepared for this event. I had watched all of the World War II movies. I had played cowboys and Indians. I had played army man! I had heard many a story from the World War II veterans as I was growing up. Every time we were taken to the IMA

Auditorium in downtown Flint, we always observed my dad's name on the wall that honored the men and women who had served their country during the war. I was ready and willing to see what I could do! Could I be like them? Could I make it?

Looking back on it, one of two things had to have happened. Either my older brother's prior military service in Vietnam or President Nixon's decision had gotten in my way. Now I would never get to prove myself under enemy fire, as had my father and my brother before me. There was a rumor in the marines that if you had a sibling who had served a tour of duty in Vietnam plus two extensions of six months each, no other sibling was required to serve in country. To this day, I do not know if this was true. My brother did serve extended time in Nam, and I believe he has paid a price for it as well.

The other piece is an order or declaration signed by President Nixon. This legislation declared Vietnam a "land" war that meant it was best suited for the army and not the marines. My understanding is that this went into effect sometime after I started boot camp, and they were now removing the marine grunts from Vietnam and inserting the army. Either way, I felt cheated for a long time. For the first part of my life, I had been in preparation to be a marine combat veteran. I lost my opportunity to become one. In retrospect, it was probably one of the better things that happened to me in my life.

Anyway, my assignment for the next long and boring twelve months was to be part of a color guard for the commanding general of Okinawa. My duties were to stand guard at the main entrance of the camp and salute smartly when the executive officers went by, stand guard duty on the base, and be part of the color detail that raised and lowered the flag each day. I say it was boring because we had one day of duty on and one day off. Time passed agonizingly slowly. There was very little to do, and I was always broke. I was a private first class (PFC) at the time, and we were paid once a month. My money did not last long even though I was frugal. I never made it to the end of the month with any money in my pocket. I spent a lot of my time at the base library reading any book I could get my hands on. Being the new recruit on the block, I was assigned to a lance corporal to show me around and assist me in getting used to things.

Shortly after I got there, I was on one of my first guard-duty watches. My buddy, the lance corporal, was on guard duty with me. He was the senior man of our detail. Our job consisted of putting on colorful belts and hard hats and walking around looking military. Not much was going on. Every once in a while, there might be a fight at the enlisted men's club, but that wasn't our responsibility. The military police, or MPs, took care of that.

On this watch, we walked out of sight of the guard shack to check out a vacant building. The lance corporal stopped when we were out of sight and pulled out a marijuana joint. He asked me if I wanted to get high. I told him I had never gotten high before, but my friends back home were now into drugs. It seemed to me the whole world was "turned on," as they said when they did drugs. He asked me if I wanted to try marijuana, and I said I wasn't so sure. He told me it was good stuff, that it came from Vietnam and was laced with heroin. I think they called it angel dust. After a while, I said I would give it a try. He taught me how to smoke it. You took a drag the same as you did for a cigarette—everybody in the marines smoked then—but instead of exhaling, you held the smoke in as long as you could. That way, you could get the full effect of the drug. I did this once, but nothing happened. He told me to take another hit. I did, and this time, all hell broke loose. Almost instantaneous to exhaling, I felt nauseous. I bent over and threw up. I had the dry heaves for a bit. Then I came around. The lance corporal thought this was very funny. He told me I was now stoned. I'll say I was stoned—stoned out of my mind. I'm not sure if I could function properly. The lance corporal proceeded to ask me if I knew about the sergeant of the guard. I did not. He said he was an anti-stoner, had a flattop haircut, and was the biggest prick in the world. On earlier occasions, he had busted people for using drugs while on duty. Oh! Fricking great! Just great! He told me in a short while he would be driving around in his van making his rounds and checking everybody out. He didn't like any screwups on his watch. Well, did I ever get the biggest case of paranoia in my life! Somehow, I thought this too amused the lance corporal. But now I was in a bad spot. *I'm going to get busted*, I thought. *I just know that I am!* Sure enough, a short time later, he spotted the headlights of the sergeant's vehicle off in the distance. He must have seen the paranoia I was going through, or maybe he had experienced it himself. Anyway, he lined me up for what I had to do. I had to pull myself together. I had to blink my eyes several times to get the stupid look off my face, and I had to straighten my posture up. He told me that when the sergeant pulled up, he would do all the talking and I shouldn't move. If the sergeant asked me any questions, all I needed to do was either nod my head or say, "Yes, sir." Well, that was easy for him to say. The sergeant pulled up and talked with the lance corporal a bit and then left the area. He never asked me any questions, thank God!

The next thing I remember is how hungry I became. Man, all I could think about was food. I thought something was wrong with me. The lance corporal said this was common and that I had the "munchies," which happened when you were stoned on marijuana. I think we walked over to the mess hall, and he got us a sandwich. I can still remember eating that sandwich. It may have been the best-tasting sandwich I had ever had. I devoured that food. I am not sure how long I was high, but it seemed like forever. The rest of the time I spent in the service, I never smoked pot again. I'm lucky; I prefer a good old beer buzz any day.

There is one other drug incident that happened in Okinawa. I am not proud of this one, and I'm probably lucky to be alive. One other time during my tour on Okinawa, I tried LSD. This is a mind-altering drug that is supposed to give you a good trip. You see, I was only nineteen years old and everybody was doing drugs. Each payday, the drug dealers would come through the barracks and take orders like a waitress in a restaurant. They would write the orders on a pad of paper and then return shortly to complete the transaction. This happened like clockwork once a month at payday. There were a few guys who went home early because they had become addicted to heroin or cocaine. This was a major problem in the Far East for the American military.

This one time, a guy asked me if I wanted to do some acid. I don't remember being real eager about it, so maybe it was something different than LSD, but for some reason, I agreed to try it. It must have been around nightfall when we took it. I believe we had tiny squares of white cardboard that we chewed in our mouths for a while. Now supposedly, this was to be one of the finest experiences of your life. You were supposed to hallucinate, trip out, and see brilliant colors. After a time, none of this was happening for us. It seemed as though the drug dealer had taken him. We decided to go for a walk. We ended up by some large gasoline storage tanks—you know, the ones like they show on television when they are discussing the price of oil. They were round cement tanks that must have been twenty to thirty feet high. For some reason, we decided to climb up to the top of the tanks to have a look around. There were no guards or fencing to prevent us from climbing up. So up we went. We sat up on top of the tanks for a while. I don't remember any railing there to prevent us from falling off the top. Then a guard vehicle pulled up to the tanks, and two people got out and lit up cigarettes. My partner and I panicked. We didn't want to get caught up there. We were looking for a place to jump down and get out of there. We thought we saw an easy jump on one side of the tanks. We came very close to jumping. Luckily, the guards left before we made up our minds to jump. We climbed down from the tank and returned to the barracks. The next day, when I looked at those gasoline tanks, my heart leapt into my mouth. It was then I realized it was straight down for thirty feet or so. There was no easy way down. That would have been good-bye, Rick! We must have been impaired to have been thinking of jumping and to have been on top of the tower in the first place. That was the last of my drug use, and I am proud to say that.

After my time in Okinawa, I was assigned to an infantry unit at Camp Lejeune in North Carolina. I enjoyed my time there. I was finally placed in the infantry, and time passed quickly. After I made corporal, I was able to afford a car. I took over payments on my younger brother's Chevrolet Nova. Having wheels opened up a whole new world for me. On nights and weekends, we were free to do as we pleased. I met a good friend named Johnny, who was from a small town in North Carolina near Asheville. We spent many a weekend up at Johnny's house. His family was good to me. Johnny was an expert at meeting girls and having fun. His enlistment was up about six months before mine. After Johnny got out of the marines, I continued to go to his place most weekends. It wasn't the same though; something had changed. The last weekend I went up there, the local police were waiting for me. It was a Friday night, and after we were dismissed for the weekend, it took about three hours to drive to Johnny's place. As soon as I hit the city limits, unbeknownst to me, the local cops were waiting. They pulled me over and ordered me out of my car. I hadn't committed any motor vehicle violations, and that probably saved me from going to jail. They questioned me for a short while asking if I did drugs and if I had any drugs on me or in my vehicle. These boys were not playing! I think it helped that I was in the military and didn't have long hair. They asked me if I minded if they searched my car. They had already started to do so. I said I didn't mind. They made me go sit down with my hands placed behind my head. They very thoroughly inspected my Nova. They pulled my trunk apart and looked over the entire spare tire area. They pulled out all the carpeting and found nothing. They searched my entire engine compartment and took off my air filter and found nothing. They searched my front bumper and rear bumper, and one cop went under the car inspecting the underbody framework. Then they started on the inside. They went through my backpack of clothing dumping the contents out onto the street. I had a second backpack that I kept all my cassette tapes in. They dumped all of them out on the ground, opened each cassette box, took out the tapes, and found nothing. They removed my backseat and inspected every square inch of that space, nothing. They looked in the glove box and under the dash and found nothing. They removed the inside panels off of each door and found nothing.

Finally, they came back over to me and questioned me some more. I told them I didn't do drugs, didn't sell drugs, and had no drugs in my possession. They told me to gather my things and I was free to go. Thank God! I always heard stories of small-town, redneck cops doing weird things and breaking the law. I felt lucky they didn't plant any drugs in my possession. I was in no position to defend myself. But having thoroughly inspected everything and having not found anything—because there was nothing to find—they were kind enough to let me go free. If I had had so much as one marijuana seed in that car, I probably would still be in jail today.

I finally pulled into Johnny's yard. I got out, and Johnny met me at his front screen door. He didn't come out. He whispered nervously to me to get the hell out of there and to never come back. He said some high school kid was caught with drugs and told the police that I was his supplier. Johnny said, "Good-bye. It's been nice knowing ya, but turn around and get the hell out of this town!"

I left Johnny's place and headed out of town toward the expressway. The police escorted me all the way to the city limits. Good-bye, Asheville area! I had very good times there. I have often wondered if it might have been Johnny who was busted for drugs. Anyway, I never saw him again. Thank God I didn't do drugs.

These experiences along with the training from the marines allowed me to resist the peer pressure that existed in the 1970s to use drugs. There was a lot of drug and alcohol use in the shop when I hired in. I was fully aware of it, but I didn't participate. I wasn't a part of it. Knowing I didn't care to use drugs and alcohol during work made it easy to say "No."

Production Injuries

Gene

One night, we were shorthanded on our assembly fixture. A replacement named Gene was sent to work with us. Gene was a good guy. He was a good worker and fit in well with the team. Not everybody did. But Gene was a stoner. Every night, he got high on drugs. On this particular night, Gene was really stoned. Normally, this didn't bother us as he kept to himself and did his job. I'm not really sure how it happened, but Gene ended up with one of his hands locked up in the fixture. I don't know how this could have happened, because after we loaded our parts into the fixture, we had to hold down palm buttons with each of our hands to prevent injury. Sometimes, guys would permanently hold down a palm button with a heavy weight to override the safety system, and sometimes, the electronics got screwed up and you could operate equipment with only one hand. In any event, we had locked up the fixture, and he let out a scream because his hand was locked in there. I had visions of his hand getting cut off or flattened like a pancake or maybe severely lacerated. Someone hit the emergency stop button, and the fixture opened up. There was no blood! He raised his hand and looked at his glove but didn't see or feel any blood. He removed his glove and looked at his hand. It was white and flattened, but it was not busted up and crushed. He laughed about it. Then he jumped off the work platform and headed up the aisle toward the medical department. We watched him walk down the aisle. Then we felt a wave of relief and laughed about it a little bit to relieve the tension. Then about three-quarters of the way down the aisle, Gene's knees buckled and he tilted to the left. He started walking almost sideways. We couldn't get to him in time because he had traveled too far down the aisle. This wasn't good because there was a five-foot-deep train well on the left. Finally, someone caught up with him and pulled him back into the aisle and walked him the rest of the way to medical. He was lucky he didn't have any major damage, and he was back to work the next night. He was placed on medical restrictions and got to sit around all night for a couple of weeks doing nothing.

Sometime after that, I saw Gene again outside a popular bar in downtown Flint. He was on a monster of a souped-up motorcycle, and he was revving the engine up. We exchanged greetings, and he asked me how things were going. His hand was fine now. He told me he was betting some guys that he could pop a wheelie with his bike and ride it down the street. Gene was stoned again. My friend and I stepped aside to enjoy the show. After the money for the bet was collected, Gene started revving his engine again. My buddy leaned over to me and said Gene was going to flip his bike right over. Sure enough, when he let go of the clutch, the front end of the bike shot up into the air and instead of moving forward, it continued all the way over. After they pulled the bike off Gene, he hopped up and started laughing. We all stood there laughing at stoner Gene. Gene paid off his bets.

Sometime later, Gene contracted some sort of neurological muscular disease that made him go out on sick leave. His friends held a fundraiser for him. A picture they posted in the plant showed Gene confined to a wheelchair. Shortly after that, Gene passed away.

Johnny

Another night, there was a substitute crewmember named Johnny. Johnny was an all-around good guy who normally filled in for the crazy repairmen at the back of the line. Johnny had been an athlete and was in pretty good shape. He was a big man, around six feet two inches tall. He fit in well with our assembly crew. He and I were working in unison on the front end loading the rails and welding them together. As we welded with our welding rods, they would disintegrate down to about one or two inches, and they would be glowing red-hot. We had thick tin bins that we would "flick" these ends into, and then we would place a new rod into our welding stinger. On this occasion, both Johnny and I needed to reload our welding stingers with new rods. I'm not sure what really happened, but as I turned to flick my red-hot stub into the metal container, I saw Johnny bend over. I must have seen his back pocket because my stub flew directly into it. Now quite a scene erupted. Johnny's eyes got as big as silver dollars, and he started moaning or maybe it was chanting. I know it was definitely not screaming. He stood up and started swatting at his rear end, and then he was running around wide-eyed. He kept moaning, "Whoa oh ho, whoa oh ho, whoa oh ho." I'm not sure why, but I erupted into a fit of laughter watching him running around and swatting at his behind. I realized I shouldn't be laughing, but the longer this went on, the harder it was to stop laughing. All of us were laughing. We laughed so hard we had tears in our eyes, and my stomach hurt. Finally, Johnny squatted down, and the hot rod burned its way out of his pants. He was now pissed off at me. He looked at me, pointed his finger menacingly, and said he was going to kick my ass when he got back. Off to medical Johnny went. He was placed on sick leave for a month or so. But soon, the day of reckoning was coming. I wasn't looking forward to it; deep down, I knew I was a dead man. Johnny was capable of tearing my little five-foot-eight-inch frame into little pieces and then handing them back to me.

One night, Johnny returned to work. Word spread quickly around the line that Johnny was back and he was gunning for me. Shortly thereafter, he came walking up to our assembly fixture. Everyone backed away and left us facing each other. It was Johnny and me all alone. He had a smile on his face and shook my hand. Whew, what a narrow escape that was for me! I apologized profusely for both throwing the rod in his pocket and then laughing as he tried to get it out of his pants. He said he understood, and he shouldn't have been near the metal container on my side of the fixture. He said it was all right because he got time off on sick leave and he enjoyed that. Besides, his lady friend thought his scar was cute. However, I think this was more for the effect on the others listening, as he grabbed me, winked, and said, "I ought to kick your ass!" Johnny, to this day, I am sorry for the incident and you are all right with me.

Rick's Injury

My only injury while General Motors employed me came while I was working on this assignment. One night, I was working the non-welding job on the assembly fixture. I went to leave the work platform. I pushed aside the parts hanging on the monorail brackets to slip in between them, but they swung back at me and I wasn't yet clear of the line. An engine cross member slammed into my right elbow. Earlier, I had talked about how these sheet metal parts were as sharp as razor blades. I wasn't wearing any type of protection. It was not required in those days. I went up to medical and received a couple of butterfly sutures. I then went out to the line ready to work and as good as new. Later in the week, the general supervisor, who was the supervisor's boss, asked me what happened. I explained the incident to him. He told me to be careful and if it happened again, he would have me penalized. This plant was notorious for penalizing people who had been injured on the job. We all thought it was for their protection in case of a lawsuit. But it did seem like everywhere I turned, there were those shop rules. Not many people told us that we did a good job.

Running Piss-Poor Quality

Cal

There are more memories of this general supervisor. His name was Cal. As we started up the 1975 model year production run, we had a "running" changeover. This I learned meant that you ran out all of the previous year's product, and then without stopping the production line, the very next part became the new or current model product. This year though was apparently different than the last few years. There were, if I remember correctly, brand-new parts that had never been run before. For the motor compartment rails, we used to add an energy-absorbing (EA) bracket that was an addition to the original design of the rail assembly. I believe it was government-mandated to limit damage to vehicles and the associated repair costs that were caused at lower speed fender benders. The 1975 rails had the EA bracket already formed in them, and we didn't need to add them anymore. I believe the engine cross member was a new configuration as well.

When the running changeover occurred, things didn't go very well. I remember waiting for what seemed like hours for all of the frames components to arrive by monorail to our fixtures. I believe some of them were hand-delivered to speed up the process. This working on and off was a production operator's worst nightmare. It made time go by slowly. Your body relaxed, and your mind wandered off thinking about things like getting out of there, rather than focusing on the job. The best scenario for a production operator was routine. That way, we could pace ourselves for the entire shift and then get the hell out of there. None of us ever came in on our own time to see how things were going; besides, it was a violation of the shop rules to be at work if it wasn't your assigned shift. This changeover didn't go well, and for me, as a line worker, it was an excruciatingly painful process.

This happened over a long period of time—I think throughout the late summer and early fall of 1974. Pressure must have been mounting because one night, we were all headed upstairs for a big meeting. I believe the production superintendent talked to us a bit about the new frame and our poor workmanship and productivity. Then Cal, the general supervisor, got up to speak. This was probably one of the worst efforts at motivation that has ever been tried on a group of willing workers. Cal didn't have the gift of gab, and he was very brief. He was in no mood to discuss with us what was going on or what problems we were encountering. He simply stated that he didn't know a whole bunch about life or anything else, but here was what he did know: "All I can tell you is that before they fire me, I'll fire every one of you sons of bitches first! Now get your asses downstairs and go to work!" Wow, did I feel motivated. I felt like going to work and achieving all that Cal wanted. Not! I felt just the opposite.

Before this running changeover occurred, I was very content running my numbers and achieving good quality. Now, I didn't understand why we weren't running, but I knew we were constantly short of parts, the ones we got fit poorly, and it took a monumental effort just to get all the parts

General Motors: Life Inside The Factory

together and then get the fixture to lock up properly. This went on all night long. We never could get in a good rhythm. Looking back, I can see some of the early fit problems must have been corrected because now the merry-go-round end of the process wasn't working properly; yet, after this highly motivating speech, we decided to go to war against Cal. The entire frame plant slowed down on second shift. There was no coordination of this effort. It was like we all understood collectively together. We searched high and low for any reason why we couldn't run. One of our highly regarded fixture buddies was a guy named Mark. He drove his daddy's big Caddy to work each night. I think he said his dad was a general foreman at the engine plant next door. Mark was an expert on coming up with ways of not running. I don't know how he did this, but the locating pins for the engine cross member had not been hardened or heat-treated. Mark could place the cross member just so, and when we locked the fixture in place, it would snap the locating pin right in two.

Not wanting to run poor quality or face the possibility of getting fired, we would sit down and wait for the foreman to come around. The foreman put up with us, so he must have understood what we were going through or maybe he was threatened as well. The foreman would go and get the die maker who would then replace the pin. After this happened a few times, the die maker started threatening us because he was tired of having to get up and replace the locating pin.

One night, as we were struggling, Mark couldn't break the pin anymore. So whenever he could, he would hit the locating pin with his hammer in an attempt to destroy it. One time, we loaded the fixture and were waiting on Mark to hold down his palm buttons. As he did this, he also swung his hammer. Somehow, the hammer became wedged between the lifters and another part of the fixture. It was wedged tight. This was not good because Mark or all of us could be written up for sabotage, which was a violation of the shop rules. Management was looking for any excuse to penalize all of us on the line. They were always looking.

If management could pin sabotage on you, you were fired and never brought back. Mark kept working to free his hammer. After a short while, he started wiggling it back and forth. It was getting looser and looser. What a relief! We were going to be okay. Then the hammer suddenly freed up and flew up into the air. Mark had placed himself over the hammer. It struck him square in the jaw. Mark was a fairly big guy. After the hammer struck him he just looked at us with a blank stare in his eyes. He stood up and then fell down onto the work platform. Mark was knocked out cold,

47

just like a heavyweight boxer! He woke up shortly after that, and we all started working as hard as we could. Later in the shift, the die maker came by and asked us if we liked the newly hardened locating pin. Hell no! He thought this was hilarious and walked away laughing. I think that pin is still in the fixture today.

It seemed like things were smoothing out, and we were starting to get our production numbers on a nightly basis. The running changeover was ending. But quality must have still been an issue. One night, we were all headed upstairs to the large conference room once again. It seemed like we were all collectively in trouble again. The production superintendent addressed us. He had just gotten back from a trip to one of our assembly plants on the East Coast. While he was out there, they found a quality issue. The steering control bracket was found to be either out of position or not fully welded to the side rail. I believe they found several hundred defects. He went out into the parking lot that was full of assembled vehicles and crawled underneath each of them to inspect this bracket. He pulled several of them off with his bare hands! Boy was he pissed at us! So here came Cal once again, just itching to fix this problem. He gave us the same old pep talk. We all knew that he knew that he didn't know much about life. But we all knew that Cal knew that before they would fire him, he would fire every one of us first. End of conversation, end of the meeting. Downstairs we went and back to work. The slowdown started all over again. Every time Cal came around the frame line, we would all start crying out, "Cal! Cal! Cal!" which was very similar to a birdcall. He didn't care much for that. Mercifully, I was never a part of a rolling changeover as a production operator again.

***

Flashback: General Motors Quality

Writing about the quality of our production parts during the rolling changeover leads me into my overall experiences with the quality of General Motors' production vehicles in the 1970s. There were many problems and they were universal and quite common.

Product quality in those days wasn't the greatest. The Big Three dominated the domestic marketplace and virtually told the consumers what they could buy and at what level of quality the domestic vehicles would be built. There were not many other choices back then. As I hired into the company, in the fall of 1973, the oil embargo opened up the door for the coming change. Soon, consumers would have ample choices, and they chose en masse any product but the Big Three's, first on each coast of the United States and then into the middle of the country.

The year my brother was scheduled to leave Vietnam, he wanted to buy a new car. Through my father's class-A discount, he was able to purchase a brand-new 1970 Chevrolet Camaro. It was a beautiful lime green with a 350-cubic-inch engine and a manual four-speed transmission. I was in my senior year of high school when my father brought it home. How envious I was of my brother's street-racing machine. I took it out for a spin, and the manual shifter came right out of the transmission. Uh-oh! *What do I do now?* My father was going to kill me. Somehow, I got the shifter back into place and got the car back home. I didn't say anything about my little incident. When my dad drove the car, the same thing happened to him. He wasn't very happy with this. My brother was due to come home soon, and he wanted the car ready for him.

One morning before school started, he drove it to Summerfield Chevrolet on Saginaw Street in Flint, and I followed him to the dealership. We were taking it in for service. I had never seen this before. The first problem we encountered was they were late opening up that morning; traffic was already out of the parking lot and filling up onto Saginaw Street. Soon, the service department opened up, and cars started pulling inside. When it was our turn, which was about an hour later, we were both late, he for work and I for school. My dad pulled her up into the service write-up area. He got out of the car as the serviceman approached us. My dad and he started discussing all of the issues that were wrong with the vehicle. It seemed like there were eight or ten quality defects that we had found. The serviceman was very interested in our case. He understood our issues. He wrote all of the defects up and took the car away to be serviced. My dad then took me to school. In a couple of days, we received a call that the car had been repaired, and we could pick it up. When we got the car home, my father discovered that they had fixed one or two things, but most of the quality items had not been touched. This didn't settle very well with my father.

The next morning, there we were again outside Summerfield Chevrolet waiting on Saginaw Street to get in for service. When it was our turn, the serviceman wrote up all of our quality issues. There was a full page. He was very interested in our problems and was very understanding. When the write-up was complete, he took the car away for service and my dad took me to school.

A few days later, we got the car back and … Yup—same old thing! By the time my father got the car home, he had found out that one or two things had been corrected, but the majority of items were left untouched. Well, this didn't go over very big this time. The next morning, there we were sitting on Saginaw Street waiting for the dealership service department to open. When it was again our turn to fill out a service report, my father demanded to talk with the service manager. He was in a take-no-prisoners mood. You didn't want to see this side of my father. The service manager, to my surprise, was belligerent right back at my father. They got into a pretty heated argument. It seemed like this was this man's service department and my father had no right to be angry. From my father's perspective, it seemed like my brother's Camaro was a piece of junk—the stick shift shifter lever wasn't even attached to the transmission and the car looked as if it had been painted with a vacuum cleaner. As I was listening to how to deal effectively with our dealership, I saw this event being repeated in what seemed like four or five areas of the service department. There was an ongoing symphony of warranty work being played out as far as my eyes could see! It seemed like we didn't build them like we used to. After this was over, my father took me to school. That car was never right.

The next opportunity I had to work with a dealership was when I bought my brand-new 1973 Pontiac Firebird. It had the same body style as my brother's 1970 Camaro, and my dad told me that they had had enough time to work the bugs out.

So mine wasn't so bad. But it wasn't perfect. With this vehicle, if I let my hands go off of the steering wheel, the car pulled hard to the left side. It was almost as if I was taking a left turn. I didn't know much about cars, but I knew if this weren't corrected, I'd soon be buying new tires for the front end. I took my car to the dealership for warranty work. We went through the write-up ritual. They kept my car. When I picked it up, the same thing was happening: the car pulled sharply to the left as if I was making a left turn. I returned to the dealer for warranty work, and we went through the write-up ritual. After a couple of days, I got my car back. Yup, same thing, no different! I took the vehicle back to the dealership and demanded to see the service manager. He too didn't accept unsatisfied customers in his service area. He told me to leave, and I did. I drove my car to the next dealership I came across which happened to be a Ford. They looked at my car and said they had never seen such a mess. They gave me a front-end alignment for free. I never had that problem with that Firebird again. Neither Summerfield's nor the Pontiac dealership made it. They both went out of business as competition in the auto industry heated up. Could you imagine if I wasn't a third-generation GM employee? Much like my experience at Sears, I would never have purchased another GM vehicle again. Having lived through the 1974 rolling changeover, I could begin to see why there were so many quality issues with our vehicles. Unfortunately, General Motors chose to build junk while our foreign competitors were focusing on quality, reliability, and customer care. It didn't take much back then to be ahead of General Motors, or the Big Three for that matter.

1976 Chevrolet Monte Carlo

In 1976, I ordered a brand-new Chevrolet Monte Carlo. This was a beautiful car. My dad again received his class-A discount because he was an engineer and on salary. I believe all salaried employees received this generous discount. In this case, my father was able to have the vehicle driven by an executive. The discount was even greater with miles driven on the vehicle. One time, while the vehicle was being driven in the Detroit area, a young man became very interested in the car. He asked if he could sit in it. The driver allowed him to do so. It turns out that the young man was none other than Denny Franklin, who was the starting quarterback for the University of Michigan. Now this car not only had a great appearance, but it had star power as well!

After the car had been driven the proper amount of miles in the company product evaluation program (PEP program), we went to Close Chevrolet in Linden, Michigan, to pick it up. I remember this well, because I wrote a check and paid cash for the vehicle. Man, was I happy. This was the first luxury vehicle I had ever owned. It had everything; it was loaded. Then I started experiencing problems with it. Being younger, I liked to have the radio loud. I blew the front speakers out. They didn't work. They emitted a terrible vibrating noise. I took the vehicle to the dealership for service. The service manager took a look at my Monte Carlo. I turned the radio on and turned the volume up. The front speakers sounded terrible. When I say I turned the volume up, I don't mean as high as it would go. It was probably a little more than halfway up. Surely, the speakers were engineered to accept this much power to them. The service manager thought about this for a little bit. Then he turned the radio station over to a classical music channel. This type of music didn't use as much bass. He turned the volume down to a barely audible level. He looked over at me and said the speakers sounded fine to him. Man, I couldn't believe this!

He refused to replace the speakers. He said because they would have to take the entire dash assembly apart to replace the speakers, it would cause more problems than it would solve. That was it, case closed! Dumb me, I went home and installed a new set of quality speakers myself. Oh, by the way, the service garage was full of drivers seeking new car warranty work just as it had been at Summerfield's several years earlier.

Imagine this going on at virtually every General Motors dealership in the entire United States. GM's philosophy of build them, get the numbers no matter what, and then fix them later was in full bloom. However, they were blind to the fact that the consumers were tired of taking their brand-new vehicles back to the dealers over and over again. They just wanted their vehicles to work like they were supposed to, like the advertisements of them portrayed. With the advent of two-income families, they didn't have the time anymore to spend at the dealerships haggling over this and that. It was a terrible practice to begin with. The Japanese took full advantage of this opportunity. They strived to build dependable vehicles that needed less warranty work, not more. They heard the American consumers' complaints about things not working as expected. They saw that the philosophy of build them with quality defects and fix them at the dealership was a money-losing business venture, both in terms of pure profit and also in terms of customer ill will. General Motors, on the other hand, in the isolated cocoon of its business world, never saw this threat to their outdated business model. The upper executives were too wrapped up in getting their bonuses and increasing the price of the stock that made them even more money! Manufacturing was a mere holding company for their banking needs.

Starting in the early 1970s, American consumers had plenty of choices they could make when purchasing a new vehicle, and they were beginning to vote with their feet. They turned their backs on General Motors in droves. The arrogance at General Motors' top levels never allowed them to fully address the paradigm change that was beginning to occur in the domestic marketplace. It was also becoming fashionable to drive foreign manufacturers' products, such as BMWs and Toyotas.

***

Now that I was an employee of GM, I witnessed firsthand how they managed product quality. My experience proved to be a valuable lesson in how not to run good quality. GM executives were experts in running poor quality and focusing the major blame on their hourly workforce. We hourly never had a chance to participate in quality problem solving. It was pretty much a run-all-you-can-or-we'll-fire-you mentality, just like Cal told us in the "big meetings" upstairs.

There are a few more experiences from second shift that I've found worthy to write about. These incidents take us back into the time I spent working on the night shift with the young and carefree guys ...

Car Wreck

One night, for some reason, we were let out of work fairly early. Being young and single, we weren't about to go home. We all went out to Kenny's house—he was a wise old product repairman—to play cards for the rest of the night. We partied long and hard that night, enjoying games of euchre and poker. There was plenty of booze flowing freely. I left Kenny's around two in the morning. Kenny lived in Mt. Rose, Michigan, which was north of Flint. I drove straight down Mt. Morris Road heading west toward the I-75 expressway. I'm not sure what exactly happened next. I was driving my 1973 Pontiac Firebird. I loved that car. It fulfilled for me the longing for a muscle car I had had when I was in high school a couple of years back. I had jacked the rear end up with air shocks. This gave the vehicle a racing-car look. I always had the maximum amount of air in those shocks. It made for a very bumpy ride. I also replaced the wheels and the tires. I had a beautiful set of Cragar mag wheels put on oversize tires. I purchased the widest set of tires for the back that I could find. They had to be special ordered, and I waited six weeks for them to come in. I was disappointed though, because after they were installed, the outer edges of the tires scraped against the inner edges of the rear wheelhouse. But I loved that car, and I was very proud of her. I had a cassette tape deck, top-of-the-line, installed at Duke's Tape Shack.

Because the rear end was jacked up, I couldn't see anything out of my rearview mirror at or near street level. The rear window wasn't very big to begin with, and I added to it to create a huge blind spot. One time, I was backing up, and I knocked over someone's motorcycle. I paid cash for the damage. From then on, someone would have to get out and guide me in as I backed up. I didn't care; I loved that Firebird.

As I was going down Mt. Morris Road, which is fairly straight, I began to push the accelerator pedal down. The car responded immediately and took off. I kept going faster. I remember my grandmother saying as I was growing up and misbehaving that it was the devil pinching me. Well, at this point, he was using his full pitchfork because I was going well over one hundred miles per hour. I was flying down that road. Then I believe I hit a dip in the road. I wonder if maybe my front end left the ground. I lost control of the car and started swerving all over the place. Suddenly, I crossed the centerline and flew into the drainage ditch. My front end somehow cleared the ditch, and I later found out my rear end caught the top of the far side. I flew past the ditch and went into a field. I was spinning, spinning out of control. It felt like I was never going to stop spinning. In those days, I didn't wear a seat belt. I don't remember anybody wearing seat belts then. Then I asked God for a deal. I told him that if I didn't die in this field, I would never drive in this condition again. He must've agreed with me because finally I came to a stop. I reached for a wad of gum and put all that I could chew into my mouth. I got out of the car. I was unhurt and very sober. I got back into the car and tried to start the engine. The engine wouldn't start. Soon, there were people there helping me. I bummed cigarettes from those people to calm my nerves and hide the alcohol on my breath. A Michigan state trooper arrived, wrote a report, and called a tow truck for me. I arrived home around three thirty in the morning riding shotgun in the tow truck. I was very lucky. If this had taken place a few years later, I would have and should have gone to jail.

Back then, there wasn't the social stigma attached to drinking and driving. I remember being at parties with my parents when I was around ten or so; as people left, they were given drinks. These were truly "one for the road." If the police stopped you then, I believe they thought it was humorous and sent you on your way.

Fixture Wars

As part of our assembly process, we had two assembly fixtures, one in the front and one in the back of the main conveyor. There were two sets of three man crews. The merry-go-round ran a production number of 120 parts per hour. Therefore, each fixture was required to run sixty parts per hour. Now our brethren on the other fixture were bigger and meaner than we were. It was kind of like the fraternity brothers versus the greasers, or better yet, David versus Goliath. You see, they had a great big stud on their crew named Skip. Skip was their enforcer. We had no one to compare to him on our fixture. Whatever Skip said, that was the way it was. Skip was so mean he hung out at Walton's Bar in Fenton, Michigan. Not many people could hang out there and live to tell about it. My only time there ended up in a big ol' bar fight.

Anyway, we got along like brothers back on the fixtures. Skip was the big brother, and we were the little brothers. Skip was king. We were on the back fixture, which meant that the front crew would have to hold their frames back to allow ours to go forward. This was supposed to happen one for one. There was many a night when Skip decided that we didn't deserve to get any frames to the merry-go-round. Skip would feed his frames onto the conveyor until he was tired, and then we would have to work like hell to catch up while Skip rested.

One night, we decided not to take it anymore. When Skip refused to let our frames pass by, we pushed them over his frames and onto the take-away conveyor. Well, this pissed Skip off royally. There were about five frames on the conveyor between our fixture and his. Skip went crazy and threw all of our frames off of the conveyor and onto the floor all around us. We conceded that night, not knowing what to do. Skip loaded his frames first for the rest of the night. He had won the battle and remained the king.

Another night, things weren't going well. Skip once again was stopping our frames from getting to the merry-go-round. Things went back and forth for most of the shift. Skip's fixture numerically was well ahead of ours. Finally, we had had enough, and words were exchanged. Suddenly, Skip got so pissed off he picked up a side rail, which weighed over forty pounds, and flung it at us like a big spear. It shot through the air and landed on our work platform. Whoa! That was the end of that. Skip could have all the spaces he wanted. It wasn't worth getting killed over. I guess we didn't match up to the physical toughness of the place. This went on for the better part of two years.

Education

Throughout all of 1974, I kept bugging the UAW apprentice coordinator to get me on an apprenticeship. Finally, out of frustration and with continual denial of the secret testing preparation being conducted at the union hall, he said if I was to take college classes in blueprint reading and hydraulics, he would see what he could do. I enrolled at Mott Community College for the second semester of the 1974–1975 school year. I took basic hydraulics, technical math one, and bowling. (I received credit from my time in the marines for physical fitness and needed one additional hour to complete this requirement.) My academic counselor selected these classes. I believe I was laid off at the time, and for the first time, I was finally ready to advance my formal education. It had not come easily for me. I had barely made it through high school, like my mother before me. My father had quit high school to begin an apprenticeship at Chevrolet in the 1940s. Then he served in the United States Marine Corps in World War II. He finally graduated from high school when my older brother was graduating from Flint Northwestern in 1967. We had a good laugh when my father put on my brother's cap and gown for a picture. My home life was not conducive to formal education. From what I remember, nobody's in our neighborhood was. If there were such people, they were few and far between.

***

Flashback: Education

I started my education in the Flint school district. I attended Selby Elementary School until the fourth grade. Then our family moved to a different neighborhood a couple of miles away. At that time, my parents enrolled us in a private parochial school. I entered fifth grade at St. Luke's school in Flint and found myself in way over my head. The private school was leap years ahead of the public one I had attended. I also think my glasses situation must have attributed to this as well. I couldn't see the blackboard clearly. How could that not have affected my academic progress? Couple that with a weakened self-confidence, and I struggled with academics in fifth grade. Looking back, I wonder if I should have been placed into fourth grade rather than fifth. Somehow, I made it through, but I was never a smart kid. I was always at the bottom of my class standings.

St. Luke's school went up to the eighth grade. After that, we moved on to one of the area's Catholic high schools. I went on to St. Michael's school, which was located in downtown Flint. I attended St. Michael's for one year. That was ninth grade. For the beginning of tenth grade, my parents offered me a choice between St. Michael's school and Flint Northwestern. I was ready to move on, so I chose Northwestern. If I could do do-overs, I would choose to stay at St. Michael's. It was a wonderful school and was very small. There were around twelve hundred kids from kindergarten through the twelfth grade. There were approximately one hundred kids per grade. It was a very disciplined place with a premium put on education. My graduation class would have been the last one for St. Michael's. The Lansing Diocese was building a larger high school, Flint Powers, for all of the area Catholic students. It was scheduled to open its doors in the fall of 1970.

Flint Northwestern

My first memory of Flint Northwestern is its large size. It consisted of three grades: tenth, eleventh, and twelfth. There were over twenty-five hundred students attending the school when I walked in the doors. That averaged around eight hundred students per grade. Not all of us made it to graduation. The school was in its fourth year of operation. This was a very new building. In fact, it was the newest high school in the Flint area. This was where I first encountered kids from other ethnic backgrounds. There was a busing program that brought kids to the school from all areas of the city. I believe my first year at Northwestern, around 70 percent of the students were white and around 30 percent were minority students.

While I still didn't apply myself, I received better grades at Northwestern because the classes were easier than at St. Michael's. This was the reversal of when I went from public to private school. I maintained a 2.4 grade point average. If I would have remotely applied myself, it could easily have been a 3.0. I was still adjusting to the new school and the bigness of it right through the first semester.

During the second semester in April of 1968, Martin Luther King was assassinated. Shortly after that, some students applied to hold a rally in his honor at the school. I remember that morning well. I was lucky that I was in biology class. The biology classroom was located in the back of the school and had a set of exit doors that led directly to the outside nearby. We were alerted ahead of time by the school that there was going to be a peaceful demonstration in honor of Doctor King. The demonstration started off peacefully but soon turned violent. Every so often, you could hear the demonstrators marching down the halls. Then they started knocking on the doors daring those of us who stayed in the classrooms to come out into the hallway. The principal came over the PA system and told us to stay in our classrooms and instructed the teachers to lock the doors. A lot of the kids left the classroom to join in the demonstration. There we were, just a small few who didn't exit the room, locked up and scared. The demonstration was getting larger and more violent. Friends told me that some of the demonstrators were opening doors and dragging kids out of their classrooms. Some were beaten pretty badly.

After about a half an hour of this, the principal, after pleading with the demonstrators to stop, authorized us to leave the school. The teacher unlocked our door and looked down the hallway. The coast was clear, and we were signaled to leave. We exited the building right there by the biology lab and ran into the empty field behind the school. We ran for our lives. We didn't know what to do. Some of us decided to get to the west parking lot to see if we could get a ride home. The closer to the parking lot we got, the more we could hear the disturbance that was going on inside. Windows were busted out. There was a lot of smoke coming out of the building, and kids were running in a panic everywhere. I found a friend who had a car, and we quickly left the school premises.

I'm not sure how order was restored at the school. The school board closed the school for a couple of days. I think they referred to this as a cooling-off period. When I returned to school, there were uniformed police officers, fully dressed in their riot gear, shotguns in hand on guard in the building. Flint Northwestern would never be the same for me. There was quite a bit of racial tension left over from the riot. At lunchtime, I entered the cafeteria. It had windows on three sides if I remember correctly. Most of the windows had been broken during the disturbance. The tables and chairs were all busted up. Many of the bathrooms had been set on fire. I don't recall any other incidents for the rest of that school year, just the usual fighting. I had not been aware of the racial tension in the school until this event happened.

Each of the following two years around the same time, there was some type of large disturbance at the school. But now we heard about it ahead of time, and we would skip school that day to avoid any altercations. The second and third incidents were not as violent or large as the first one. By my senior year, the ratio of minority to white had reversed itself. The student makeup of the school was now 70 percent minority and 30 percent white. That ratio had reversed itself in a short three years' time. When I graduated from Northwestern in June of 1970, I walked off the football field where the graduation ceremony was held and have never returned. When I walked out of the school building, it had been operating for six full school years. It looked like it was twenty to thirty years old. They never fixed all of the broken windows in the cafeteria after the second disturbance. Some of them were still boarded up. We also had tables with large holes in them and chairs that had been piecemealed together. Again, after the second racial disturbance, they never replaced the tables and chairs as they did the first time. The bathrooms were a wretched site, and some of them were off limits because there was too much violence committed in them. No wonder my degree from that place wasn't very valuable.

Hanging Out with the Wrong Crowd

While I was at Flint Northwestern, I hung out with some unsavory characters (not all of the people I hung out with were, though). We skipped a lot of school and drank a lot of beer. Sometimes in my senior year, we did that first thing in the morning before going to class. I thought this was pretty cool at the time.

On nights and weekends, we were always in someone's car driving around drinking beer. One night, we decided to drive up north. So away we went listening to the radio and bullshitting all the way up there. Once we were up there, we didn't know what to do. The common saying for up north was that they "rolled the sidewalks up at eight o'clock at night." This was in the wintertime, and it was cold that night. We decided to go driving around on one of the local lakes. This was very common back then. The ice fishermen did it all winter long. We did this for a while, spinning the car around in complete circles. Then this also became boring. We were looking for other things to do.

We then had the bright idea to get more alcohol. It was late, and all the stores in town were closed. Besides, of the four of us, no one was even close to the legal drinking age of twenty-one. I had been buying alcohol since I was sixteen years old though. We would drive to a party store located in the "bad" part of Flint near the Buick complex on Industrial Boulevard. We would walk in and purchase whatever alcohol we wanted. No questions were asked. The first time I did this, I was extremely nervous, but I placed my six-pack of Colt 45 malt liquor on the counter, took out my wallet like I had done this for years, and paid for my purchase. I remember feeling shaky on the inside though, and at any time, I was ready to pee my pants. The lady at the cash register rang me up, and off I went. I didn't even know what Colt 45 was at the time, but that was what the other customers were buying that night and they had great commercials on television. I soon learned that Colt 45 packed a hard punch! By the time I was a senior in high school, I was an old pro at buying alcohol.

So there we were driving around with nothing else to do, and we were out of alcohol. We decided that if we couldn't buy beer, we would take some. The guy driving spotted a party store that was in a remote location near the lake we were driving on. They started making plans to break into the place. I think it was at this point that my life changed. I realized deep down inside of me that I wanted no part of breaking into a store and committing a robbery. The only thing I could think of was to fake passing out, so I wouldn't have to participate in the event. I couldn't imagine my father's reaction to this if we were caught. I knew I was guilty by association. They did stop at the store, and the driver pried the rear door open. I could hear them talking. The other three took turns carrying liquor and beer to the car and filling up the trunk. We then took off and made a hasty retreat back to Flint. I knew then that I was hanging out with the wrong crowd. I probably couldn't explain who the right crowd was exactly, but I knew this wasn't it. I signed up for a three-year hitch in the marines shortly after this episode. I knew I needed to get away from these guys; otherwise, I wouldn't have the willpower or the guidance to separate myself from them. So I graduated from high school June 17, 1970, and left for Marine Corps boot camp August 3, 1970. This was the best thing I accomplished in my younger life. The marines were good for me at the time. They gave me a stable life, taught me how to set and achieve goals, and provided much-needed self-discipline.

I thought about staying in forever, but I knew this lifestyle was not what I was seeking long-term. When my enlistment was running out and I was a "short timer," the wife of one of our sergeants had a baby, and she was named Marina Cora. Whoa! That didn't settle well with me. Then I came across an officer who had been badly wounded in Vietnam. One of his eyes had been shot out. I was told to look at his glass eye closely, and I would see it. The "it" was the Marine Corps insignia: the eagle, globe, and anchor. It was the retina replacement in his glass eye. I knew long-term I had to get the hell out of there. So after my enlistment ended, home I went. I signed up for a full schedule of classes at the local community college. After three weeks of attempting to go to college, I knew I wasn't ready for it yet. I dropped out of college and signed up to work for General Motors.

***

Telling the story of my education leads me into the subject of the city of Flint. Flint was a wonderful place in which to grow up. Life was good in Flint during the 1950s and 1960s. There was plenty of everything. There was plenty of money, resources, and people. The Genesee Valley Shopping Center opened its doors in 1970. This was the first enclosed mall I had seen. It was one of the highest revenue grossing malls in the country for several years, a sign of the seemingly unending good times that had gone on for years. In the early 1970s, it seemed to begin to change.

***

Flashback: Flint Childhood

As I said, Flint was a wonderful place in which to grow up. During my childhood years, it was a land of plenty. There were plenty of people, plenty of jobs, and plenty of money. Flint became a symbol of the success of the entire country leading into the 1960s.

When I was born in 1952, my parents lived in a popular section of Flint called Flint Park. We lived on Flint Park Boulevard near Dupont Street. I really don't remember the house. We must have moved out of it when I was around three years old. I do remember driving past the house later, and my parents showing us the old house. It had a coal furnace, and my dad had to shovel the coal into it to keep the house warm in the winter. It sounded like a lot of work. Two things stick out in my memory of that place.

There was a very popular meat market called Stanley's Market. For years after we moved, my parents would always crave the meats from Stanley's. I remember the different types of sausages and fresh cut meat we bought from there. I can recall the different smells that were in the building. For some reason, I distinctly remember the highly polished wood floors.

There also was an amusement park located nearby. It too was called Flint Park. I vaguely remember riding all of the rides in the park. It was a pretty old place by then. It must have shut down before I was too old. After it shut down, it still had a roller rink that remained opened. When I was around seven or so, we would skate there quite often. At the end of the skate time, the operators would hold races by age group to see who could skate the fastest. One time, I won my race! I must have been a fast skater. For my prize, I received a Snickers bar. Man, was I proud of that.

There was a small lake adjacent to the park's property. It was called "Devils" Lake. Local folklore had it that it had no bottom. It was claimed that many a person had gone swimming in Devils Lake and never returned. The bottom of the lake was full of muck. My grandfather told me that when he was younger, the circus would come to town once a year. The promoters of the circus would make the elephants swim across the lake to attract attention for the show. Later, when I was twelve or thirteen, my friends and I would ride our bikes to the lake and float on rafts that we had put together across the water. There were two problems with this. If the Flint police came by, they would make you get off the lake and may take you home to tell your parents. And that was the second problem, if your parents found out that you had been floating on Devils Lake, you'd never hear the end of it. Occasionally, I'd see an article in the *Flint Journal* about a drowning in Devils Lake. It must not have been a nice place.

My parents moved to a small, modern ranch home located in Manly Village when I was around three or four years old. I say it was modern because it had a natural gas furnace. No more shoveling coal for my dad. It was probably a good thing for me as well, because it wouldn't have been too awfully long before I probably would have been shoveling right along with him. It was a very small house. I believe the most it could have been was eleven hundred square feet. This included three bedrooms, one bathroom, a kitchen, and a living room. I remember the one bathroom being a problem. At the time, there were three of us boys in the house. It seemed as if every time my parents would get in there, one of us kids would have to go really bad. This seemed to happen a lot.

The house came with a built-in milk chute. Back then, the dairy company would come by and deliver fresh milk and pick up the empty bottles. But that's not what I remember most about the chute. Whenever my parents would lock themselves out of the house, they would send one of us kids through the chute to open up the back door. This didn't happen often, but it happened a couple of times. The chute must not have been very large, because I don't remember my older brother going through it. It wasn't too long after that that the milk companies stopped home deliveries.

Some of my memories of Shamrock Lane include a picture of me in a cowboy hat sitting on a horse. Apparently, a man would come down the street once a year to take these pictures. I believe all of the kids from the village have one of these pictures in their photo albums.

Flint School System

I remember the school system. It was strong at the time. It must have been around 1957. During the summers, we attended Tot Lot. This was a program designed to keep us kids occupied while we were out of school. We sang songs like "Found a Peanut" and played games like Red Rover. Tot Lot was held in the primary units. These units were smaller buildings that held one classroom of children. They were built across the street from the big school building. The big building was named Selby School. At the end of Tot Lot, the school held a potluck dinner or an ice cream social. All the kids and parents would come to the school, eat dinner, and have ice cream for dessert.

Also in the summers, the Flint school system had a full-blown recreational program, mainly sporting activities. I remember playing Little League baseball. I also remember not being very good at it. The baseball fields would be packed full of kids. There was always a ton of kids everywhere you went in Flint.

I went to the primary units from kindergarten through the third grade. For fourth grade, I was transferred over to the big school, Selby. That was a scary first day "in the big school." I believe Selby School housed fourth, fifth, and sixth grades. That year would be my only one spent at the big school.

Once a year, the Shrine Circus would come to town. The Flint school system supported this activity. They would load all of us students up on the city buses and take us to the circus on school time. We got a day off to attend the show. This was a really big deal. I can remember squealing with delight during the circus.

Flint had a planetarium. The school system actively supported it as well. Once a year, we would be bused to the planetarium to see the current celestial show. We learned a lot about the stars, planets, and solar system.

During this time, the City of Flint developed a very good library system. I believe it was one of the first of its kind. Rather than having independent libraries, the local libraries joined forces. Everywhere you went in Flint, it seemed as if there was a neighborhood library. These buildings were full of books. Books were everywhere. I can remember reading and reading and reading. The school system did a good job of providing plenty of books for everyone to read.

Mott Camp

One summer, I was able to attend Mott Camp. This camp was available to kids from the Flint area. I do not know exactly where it was located. I remember the day we left. We went to the Selby School parking lot and waited for the truck to arrive. The truck was a stake-bed model. All of our gear and all of us campers were packed into the back of the truck, and off we went for two weeks of camping.

I remember two full weeks of activities. It seemed I became very good at making leather belts. You could purchase an unfinished belt from the camp store, and the counselors would help you complete the final product. Usually, we stamped our names into the leather. On the first weekend, our families would come to visit us. Many of the campers would cry when their parents left because they were homesick. Not me, I enjoyed my stay, and I knew it would only last one more week.

The last night at the camp was a thriller. As dusk began to fall, the counselors rounded all of us campers up and led us to a huge bonfire. There was some type of treat provided to us. Then when it became pitch-dark, the counselors began to tell us spooky stories. As the evening progressed, I became scared out of my wits. I just knew that lurking in the darkness a few feet away were terrible creatures just waiting to tear me apart.

For the grand finale, they told us a story about the hermit who lived on Mott Lake and how he tortured children just like ourselves. This went on for about an hour. They built the story up to a resounding crescendo. Then out of the darkness from the lake here came the hermit. You couldn't see his face because his coat covered it. He was all in black and wore a stocking cap. He was hunched over like the hunchback of Notre Dame. Holy shit was I scared!

The entire assembly took off running. We were all running for our lives. We ran all the way to our sleeping quarters and shut the door. It was hard to fall asleep after that. The next day, we packed up our gear and headed back home.

Local Drug Store

During this time, we didn't have the huge mega stores like we do today. We had grocery stores, but they were single-purpose stores. If we needed prescriptions filled, we went to Kilbourn's drugstore located on Fleming Avenue. Kilbourn Drugs was a little specialty store. It had an old-fashioned soda fountain in the back. You could go there and get a homemade milk shake or cherry Coke. That was pretty cool. If we needed specialty meats, we either went to Stanley's Market or to the new Quality Market that had just opened up adjacent to Kilbourn Drugs. The city of Flint had all of the amenities readily available and in close proximity to your house. Back then, we only had one car. When Dad went to work, you had to walk everywhere. And walk we did. We walked everywhere.

Movie Theaters

On the weekends, we kids were dropped off at the local theaters to enjoy watching the matinees. I remember nothing but kids at these movie houses. There were hundreds of kids. I remember finding it difficult to find a drop-off point near the theater because of all of the kids being dropped off or picked up. This was a big deal. We didn't have the entertainment sources we have today. The two movie houses I remember going to were the Delta and the Capitol theaters. One of them must have been a throwback to the vaudeville days. It had a stage and a huge organ. I remember some old lady playing the hell out of that organ while seemingly hundreds of kids were running around in chaos in the theater. The more she played, the more we ran around throwing our candy at each other.

Once the show started, the ushers restored order and were very strict. You were a dead man if they shined their flashlight on you during the movie. If they shined their flashlight on you a second time, you were unceremoniously escorted out of the theater. You didn't want your parents to discover you had misbehaved.

The movies themselves were mostly Westerns. They were the classic cowboys-and-Indians movies. The cowboys always won. There was Rin Tin Tin and the Lone Ranger with his faithful sidekick, Tonto. There was Gene Autry, the singing cowboy; Roy Rogers; and Dale Evans. We kids spent many afternoons at the movie matinees.

Next House

Around this time, my parents moved once again. They moved about two miles from our Shamrock Lane home to a house on LeErda Street. This is the home I remember most while growing up in the city of Flint.

We were clearly moving on up with the new house. This house was around fourteen hundred square feet. It was a Cape Cod–style home. It had four bedrooms. The upstairs was huge compared to that of the tiny house on Shamrock Lane. The biggest feature was it came with one and a half baths! Now my father could sit on his throne and not be disturbed.

I had just completed the fourth grade when we moved that summer of 1962. I remember walking home from school on the last day. There was the moving van packing up all of our stuff. My mother was quite happy because she was remaining close to her parents. My dad had wanted to move to the new suburb of Grand Blanc, but my mother wouldn't hear of it. There was no way she would live with her parents that far away from her. I remember my father arguing "far away from what?" The "what" was my grandparents, who lived on Kermit Street just off of Pierson Road.

There was no way my grandparents were going to move away from the church, Saint Michael's Byzantine that was located on the corner of Pierson and Fleming Roads. My mother was part of a large family. Both of my grandparents' families were quite large. I believe there were ten or eleven siblings on each side. They all mostly attended Saint Michael's church together. Saint Michael's was a Byzantine Catholic church. It followed the Eastern Orthodox Catholic traditions. My father was a Roman Catholic, who followed the Western Catholic traditions. I believe it wasn't fondly looked upon when my parents first got together because of this. After my parents were married, we followed the Roman Catholic traditions of my father.

My grandparents' families on my mother's side were from what was then Czechoslovakia. They were the first generation born in the United States. My grandfather's family came to Flint from Pennsylvania. In his early years, my grandfather had worked in the coal mines there. The families moved to Flint because of the jobs the auto industry provided.

Weddings and Such

I remember a lot of my early life revolved around family activities associated with the church, mainly weddings and funerals. Weddings were the best back then. The wedding Mass would take place on Saturday morning around nine or ten. Then we would all proceed to the church hall where the ladies' auxiliary would serve up a huge breakfast. It consisted of eggs, potatoes, sausages, and bread. This was truly a feast. The food would be in large bowls and placed on the tables by the servers, usually young girls in training for the auxiliary. My dad would wink at them, and we would get served first most of the time. After the breakfast was over, the assembly would break up for the rest of the day. We were on our own until it was time for dinner. Then once again, we would all head back into the church hall for a dinner. This too was very good and served by the ladies' auxiliary. They cooked all of the food themselves.

After the dinner was over and the tables were cleared, the reception would start. This consisted of a polka band and plenty of booze. The booze that was served back then was draft beer and Seven and Seven's. This was Seagram's Seven whiskey mixed with 7-Up pop. Some of the men would volunteer to man up the bar for the night. They would pour the beer into pitchers and place them on the serving counter. Guests would come up and exchange empties for full pitchers. The men would mix the Seven and Seven's and place them in large commercial coffee containers, and the guests would pour their own drinks. I remember us kids getting a taste every so often.

Later in the night, the bridal dance would be held. Here you could dance with the bride or the groom for a small donation to help them get started in their new life together. For your donation, you received a shot of whiskey. I remember both the women and men taking the shot. It was considered good luck for the bride and groom. On some occasions, people got a little carried away. I saw the attendants hold a special for the dance. Usually, the guests donated one dollar to dance with the married couple. If a special were held, the donor would get six shots for the price of five. What a deal this was!

This party would go on until one or two in the morning. There would be a dance floor full of adults and kids. There were kids everywhere. All the guests brought their kids. We played the entire night at the reception. If you were close family members, there would be a breakfast the next morning where the last day's leftovers were served. Weddings were a big deal back then.

For funerals, all of the families would go to the funeral home to pay their last respects to the deceased's family. This went on for three or four days. The day of the funeral, we kids were taken out of school. There would be a morning Mass said in the church. Then we would all proceed to the cemetery for the final rituals. After the cemetery, we would all go back to the church hall for a luncheon, a massive luncheon served by the ladies' auxiliary. Once again, the food was extremely good and plentiful. After the lunch, the assembly would break up. If you were a close family member, you would head over to the family's house for drinks and more socializing. These funerals took up pretty much the whole day. I can remember the long lines of cars in procession on the way to the cemetery. They placed neat little flags on your car, and you had to drive with your lights on. We got to run all of the red lights and stop signs on the way. No other cars would cut into the funeral procession—not only was this disgraceful, it was considered bad luck.

Church gatherings occurred for baptisms, first Communions, and confirmations. Graduations from high school were a big deal as well, but they were not church functions. But once again, the families would all gather and celebrate the event.

Some of the other events that occurred at my grandparents' church were just as rich in enjoyment and family. Every Friday night, the men put on a fish fry. They did all of their own cooking. All of the money raised went back to the church coffers. People would come from miles around to buy their fish. It was very good. When my grandfather came home on Fridays after the fish fry, he would sometimes bring with him leftover bits of fish. This was another feast in itself.

The church had a thriving men's club. This was a private place where the men of the church could gather, socialize, and nip a few drinks (thank goodness for confession). I remember at first, the club was located in a dingy room in the church's basement. Later, as the congregation built a modern social hall, it included a very nice men's clubroom. Occasionally, my grandfather would take me with him to the club. I remember him drinking beer there, and I had to promise him I wouldn't tell my grandmother (as if she didn't already know). My grandfather would get a small glass from the cupboard and pour me a sip of beer to drink. I still remember him telling me not to let the alcohol control me. I was to control it. Hey, Gramps, I still control "it" today. Thank you for your patience and teachings so many years ago.

Downtown

One of the other things we used to do as kids was take the bus downtown on weekends. This started for me when we moved to our house on LeErda Street. We would step up into the green-and-yellow bus's compartment, deposit five cents into the coin slot, and on our way we would go. I never remember any threats or physical danger. We would soon arrive downtown to a sea of people. There were people everywhere. You couldn't walk down the street without constantly bumping into people, mostly kids. We would shop around for hours. We would always go to the Smith Bridgman's department store to look around. This is where my mom always took us to buy our school clothes. I don't remember having much money, but I remember purchasing a few things now and then. What I remember most is waiting for the bus to come and take us home. We always waited outside of Kresge's dime store. In Kresge's, they sold caramel corn. This is fresh popcorn with caramel poured over it. It was the best popcorn I'd ever had. We would buy a bag and devour it on the bus ride home.

Holidays

Holidays were huge events back then as well. I especially remember Halloween in the city. The night of Halloween, all of us kids would put our costumes on and go trick-or-treating. We would go house to house and receive our treats, which were for the most part candy. Here and there, a dentist might give us an apple or a toothbrush. We would receive tons of candy. It didn't take too long to fill up our bags as the houses were packed closely together. If we covered two square city blocks, we had more candy than we could ever eat. I remember spilling my candy on the living room floor and going over it to see all of my treasures. This was the time before people placed needles or drugs into the kids' candy. I never heard of any child abductions. I believe it was still a time of innocence in our society. I mostly remember the thousands of kids who were out in the streets trick-or-treating. It was a fun time.

Mainly though, the holidays revolved around the church and its traditions. Christmas was a huge holiday time for us. Not only did we receive presents, but we spent a great deal of time in church celebrating the birth of Christ. The days before the celebrations were the time to get ready. There was always plenty of food during the holidays. To get the food, we went to the grocery store. The local grocery store in Flint was Hamady Brothers. They were everywhere by the time I was in grade school. They opened up a new store in the Northwest Plaza, which was close to our house.

Hamady Brothers was the symbol of plenty. Its shelves were stocked full of every grocery item you would ever need. I can remember going there with my mother to shop for the holidays, especially Christmas and Easter. Upon our arrival, the parking lot outside the building would be packed full of cars. On the inside, it was hard to find an unused shopping cart. Once again, there were people everywhere. The store was crammed full of shoppers whose shopping carts were overflowing with holiday goodies.

For the holidays, my mother always bought a bag of nuts. I think this sticks out in my mind because we had to open the nuts with a nutcracker. I don't remember having nuts around other than at the holidays. Mom always had plenty of nuts around for our guests during that time.

Once we were done shopping, we had to stand in the checkout line to pay for our groceries. This was so boring to me when I was young. I didn't mind walking around the store and helping Mom by putting stuff in the cart, but standing in line was so boring. It felt like it took hours to get checked out. The lines were long. As we checked out, the carry-out boys would place our groceries in brown paper sacks. These sacks were typical back then. They were all printed with the Hamady Brothers logo on them. Around Flint, these bags came to be called "Hamady sacks." All of us old-timers from Flint knew the meaning of the term *Hamady sacks.*

The biggest Christmas celebration occurred for us on Christmas Eve. We would pack up and head over to my grandmother's house in the early afternoon. It seemed as if the whole world ended up over there. Their house wasn't any bigger than our eleven-hundred-square-foot home on Shamrock Lane. My grandparents had had this house built, and to them, it was a palace. With the entire extended family invited over for dinner, there was little extra room in the house. They would have to open the windows and doors to cool the house down later in the day, even though it was early winter in Michigan.

My grandfather had partly finished off his basement, and he had built a small bar in the room. This served as the main gathering place until dinner was served. All of the adults would begin socializing around the bar. Looking back, I realize this must have cost my grandparents an arm and a leg, as I don't remember anyone bringing food or booze with them to the celebration. This night was filled with lots of laughter and family bonding.

Then dinner was served. What a treat it was! My grandmother literally slaved away for about a week preparing for this meal. Most times, my mother would go over and help her out. When we were younger, my mom would bring us kids over with her. My grandmother prepared many of the traditional Czechoslovakian dishes. She made many types of breads, including nut bread and poppy seed bread. She also made nut cookies and sheregi (pronounced "she-deg-e").

She made homemade cheese and several other dishes. She also made a variety of pirohi's (they are better know as pierogis). This was the main dish of the night. These delights were filled with potato, sauerkraut, sweet cabbage, cottage cheese, and prunes. The sweet cabbage was the most popular. There were hundreds of these little pies there for the taking (you can now buy frozen pierogis from the grocery store. They are very good to eat, but they in no way compare to a grandma's home cooking). This meal was to die for. For us kids, she rolled some of the dough into small, round pieces that she called "worms." She also made a couple of different soups. The main one was potato with a few peas sprinkled in. One time, she told me the peas were her own addition to the recipe. I couldn't get enough of her potato soup. She served meats like ham, lamb, and sausages. Nobody cooks like that any more.

On the day before Christmas Eve, she would pack up a large basket of food and take it to the church to be blessed by her priest. She always left some food for him.

For some reason, my writing in this chapter doesn't begin to describe the food my grandmother always tirelessly prepared for all of us. This was a feast the whole extended family looked forward to for the entire year. Bless her heart!

After the dinner was cleared away and the dishes cleaned up, it would be getting near time to open the presents. We kids started going crazy. We couldn't wait; the anticipation was killing us. All of the adults were waiting nonchalantly telling us kids to calm down. Calm down, hell, we wanted to open our gifts! Finally, after what seemed like many tortuous hours, the adults were ready to open the gifts. We would all try to cram into the small living room. The living room was decorated with a live Christmas tree. They always put only blue lights on the tree. There wasn't much room left with the tree and all of the gifts that were stuffed—and I mean stuffed—under it. I couldn't wait to get my hands on my presents. I always felt that I had already waited long enough. Couldn't we hurry this up? I always eyeballed all of the gifts up earlier in the evening. We were not allowed in the room before time to open presents, but we always managed to sneak in there and eye up our presents when the adults weren't looking.

When the adults finally all got into the room and the anticipation was at a feverish crescendo, one of them would get the bright idea to sing Christmas carols before the present opening could begin. Man, were these people nuts? My hand would be right there, close to my prize, and they felt the need to sing. My older cousin said this always got him in the Christmas spirit. Christmas spirit, hell, I wanted my gifts.

So the singing would begin. It was made clear to us kids that if we didn't sing, we wouldn't receive our gifts. They could be given to the poor, thankful children at the Whaley orphanage. *Yuck!* So off we would all go, singing our little hearts out so we could receive our presents. We usually sang three or four carols. After we got started, it wasn't so bad. I can still see everyone's faces dimly lit by the Christmas tree lights as we sang Christmas carols.

Finally, it came time to open the gifts. Then some other adult would get the bright idea to call off one name at a time so we all could watch and see who got what. What the hell? It seemed that none of the adults could remember who got what last year, and it was a madhouse of confusion while the gifts were being opened. What the hell had they been drinking? Oh yeah, they'd been at Grandpa's liquor for a couple of hours by then. So they would begin calling off one name at a time while everyone had to watch what that person got. It didn't last too long, and then all hell would finally break loose and we all got to open our presents. If they had waited and gone one person at a time, they would have missed midnight Mass, as it would have taken so long. Finally!

After the gifts were opened, the night became anticlimactic. We never could play with our toys because we either lost all of the pieces to them or they would get broken. So then we had to wait until the adults were ready to leave. We usually broke up around nine at night or so. This happened pretty much every Christmas Eve until I went into the service.

Easter was an offshoot of Christmas. It was the biggest holiday of the church. We would again all assemble at my grandparents' house and eat a huge, home-cooked ethnic meal. At Easter, my grandfather would meet us at the back door when we arrived and say to us in Czechoslovakian, "Christ is risen," and we would repeat it back to him. That was about the only Czechoslovakian I ever learned. My grandfather was fluent in it.

Thanksgiving closely resembled the two religious holidays. The one exception was that it was not a religious day. We once again all assembled at my grandparents' house. Most of the men arrived later because they attended the Northern-Central high school football game. It was the high school football game of the year in Flint. It was held at Atwood Stadium. The place was packed with fanatic fans from both sides. It was usually a slugfest. Most of my family had attended Flint Northern. Their colors were gray and red. On Thanksgiving Day, you would see a lot of these colors around town and at my grandparents' house.

One note about my extended family: 99 percent of them worked for General Motors in some shape or form. General Motors provided the income for all of these events and this way of life. We had a mix of hourly and salaried employees. There were supervisors, engineers, and office workers in the family. On the hourly side, there were production workers and skilled tradesmen. These hardworking, dedicated people are the people who raised me. They were much more than the non-value-added status that General Motors attached to the majority of them. We all drove General Motors products. We hadn't heard about the Japanese yet.

IMA Auditorium

A group that had its ties to GM built the IMA Auditorium. It was a central gathering place for the people of the city of Flint. It could house around five thousand people in the arena. The IMA held many events in it. I have already written about the Shrine Circus being held there.

When we got older, my father would take us boys there to see the Golden Gloves. This was a yearly event held to determine the boxing champions of the greater Flint area. The contest was held over three or four sessions to crown the winners in each weight division. Typically, we would get to see one of these sessions. On fight night, the place was packed.

Tobacco smoke filled the arena. It was proper to smoke in public in those days. As the night progressed and the lights were turned down, you could see a smoke haze over the entire boxing arena.

The bouts were something to behold, as the young fighters displayed their talent. There were many knockouts that we were able to witness. One night, some poor kid was knocked unconscious by his opponent. He fell over backward. He was out cold. His head made a sickening thud as he hit the canvas. They had to take him out of the building on a stretcher, put him in an ambulance, and take him to the hospital. He died the next day from the blow to his head when he fell. An investigation revealed later that his head hit a metal brace that held the canvas floor in place. The fights were never the same intensity after that. At least that's how it appeared to me.

The IMA was one big party place on New Year's Eve. It seemed as though the entire town would pack up all of their party favors, hor d'oeuvres, and booze and head to the IMA to ring in the New Year. I know my parents did this religiously every year. To increase the seating capacity, they allowed the partiers to set up down on the main floor. That way, they got everybody inside. It was a huge event.

The IMA was getting older and more expensive to maintain. It was torn down, and Auto World was built in its place. This turned out to be an ill-conceived idea. It wasn't too long before it shut its doors for business. The property was donated to the University of Michigan Flint campus. It now houses a school building on its site.

A&W

There is one other Flint specialty that I need to bring up. That is the local A&W. There were three or four of these drive-ins located in the city. When we were younger, my parents would take us there on hot summer nights. We would park our car and turn our lights on for service. A waitress would come out to the car and take our order. We all got the famous A&W Root Beer. At first, I got a children's frosted mug. It was pretty small. Then I graduated to a full mug when I got bigger. That was the best root beer I've ever had. As the waitress served us our drinks, my dad would roll his window down halfway. The waitress would place the tray on the window, and my dad would distribute the glasses. Sometimes, we also got their hot dogs. These, I believe, were the best hot dogs in the world. They were Koegel Vienna's. Koegel's is a meat company located in the Flint area. Their Viennas are the best hot dogs you'll ever taste. The

Viennas have a skin encasing the hot dog. The A&W would steam cook the dogs and then heat up the buns so they were nice and moist. Then they would top them off with ketchup, mustard, and onions. I can still taste those hot dogs today. We frequently buy the Viennas and cook them on the grill. These are close to but not quite as good as the hot dogs we got back then from the A&W.

As I grew older and began to drive, I frequently made night trips to the A&W in the summer. In fact, it became a popular hotspot for all the kids from Flint. The one I'm talking about was located at Clio and Pierson Roads. We would go there, pull into a parking spot, get served, and then sit there for hours talking with our friends. Soon, this place became too popular. The parking lot would fill up, and the waiting cars would get backed up onto Clio Road. It seemed like the line to get into the place was a mile long. Once we got into the parking lot, we often couldn't find a place to park; they were all taken. I think this was a sign of the affluent lifestyles we were leading at the time. A lot of the kids now had their own cars. These weren't shabby cars either. These were newer ones. We had gone from the one-car family to a society that now had two or three cars per family. Now we even had one for the kids. This was where I would see all of the souped-up street machines. They were on display at the A&W every night all summer long. I believe the A&W also became a victim of its success.

It evolved to the point where they had to hire off-duty Flint police officers to maintain order. They had to police the place in essence. Once you finished your order, out you went so the next customer could find a spot to park. No more long conversations with the cars around you. This seemed to reach its peak the summer I graduated in 1970.

We kids managed to give the cops a hard time. You were never supposed to use your horn for service, only your lights. When we got a little rowdy, we would all start laying on our horns. The owner didn't like this. It tended to chase the families away. Younger families like mine a few years earlier had to come before dark to get proper family service. They had to get in and get out to escape the crazy kids who were coming.

The highlight of our summer was when one crazy kid jumped out of his car with a small tricycle. He had a yellow rain slicker on with the accompanying large yellow hat. He was mimicking Arte Johnson's character from the popular television show *Laugh In*. Arte Johnson would attempt to ride his too-small tricycle and always fell over into some precarious position. That's what this kid did. He hopped out of his car so fast the cops didn't know what he was doing. He pedaled his tricycle until he lost his balance and fell over. Then the cops reacted and caught up with him. I can't remember if they took him to jail or not. I wished I had the balls to do something like that back then. We were all amazed and had a good time over this.

This was the Flint that I grew up in. These are the memories I have from the place. It was all beginning to change back in the late 1960s, but we didn't recognize what was happening. We all assumed that the way it had been all of our lives was the way it would continue to be. Not so. General Motors did catch a cold, and Flint caught a serious case of pneumonia.

This takes us back to my story on my educational background. I was reviewing how I received my background in education. I have written about my high school experiences. With that time frame in mind, it's now important to write about how we came to move out of the city of Flint.

Moving out of Flint

Around the time of the disturbances at school (1967–1970), the neighborhood I grew up in was beginning to change as well. It had always been a wonderful place to live. Most of the occupants were the original homeowners. It was a very clean and safe place.

I can remember riding my bicycle for what seemed like hours and miles all summer long every year we were there. We used to ride down to Sarvis Park and play there quite often. At night, during the hottest part of the summer, we always left all of our doors and windows open to cool the house down. There was no crime or fear of violence. Every once in a while, there might be a fight, but it was just kids' stuff. As I said, it was a wonderful place to live and raise a family.

On the south side of our house, there was an empty lot. No one was allowed to build a house on it. My father inquired with the owner of the lot about purchasing it the first year we lived in the new house. The owner wouldn't sell. My father attempted to purchase one half of the lot, but he wouldn't do that either. My father wanted to purchase the lot so no one would ever build next to him. The owner assured him the lot was too small to build on according to the local building codes. There was nothing to worry about. My father never pursued the purchase of the lot again.

I believe it was in 1968 that the Flint City Council passed a fair housing act, which began to change everything, or a least change was coincidental with it. They started constructing what we understood to be 235 HUD homes on the lots that used to be too small to build on. In our three-block area, they built five of them. This started happening just before I left for boot camp in June 1970. They put up a 235 HUD home in the vacant lot next to our house. The lot was so small that there was no place for a garage. Our lot wasn't very big to begin with. I remember my father sitting on our porch in the summer and watering the entire front lawn with the hose nozzle held in his hand. In the backyard, we had a two-car garage and a sixteen-foot round, above-ground pool, and that was it. There was no more room. The vacant lot to the south was as deep as ours but much narrower.

The house was completed after I left for the service. A single mother with a four- or five-year-old child moved in. She had gotten a good job with the post office and a brand-new house in a good neighborhood. Well, this didn't last too long. She enjoyed the nightly bar scene more than working. Her car must have been a little old, and her muffler wasn't working right because you could hear her car coming from way down the block. Her parking spot was right next to my parents' bedroom window. She liked to get home late at night and for some reason leave the car running a while. My dad spoke to her about this, but that didn't go over very big. He was told to mind his own business. The next summer, my parents purchased a room air conditioner, so they could keep the windows closed. It was a minor inconvenience.

The lady's child was left alone frequently, and apparently, it was okay back then. My father struck up a friendly relationship with the little boy. He was stunned one day when he discovered that the little five-year-old child didn't even know his own last name.

The lady must not have been the greatest employee. She didn't last one year at the post office. She told my father she made better money on ADC. ADC is government aid for dependent children, which is a form of welfare. Now there was no restriction on the bar scene, which occurred every night. There were some late-night altercations with men as she arrived home from her night out. Our neighborhood was never the same. When I got home from the military after a three-year tour, there were not many of the original owners left. Probably 90 percent of the houses had changed ownership. I later learned that as soon as the 235 HUD homes were constructed, most of the neighborhood homes went up for sale. Including us, there were around five of the original families still there. Some homes had turned over two and three times already. The neighborhood was a mere shadow of what it had been a few years earlier.

This woman was evicted from her home after about eighteen months. When a building inspector was checking the house, my father went through it with him. The house was totally destroyed and was unlivable. The toilets and sinks had been ripped out and broken. The kitchen was all busted up. The house remained vacant after that. Years later, guys in the shop would buy homes like this for one dollar with a promise to fix them up and rent them out.

It must have been shortly after I was home from the service that my sister witnessed a strange event. She woke up early one Sunday morning to loud noises. When she looked out the front window, she saw vehicles pulled up to the neighbor's house across the street, and strange men were carrying out their possessions. This didn't seem right to her, so she called the police and took down the license plate number on one of the vehicles. When the police finally arrived, the intruders had left the house. The police took a full report from my sister. They were thankful and took the license plate number. Later, they reported back that they had traced it to a stolen vehicle in Michigan's Upper Peninsula. So much for that.

When we finally talked with the neighbors, they were devastated. Many items were taken during the burglary. They took all of their valuables, the couch, and the TV. They had been out of town attending a parent's funeral. They had been getting a lot of phone calls before the trip where the person on the opposite end would simply hang up. This happened frequently. The police told them there had been a lot of this lately and that the phone calls were the burglars checking to see if somebody was home. When our neighbors left to attend the funeral out of state, it triggered the burglars that the time was right. This greatly upset my father because we were frequently getting these same types of hang-up phone calls.

That was enough. That was the final straw, the one that broke the camel's back, as they say. My father had wanted to move for several years. My mother was content to live in the city. She was very close to her parents who lived a few short miles away. There was no way my grandparents were going to move away from their church, which was located within walking distance of their home on Kermit Street. They were very active in the church.

Despite the objections from my mom, my father decided to move. He put his house on the market for sale. He was very disappointed in the selling price. It was selling for the same price he had purchased it for after fourteen years of ownership. It seemed like if his house was located in the Grand Blanc area, it would have doubled in value during this time. The house was very nice and in good shape. It sold for the asking price to the first person who came through.

Now I saw my father do one of the coolest things he had ever done. Over the strong protest of my mother (he said he could still see her high-heel spike marks in the lawn as they moved out), he put up a map of Genesee County. He studied that map for days to determine where he would live next. There were the two most popular suburbs: Flushing and Grand Blanc. Looking at the map, he noticed Flushing didn't have an expressway running through it. For him, that was a large negative. Grand Blanc was a thriving suburb, and they had just completed I-475, which took you into downtown Flint. I-75 ran right through Grand Blanc. Grand Blanc was in contention, but the housing values were double the prices of the houses in the city of Flint. Grand Blanc was too expensive.

Then he started focusing in on Fenton, Michigan. Fenton had the US-23 Expressway running right through the middle of it. As a matter of fact, the first expressway that I remember was the Clio to Fenton Expressway, which is now part of US-23. Fenton also had numerous lakes, which could help protect home values down the road. His real estate agent advised him on the three most important points in home ownership: location, location, and location. He settled on the Fenton area and soon purchased a home off of Torrey Road. The house he purchased had a lot of land. He had over four acres. He also purchased a vacant lot to his north giving him a total of eight acres. He used to brag that now in his front yard alone, he could place six of his Flint homes. I have lived in Fenton ever since.

This exodus from the city of Flint continued. A few years later, as I was serving my apprenticeship, a guy I was working with in the machine room got a phone call one night from his home alarm company. He had had a home invasion. The intruders came in through the small window above the kitchen sink. It was the only one without an alarm. When the intruders left, they exited out the front door triggering the alarm. The guy rushed home to find his house ransacked. I was talking to him about this, and come to find out, it was on my old street less than a block from where I grew up. It probably was the right thing to do to pull up stakes and escape while we still could. Today, Flint is a very bad place. General Motors has gone from around eighty thousand employees to less than ten thousand in the city. You can't take those kinds of hits and maintain your way of life as a community. Things have gotten so bad in Flint they are now talking about cutting off city services in several areas to save money. The elected treasurer of the county has talked with the Obama administration about this. They are also finding dead bodies in the parks we used to play in long ago. There is a notorious gang that has formed near the area of my grandmother's church. They call themselves the Pierson Hood Posse. They deal in drugs and crime. They have been accused of multiple murders.

***

This was pretty much what I remember about growing up in the city of Flint. It was a time of innocence for me. I assumed it would always be the way it was for me growing up. The only difference was now I lived in the suburb of Fenton instead of the city. I find it sad that Flint has deteriorated so badly.

Mott Community College

While I was working in the fall of 1974, I continued to take courses at the local community college. In January of 1975, I was again placed on permanent layoff from the shop. It worked out to be good for me though, because I had enrolled for more classes at Mott College, and this provided me the opportunity to concentrate full-time on my studies.

I threw myself into my studies. All I did was study. I let everything else go or put stuff on hold. I didn't do a whole lot of socializing or partying. I remember people saying to me as I started school, "Is it all coming back to you?" Coming back, hell, it was never there in the first place. I pretty much had an empty plate from my past educational adventures. I completed those first three classes and received A's. Wow! I had never done that before. I was beginning to develop an insatiable appetite for education.

There is one other flashback from my childhood education that I desire to write about. It helps to explain where I was headed in my early years. I believe this exercise helped me get on track educationally at this point in my life.

***

Flashback: The Nun's Assignment

When I attended St. Luke's grade school, one of the exercises the nuns had us do was to study and write papers on our patron saints. For your namesake, there were saints in the Catholic Church. We would study their lives, write a paper about them, and then try to emulate their lives with our own. With my first name being Richard, I was like the odd man out. There is no St. Richard. Figures! I would always gravitate toward Sir Richard the Lionheart, who was a Crusader king from England. That didn't go over very big with the nuns. They insisted that I go with my middle name, Thomas. St. Thomas was a gentleman and a scholar. That didn't fit my profile of myself, and so we had a point of contention. I had to go along with my teacher; I would complete my assignment on St. Thomas the scholar. But secretly, I yearned to emulate Sir Richard the Lionheart. I took this as a sure sign from above that this was the direction I was supposed to go. I became a warrior at heart. As a matter of fact, some of my earliest memories are of watching World War II movies with my dad. But I had completed my warrior desires by voluntarily spending three years of my life in the marines. I now had that desire out of my system. For the first time in my life, I was ready for school and actually saw some benefits in it for me.

***

I took college algebra during the summer break. I liked it. I earned an A! Now I was developing the itch to do this full-time. I did register at Mott Community College as a full-time student for the fall semester of 1975. I earned a 3.6 grade point average and completed sixteen credit hours. I was the first and only one in my immediate family to ever go to college full-time. What a great experience this was for me! I was receiving the GI benefits, which I had earned by serving in the military, while I attended school and was on an educational leave from the shop.

I also completed one more full-time semester, the winter term of 1976. I completed thirteen credit hours. I returned to work after this semester was completed. Things were looking up! I now had completed forty credit hours at Mott College, I was working full-time, and the overall economy was picking up. It was coming back strong, and General Motors had called everyone back to work. This included all of the existing apprentices who had been cut back. Things looked so favorable there was talk of putting more apprentices into the apprenticeship program. I took the pre-apprentice test again. This was the third time. I scored eighteen points out of a possible twenty-one. Now all I had to do was score highly when and if the plant conducted apprenticeship interviews.

Around this time, I was also starting to realize I wanted to go on supervision. I wanted to take my place as a first-line supervisor and see what I could do. It was still too early to do anything about it just yet, but it helped me to lay out my future plans. They were to complete an apprenticeship, complete my college degree, and then go on supervision. It was a good plan, and I felt on top of the world. The future looked bright to me.

3
1976–1979 Apprenticeship Years

Apprenticeship

I was interviewed for an apprenticeship in the late spring of 1976. I did well. I had now earned enough points to be placed on the approved apprentice list. In July, I began an apprenticeship to become a machine repair machinist journeyman. I was surprised that I was selected for machine repair. During my interview, the salaried apprentice coordinator had asked me about this trade, and I had had no clue who they were or what they did. Back on my little assembly fixture, I only saw die makers, electricians, and welder repairmen. He coaxed me through the answer. Looking back, I should have known he was tipping me off because the salaried coordinator spoon-fed me enough information to give a really good answer about machine repair. I think this had something to do with the UAW apprentice coordinator. This was the guy I had been bugging for two years to get on an apprenticeship. Turns out, he was a machine repairman as well.

I signed my apprenticeship-indentured papers and started my apprenticeship on July 26, 1976. My apprenticeship would last for 7,328 hours broken up into eight periods. There was a required amount of job training for each period. A typical apprenticeship lasted four years. I completed mine in a little over three years with the heavy overtime I worked. The apprenticeship also required 576 hours of classroom training. These courses were held at the community college I had been attending. My record shows I took twenty credit hours of apprentice classes. Some of the college work I had completed before my apprenticeship counted toward my apprenticeship training.

I remember my first morning as an apprentice well. I was picked up by my supervisor and introduced to the guys. These were the journeymen who worked out of the west plant machine repair bullpen. They did mostly machine overhauls, new work, and filled in for the guys stationed on the production lines as needed. Man, I was excited to be there and eager to get to work. I wanted to be a really good apprentice and learn all I could from these guys. I was assigned to a journeyman named Jack. Jack told me to have a seat on the bench next to him, and so I did. We sat there until lunch. After lunch, I asked Jack what I should do? He said, "Sit down on the bench." I was flabbergasted! This was my first day as an apprentice, and I was eager to go to work, but all I was doing was sitting on a bench.

You see, I had just come off of my production assembly fixture. In those days, I worked all day long. We might have gotten off forty-five minutes early most days, but when we were running production, we were hard at work. It was a brisk pace. We were always moving.

I finally asked Jack why we were sitting so long. He said we were waiting on the overhead crane to come over and give us a lift. We waited the rest of the shift. Some apprenticeship! I was sitting on a bench going stir crazy.

This was the same area of the plant I had started in two and a half years earlier. Now I had a whole new perspective of the place. The west plant consisted of about fifteen major press lines and numerous other operations. We had a department called "automatics." Here, an operator loaded a coil of sheet metal into a decoiler and fed it into a "prog die." A prog die (which is short for progressive die) is a longer, rectangular die that has many stations in it. On the front end, you started with sheet metal, and at the back end of the die, you had a finished product. Usually, we made all types of brackets in these operations.

We had quite a few "blanking" operations. This is where an operator places a coil of sheet metal into a die and cuts a blank into its configuration. It is then stacked, banded, and sent to a major press line to be used. A blanking operation is much like a cookie cutter—you know, the kind they use at Christmas time to make different configurations of sugar cookies.

All of this machinery needed tender, loving care—you know, maintenance. All of it was sitting there waiting for me to learn how it ran and to discover what type of maintenance it needed. There were hundreds of pieces of equipment in the west plant. My brain began working overtime trying to learn everything I could about these machines. This was fascinating stuff. Just when you thought you were beginning to get it, even more complexity would be introduced.

I was provided with a used toolbox that was scrounged up from somewhere in the plant. These toolboxes were on wheels so we could push them anywhere in the plant that we were assigned to work. To help us fill our toolboxes with tools, we were given a tool allowance. Some guys went straight to Sears, Roebuck, and Co. and bought one of their preassembled toolkits. My journeymen suggested that I not do this, as there were many tools included in the kits that you'd never use on the job. I was very tempted to go purchase one of those kits. I didn't, however; I listened to the journeymen and waited. They had me inventory their toolboxes to determine what tools I needed. I would then go shopping at the tool section at Sears to purchase my hand tools. Sears has a great tool guarantee. They will repair or replace their top-of-the-line Craftsman tools, no questions asked, for the life of the tool. I still have these tools today. It seemed like every Friday night, which was payday, I'd go shopping for tools and drool over the ones I had not yet collected and didn't have the extra money to purchase right then. The shop provided a lot of what we needed, especially the specialty tools and the power tools. We had to purchase our own hand tools.

Some of the highlights from this period were in building new production automation. We would receive a set of blueprints from the engineering department showing us how to fabricate the different sub-pieces of the automation. They further detailed how to fully complete the machine.

Once we had studied the blueprints, we began to order all of the individual pieces of steel—the tubing, the nuts and bolts, etc.—to complete the project. Next, we would send the steel that needed to be cut to the machine room, and then we would begin to build up the individual details. Finally, when all the small items were completed, we would assemble them together and end up with a completed piece of automation. Working under the tutelage of a journeyman, I built scissor jack tables, overhead transfer units, and index conveyors. It was a blast. I received quite a feeling of accomplishment from the successful completion of these projects.

Political Parties

In the fall of 1976, there was a presidential election. Being born and raised a Democrat, I voted for Jimmy Carter. Being Catholic, it was a really big deal for our family when John Kennedy was elected president. My parents and the Catholic Church were ecstatic with the election results. It was even more traumatic when he was assassinated. The Catholic community went into shock. I remember being in grade school on the day he was shot. I believe I was in the fifth grade. The priest came around to all of the classrooms, opened the door, and announced the president had been shot. We were then ordered to get up and say a prayer for him. They let us out of school early that day. School was canceled until after the president's funeral had taken place. I remember watching all of the events on television. My family was riveted to the TV. It was one of the most significant events in my young life.

My parents and my grandparents and most of my other relatives were all staunch Democrats. I made the mistake of telling the journeymen about my vote. They had a conniption fit. They took me out back, out of the way, and proceeded to tell me how wrong I was. I couldn't believe my ears. I told them as good UAW brothers, it was our obligation to vote for Democrats. They were really upset with me. They told me, "You wait; he'll raise our taxes and screw the economy up. We always vote with our pocketbook." I believe President Carter did just that. That was a shock to my system. I had assumed that everyone in the shop was a Democrat. Turns out a fair share of at least the skilled tradesmen were closet Republicans.

I thought about what these journeymen told me quite a bit. I thought about events that had already happened in my young life. I thought about the lady in the 235 HUD home that was built next to our house in Flint. She was on welfare and had been provided a good job working in the post office. She quit that job because she made more money on welfare. I did not believe in this system. Welfare, like unemployment, should help you for a short period of time until you can get back on your feet. In the United States, we had chronic welfare cases, where three generations of the same family had been on welfare. There were also cases in Michigan where welfare recipients fed their dogs ground beef rather than dog food. This was because with the food stamps they received, they were not allowed to purchase dog food. So to beat the system, they bought ground beef and fed this to their dogs. Something was just rotten about this system long-term.

I remembered when I was in the military, it was the first time I encountered personnel quotas. When it was my turn to make sergeant, there were eleven openings in the Second Marine Division, which consisted of fifteen thousand men. Six of these had to be filled by minorities. That left only five positions for a guy like me to compete for.

I remembered this as I signed up for school at Mott Community College and I was paying my tuition bill. At the paymaster's office, there were two lines. One line was for regular paying students, and the second line was for those students who received grant money. I found out that you didn't have to pay back grant money. So I stood in line for the grant money. When I got up to the window, I inquired as to how I could receive it. I was told I did not qualify. I asked why, and they said because I made too much money. Now I confess, I did receive the GI benefits, but I felt I had earned those benefits. But so did a lot of other people standing in the grant money line.

I remembered when it was time to buy my first house. I inquired about a low-interest loan. I was told I made too much money and didn't qualify. My thought was how could I make too much money when I am in an entry-level hourly position? I paid a lot of federal and state income taxes. I wasn't sure that the governmental agencies were the best at spending my money.

I remembered as I was trying to get on my apprenticeship being shut out of taking the pre-apprenticeship classes at the union hall. I began to fall away from the Democratic Party. Every time I needed their help, they told me I didn't qualify for their support. To this day, they do not support people like me. Really, reading this and rethinking it, I believe the Democratic Party left me. I voted Democratic and for Jimmy Carter when he ran for reelection in 1980. It would be the last time. Ronald Reagan soundly defeated him. For the first time, I voted Republican in the 1984 presidential election. I too had become like those journeymen who had schooled me. I began to vote by my pocketbook.

This is my favorite quote from Abraham Lincoln. I think these thoughts still ring true today:

> You cannot bring about prosperity by discouraging thrift. You cannot strengthen the weak by weakening the strong. You cannot help the wage earner by pulling down the wage payer. You cannot further the brotherhood of man by encouraging class hatred. You cannot help the poor by destroying the rich. You cannot establish sound security on borrowed money. You cannot keep out of trouble by spending more than you earn. You cannot help

men permanently by doing for them what they should do for themselves.

I realize that racial injustice has occurred in America. However, I have never partaken in it. In fact, neither has my family. Our grandparents immigrated to this country around the turn of the century. All of us are either blue-collar or middle-class workers. We didn't contribute to the racial system in America, nor did we create it. We are victims of it. I've always felt it was unfair to me that I have to pay the price for something that was done years before my family came to this country.

Not-So-Quick Press Line Changes

Things were beginning to change during these years at General Motors. General Motors had come out with the Chevrolet Chevette after the 1973 Arab oil embargo. Typically, in the Chevrolet stamping plants, they would only take on high-volume jobs, like the truck fenders I worked on earlier in my career in the west plant. The west plant was full of hoods and fenders for most of the Chevrolet product lineup. Once a line was set up and in place, the dies only came out if there was a major emergency breakdown. Otherwise, these lines would run over three hundred parts per hour for two shifts every working day of the year. This was the norm; it was what the plant was built to do. It was the General Motors way.

For some reason, the plant decided to run the front fenders of the Chevette in one line. This meant we had to change the line setup from right hand to the left hand or vice versa whenever production called for a line change. Now, our soon-to-be world competition was already doing this. They were light years ahead of us. I worked on one of the first line changes of this type in the plant during this time, and it took us three full days of three full shifts to get it done. That's over seventy-two hours of time. None of our equipment or the dies were set up back then for rapidly changing over from die set to die set. As we changed over more often, we got a little better at it. I believe we could get the entire line changed over in one full day or three shifts. Today, in a modern double-A transfer press, these parts changes are accomplished in less than five minutes of run time. That's if everything goes correctly. That is a far cry from the line changes of the mid to late 70s.

As time passed, I got in the groove of being an apprentice. I had never been around anything like this industrial repair business. I was as raw and green as you could get. I earned the trust of the journeymen by being as good of an apprentice as I could be, always doing the menial tasks in the beginning until I could catch on. The trouble was there was almost a lifetime of learning to be done. There was more variation of job assignments than I was used to. On production, once you got used to a job, you would work it until a higher seniority employee bumped you or you bumped someone else. This was done infrequently. As skilled tradesmen, once you received an assignment, you followed it until completion. This could take a couple of hours, or it may even take a couple of months. It all depended on the scope of the job assigned. A large press overhaul could take three or four months. But the beauty of this job was that there was far less repetition than in production work and you were able to utilize your brain a little bit. The company still didn't let you into the decision-making process for your area, but there were little decisions you were allowed to make. I enjoyed making decisions and using my brain. I could now determine what size screw holes were appropriate for a job or maybe determine a small redesign of a machine part to make it better. I was moving up. I was very humble. I got along well with the journeymen. Some apprentices who came on were already knowledgeable about industrial repair. Some of them had a hard time with the journeymen. They already had a hardened attitude. No one could tell them what to do.

The Big Decision

One morning, our supervisor, Louie, assigned my journeyman and me to go out quickly and troubleshoot a stand-alone press operation that would not run. This was considered an emergency breakdown situation. The plant needed these parts. Things were a little different in the shop when there was a genuine emergency. The petty bullshit was put aside, and it was an all-hands-on-deck philosophy until we found a way to get production going again. Production has always been king; it still is today and rightfully so.

The journeyman and I did some preliminary investigation to determine why this press wouldn't run. We made a couple of air pressure adjustments and asked the operator to turn the press over. (This is one cycle much like your car engine makes a cycle.) The operator did so, and we heard a loud banging noise from the top of the press. We climbed on top of the press to have a look. We didn't see anything that immediately stood out. We began removing the inspection covers that provided us access to the drive train. We looked around some more but still didn't see anything. We climbed back down to the floor. We removed our safety locks and had the operator cycle the press again. As the press cycled, we still heard this same loud banging noise. This wasn't a good sign, as it was looking like a drive train issue. We climbed back up to the top of the press. The journeyman had a very long steel pry bar. He placed it between the gears and applied force. He kept doing this until he saw movement. He asked me if I saw the movement, and I said I did. This movement was very slight. He asked me what it meant, and I said I didn't know. He said that being able to flex the bull gear meant the main shaft had to be broken. This was determined to be a major breakdown that could take as long as six weeks to repair. The journeyman signaled for us to go back down to the shop floor.

Once on the floor, he told me to sit down and wait for the "big" decision. Unsure of what he meant, I asked him what he was talking about. He told me to grab a seat and wait and see. Shortly thereafter, here came Louie to see what was going on. The journeyman told him, and he said to take him up there so he could see for himself. We did so. Louie told us to wait there until he got back to us. We sat back down. About two hours later, Louie and the general supervisor showed up. They asked us what was going on, and we explained the situation. The general supervisor asked us to take him to the top of the press so he could see. We took him up there and showed him the broken shaft. He asked a few questions, and then we went back down to the floor. He told us to wait right there. We sat back down. We waited until lunchtime and then took off.

After lunch, the general supervisor brought the superintendent to the job. The superintendent was not happy. He told us this was not acceptable; we had been wasting time all morning and we'd better get that press running. The journeyman told him to go screw himself, as there was no way the press was going to run; the main shaft was broken. The superintendent went to the top of the press with the general supervisor, and they looked around and then came back down. They told us to stay right there. We continued to sit on our toolboxes.

Just before quitting time, the general superintendent arrived at the job. He had the superintendent, general supervisor, and our supervisor, Louie, with him. He asked several questions about the situation. My journeyman must have had some previous experience with this guy. After a couple of minutes, he looked at his entourage and said, "Pull it." This meant to pull the die out of the press and make the necessary arrangements to run it elsewhere while we made the repairs to the press. Boy did my journeymen receive some evil stares. That night, the die was pulled, and we started the press repair the next day. I learned now how the big decisions were made. What a waste of a day!

Louie

Louie, our supervisor, was a pretty good guy. Louie was a good forty pounds overweight and constantly had a large, lit cigar in his mouth. The guys nicknamed him "Boss Hog" after a popular TV character. Louie was the sheriff in town. He did resemble that character. Louie loved his three-wheeled scooter. These were small electric vehicles that could carry two people, one on the front and one on the back. It had handlebars for a steering wheel. Hourly personnel were not allowed on any of the shop scooters. It was a violation of the shop rules. They were for salaried personnel only. Louie was overly zealous about protecting his little perk, and if any of us hourly people came close to his scooter, we heard about it. Louie's scooter came up missing frequently. Sometimes, it would take him days to find it. But he always did find it. The third-shift crew was notorious for stealing the supervisors' buggies. Usually, they were chained and bolted at the end of each shift. The third-shift workers were a different breed; nothing got in their way.

One morning, we were tipped off by the third shifters to stand by and watch the show in the bullpen. They had spent the night fixing up Louie's buggy. They had painted the entire thing white and had installed a horse's head on the front and a tail in the back. Boss Hog was stenciled in bold letters across the vehicle's body. They had a special cowboy hat ready for Louie. Well, let me tell you, Louie really blew his top that day when he saw his buggy. As he sat down in the seat, someone placed a ten-gallon cowboy hat on his head. He ripped the fluorescent streamers right out of the handlebar grips. Boy was he pissed! He did look good in a ten-gallon cowboy hat. He took the scooter to truck repair for a complete overhaul and a new paint job. Everybody had a good laugh at Louie's expense.

Louie always aspired to make it to general supervisor. He worked hard and put up with a lot of crap to stay in the spotlight for promotion. Louie had been a machine repairman as well. He had come up through the ranks. Years later, Louie finally achieved his goal of becoming a "general supervisor." After his promotion, he was reassigned to the second shift. Within one month, Louie had a massive heart attack. He was off work a very long time. When he came back, he wasn't the same man. He was now very skinny for his size and weight. He retired a short time later. Maybe the third-shift guys were doing him a favor by hiding his beloved buggy and making him walk, which provided him some exercise.

Working in the West Plant

We had a lot of fun during this time, but we did do a lot of work. A common activity was the overhaul of a clutch and brake system for a stamping press. I spent many hours pulling them apart, cleaning them up, and making the necessary repairs. Then we would reassemble them and install them back in the press. I learned a lot. This was a very dirty job. The parts were full of brake-shoe dust, grease, and grime. At that time, the physical atmosphere inside the plant wasn't very clean. A general oil mist hung over many of the presses. If you looked out into the distance, you could clearly see this mist. We took most of the stripped-down parts to the steam-cleaning booth. Here, they were thoroughly cleaned. A lot of the parts we cleaned ourselves using trichloroethylene. The solvent was very effective on grease and grime. It put off a strong odor. Years later, they banned the use of it in the shops. I hope it doesn't have any long-term health effects on my lungs. I breathed in a lot of it during my years on machine repair. So far, so good. I became very good at clutch and brake overhauls.

One time, we were working on one of these jobs. We were in the process of putting it back together. When we installed ball bearings onto a shaft, we had to heat them up so they would expand. As the bearing races were expanded, we had a short time in which we could place the bearing on the shaft. We had to do this very quickly, because as it cooled off, the bearing race would shrink down to its original size. Once in place, it was supposed to shrink because this then became a "pressed" fit, and there was no way the bearing was going to come loose. There were many large forces that were placed on this equipment and these bearings.

We had recently received a new bearing heater in the department. Previously, we had used a bearing heater oven to heat the bearings. We would turn the oven on to 350 degrees and place the bearings inside for about an hour. The expansion that took place would make them the proper size to place on the shaft. One of the machine repair supervisors had purchased a bearing heater that used oil as a bath for the bearing. I'm sure there was some value to this, but I don't remember. That was the one we used that day. We turned the heater on and placed the bearing in the oil. Larry, the journeyman I was assigned to work with that day, closed the lid. Then he went into the adjacent welding booth to take a snooze and told me to keep my eye on things. Now generally, you had to heat one of these bearings for at least one hour. That provided ample time for the entire bearing race to heat up and expand properly. I sat down on a nearby bench and waited. After a short time, a little flame shot out of the bearing heater cover and then it stopped. This bearing heater had a flip-top lid. Then it did it again. A small flame shot right out of the top lid. This didn't seem right to me. But I wasn't sure because we'd never used this bearing heater before. I went into the welding booth and got Larry. I had to wake him up. When I woke him up and used the word *fire*, did he ever jump out of his chair! He immediately unplugged the bearing heater, but it was too late. A large, steady flame was now shooting out of the heater. It was a very narrow and wickedly high flame. It kept leaping higher and higher into the air. Now there was a crowd of people all around us. Someone had grabbed a fire extinguisher. The person approached the heater and opened the cover. Now the flame was shooting up to the ceiling almost twenty-five feet above us. Things weren't looking very good. When a guy fired a CO_2 fire extinguisher at the flames, the fire immediately went out. Whew, that was a close call! Everyone was feeling pretty good about this near misfortune that didn't happen. Then, poof, the fire started all over again, and the flame went right up to the ceiling. The same guy applied the CO_2 again with the same results. The fire went out for a few seconds, and then it started right back up again. Finally, plant security showed up. A security guard had a fire extinguisher with some type of green liquid material in it. He applied this to the fire, and it went out. And this time, it stayed out.

By this time, it seemed like half the shop was in our department watching the show. There were enough white shirts in the area to choke a horse. They wanted to get to the bottom of what had happened. They assigned our supervisor, Louie, to do a thorough investigation. During Louie's investigation, he found out someone had put the wrong oil in the heater. This situation required oil that had a flame retardant in it. No shit! The bearing heater was hauled outside and destroyed. From then on, we heated our bearings in the oven just like the old days.

While reliving the bearing heater incident, it brought up a lot of safety issues that came up while I worked in the shop and especially when I was on skilled trades.

Safety

The shop is a very dangerous place to work. Shortly after I hired in, our supervisor reviewed a safety incident with us. A second shift operator was going to load a coil of steel into his decoiler. He had picked up the heavy coil of steel with the small area crane. When he got the steel a few feet up in the air, it came loose and fell off the chains that were used to secure the load. The coil of steel fell and ended up striking the operator in the lower leg just above his ankle. I believe he had to have his leg amputated below the knee. Ouch!

I vaguely remember a fatality the plant had sometime in my first year or so. Inside the train boxcars that the company used for shipping its sheet metal parts to the assembly plants, they had installed metal dividers. These dividers separated the different types of shipping containers in the boxcars. Somehow, one of these heavy metal dividers came loose and fell onto an employee crushing him to death. I don't remember if this was a General Motors employee or a railroad employee.

One time, on third shift, two electricians were up in the building steel adding a switch to the electrical buss. The electrical buss contains the main electrical arteries in the plant. Very high and extremely dangerous electrical current runs through them. In those days, the electricians added plugs while the buss was "hot." This means the energy was still turned on. This was a common practice, and usually, the work was completed without incident. This night, things didn't go according to plan. As the electricians went to place the switch into the buss, they somehow missed their target. This caused the buss to arc, and one of the electricians received an electrical shock. Further, the arc flash caused the electrician to catch on fire. Now, these guys were some thirty feet up in the air working off of an aerial lift. The slang term for these lifts in the plant was *JLG*, which is the brand name of the vehicle. The quick thinking of the second electrician saved his partner's life. He somehow kept his partner in the JLG, started it up, and returned to the floor. He then doused the fire on his partner with dirty mop water that happened to be right in the area. The electrician received third-degree burns. I'm not sure he ever returned to work. The guys in the area said they could smell burnt flesh for a long time that night.

One Saturday, as I was reporting for work, there was a sadness in the air. On day shift, a tinsmith had been working up on the plant roof. His assignment was to remove old, unused ventilation stacks. As he was doing this, he would throw the stacks off of the roof so they could be disposed of. Somehow, a cable from one of the stacks wrapped around the tinsmith's leg. As the stack flew off the roof, it dragged the tinsmith with it to the ground. The guys in his work crew felt lucky though, because he maintained consciousness as he was placed in the ambulance. Unfortunately, the tinsmith died from a heart attack on his way to the hospital. This was a point of contention with the skilled trades guys. They felt the cause of death was the fall, and the company was trying to cover its tracks by using the heart attack as an excuse.

Another time, we were having an open house in the plant. This is where the general public can come into the shop to see what we do. Mostly family and friends show up. On this day, an operator was guiding sheet metal through his prog die. It wasn't loading correctly. He overrode the safety system so he could get the steel loaded. He ended up turning the die over with his hand inside it. He severely crushed his hand. This wasn't a pretty sight on a normal day, but now we had all of our guests walking around in the plant. Later, this guy would review his accident with us hourly and admit his mistake in the hope that we wouldn't do what he did. He later went on supervision.

Now I bring these safety incidents up because being on skilled trades is more dangerous than working production. General Motors has always been an industry leader in employee safety. My plant had set safety records for going many hours without major injuries. But the safety culture on the plant floor was conducive to injury.

Each morning, the machine repair journeymen took their work break around eight o'clock. We would all go up to the cafeteria to drink a coffee. The table I sat at had around fifteen to twenty guys sitting around it. There was always good conversation at the table. Occasionally, the guys would get to talking about their accidents and injuries. There was a lot of ribbing between the guys. One journeyman would say, "Remember when I had my finger inside the clutch plate and you let go of the air valve? You ended up whacking the top of my finger right off."

Then they would all have a good laugh. Or one would say, "Remember the time you were swinging that hammer and smashed your thumb? It still isn't right today." Again, there would be laughter.

Or one would say, "Remember the time the iron hand cycled and caught my arm?"

It seemed that these stories were endless, and the guys talked about them like they had earned a badge of honor. Then it hit me! Somewhere along the way, to be included as one of the guys, you had to have some type of serious injury. It seemed as though everyone was missing a piece of a finger or toe. I remember thinking I really didn't want to participate in that honor. I didn't want to belong to that club. I liked my fingers and toes just as they were.

One job we were working on had to have a tall wooden platform built so we could have access to our work area. A main shaft in the press was broken, and we couldn't get it out. We had to use all of the hydraulic pushing and pulling pressure we could muster. On the platform, we had a three-eighths-inch chain wrapped around a Stanley die puller. We applied all the pressure to the shaft that we could get. The chain must have been weakened, because all of a sudden, it gave and came flying off the platform. One of the journeymen looked at us and spit a piece of chain out of his mouth. His face was all bloody. We got him down to the floor, and he went to medical.

One time, we had a sheet feeder up in the bullpen doing modifications to it. Something was stuck, and we couldn't free it up. We had chains attached to the sheet feeder holding it up in the air, and we had hydraulic jacks attached trying to free up whatever was stuck. We had the bright idea to get the welder over to cut a piece of metal off. We didn't realize the pressure we had on it. We didn't think to release any of the pressure that was on the sheet feeder. All of a sudden, as the welder was doing his cutting with the torch, the piece came free. There was so much energy stored up in the piece that it shot forward about fifty feet and embedded in the door of a metal cabinet that was in the department. We were all stunned by this. It was as if we had created the world's largest slingshot, pulled it back as far as it would go, and then released it. Man! That was a close call. If that metal had hit a person, it would have taken his head right off. We didn't tell anyone about our little incident.

When I was in the machine room, I had my personal near miss. I had been working in the grinder section for a while. I enjoyed this work. Grinders were very precise and left a smooth, finished surface. It was usually the last machining operation performed on a piece of metal.

When we would work on machines as part of our apprenticeship training, we would work with a journeyman until we learned how to operate that machine. Then we would work on our own with the journeyman nearby. I was well into my machine room training and had learned to run many machines. You were put in the grinder section near the end of your machine room time. I was not a novice. The machine room supervisor was a per diem who was trying to make a name for himself so he could become permanent salary.

This supervisor told me to run a large Madison grinder. I had never run this machine before, nor had I seen it run. This was a dangerous situation. With the help of this supervisor, I ran the machine successfully on and off for a couple of days. Then a hot job came in that we had to have. I didn't know how to run it. The supervisor helped me with the setup of this job. Then he left and said he'd be around later. I started running the machine just as he had told me to do. This machine had a stationary grinding wheel overhead and a large table that traveled back and forth underneath it. As the grinding wheel contacted the steel parts, it removed a very small amount of metal. The grinding wheel itself was around twelve inches in diameter and about ten inches thick. This machine was made to work on very large pieces of metal.

While I was running this job, the metal hold-down clamps began to rock back and forth. I didn't know it then, but that was a bad sign. I had my face right near the job watching what was going on. Then the metal piece rocked again and dug into the grinding wheel. There was one hell of an explosion. The grinding wheel disintegrated right in front of my eyes. The metal piece went flying off the worktable. I was stunned. I couldn't move. People started gathering around the machine and me. The journeyman led me off the work platform and sat me down in a chair. I couldn't move. I couldn't do anything. As the effects of the explosion wore off, I took inventory of my body parts. Everything was still there—no cuts, no bruises, and no amputations. My face was wet from the water coolant. There was quite a commotion with all of the activity in the area.

The next thing I remember, all the journeyman were yelling at the temporary supervisor. The journeyman felt I had been wrongly told how to set the job up. They called the committeeman. I was given the rest of the day off to collect my nerves and myself. The per-diem supervisor was placed back on his tools. I was very lucky that I hadn't sustained a serious injury. I never did run that machine again.

As a young and inexperienced apprentice, I did have two incidents that I can recall in which I injured my journeyman. The first time, I was working with Lee, a seasoned veteran of machine repair. We were installing a permanent extension ladder on a draw press. This was a heavy ladder that was configured to be raised about four feet in the air when not in use. This was for safety purposes. They didn't want any unauthorized personnel gaining access to the top of the press. So we were working on installing the new ladder. It finally came time to lift the ladder up into the air and place it onto the holding brackets we had attached to the press. When Lee said, "Go," I grabbed the ladder and lifted with all that I had. The problem was where I grabbed it allowed the hinges to move forward pinching his fingers between the two pieces of the extension ladder. Boy did he start to scream at me! I felt like shit. Lee examined his fingers and walked up to medical. He had to have some minor repair work done on a couple of fingers. I felt really bad.

The other incident I recall happened as I was working on making a brake adjustment to a draw press. Some of our draw presses were of the under-drive style. This type of press has its power train located in the plant basement. The journeyman I was working with that day, Cecil, was being very patient with me. He allowed me to crawl up to the brake assembly, loosen the retaining bolts, and begin to remove the shims that were in place. The brake shoes had worn down so that the press wasn't stopping at the top of its stroke. The ram was beginning to drift down a little bit. By removing a shim, we lessened the amount of travel the break spider had to make. With less travel, the brake system worked properly again. This was a routine occurrence in a stamping facility. Anyway, I had crawled up to the top of the power train and was working on the brake adjustment. Cecil had given me a trouble light to use while I was up there in place of a flashlight. There was very little light in the dark and hot industrial basement. Somehow, I managed to kick the trouble light as I was moving about making the adjustment. The trouble light fell from my work area and smashed Cecil right in the face. He was standing at the bottom of the ladder, holding it in place so I didn't fall. Well, he wasn't too happy with me. I don't remember too much damage to his face, but I think I bruised his ego some. If I remember correctly, he had a minor burn on his forehead from the heat of the lightbulb.

Supervisor Bob

About one year into my apprenticeship, I was reassigned from the west plant over to the east plant for further training. The plant did a good job rotating the apprentices around to the different areas so we could see what was going on and learn our trade. The east plant was very similar to the west plant. It had about thirteen major press lines. There were lots of machines and equipment that needed tender, loving care.

The machine repair supervisor on this side of the plant was an older guy named Bob. Bob loved to be taken out to lunch by the vendors who called on our plant. Bob got his share of free food and drinks on a regular basis. Sometimes, Bob wasn't around much after one of his free lunches.

Bob was hard on all of his apprentices. He must've been treated poorly somewhere down the line. You kind of felt like Bob's personal slave after a while. Bob had you over a barrel. After each of the eight periods that made up your apprenticeship, the supervisor was required to do a written evaluation of your performance. If you received several poor evaluations in a row, you could be removed from your apprenticeship. In the old days, this meant something, but by the time of my apprenticeship, this evaluation was rarely filled out. With all of the government regulations, these ratings didn't hold much water anymore. But Bob still took them seriously, and it gave him great pleasure to watch his apprentices squirm a little bit in anticipation of his performance review. I was in Bob's sights as his next victim. I could tell that Bob didn't care too much for my performance or me. He always found one apprentice to pressure.

Then I met a younger journeyman named Herb. Herb took me under his wing and showed me the ropes on this side of the plant. He taught me how to get around Bob. He told me to always carry around my machinist hammer wherever I went. If and when I saw Bob coming toward me, I was to immediately start hammering on the closest thing I could put my hands on.

You see, there are two types of hammers. One is a carpenter's hammer. And the other is a "machinist'" hammer. In machine repair, we always used a "machinist's" hammer. We were not carpenters! If Bob caught you with a carpenter's hammer, he would note that on your review. Herb told me to always hammer intently and to use only my machinist hammer.

When Herb was an apprentice, Bob had been giving him very poor ratings. Herb protested because one time when Bob did this, Herb didn't even have a job assignment. Bob didn't care whether Herb had a job assignment or not, his apprentices were to be always busy and they better be doing something constructive. So Herb got the bright idea to start carrying his machinist hammer wherever he went. Every time he saw Bob, he started hammering away. One time, he got a little nervous because Bob was coming toward him out of nowhere. In a panic, Herb started hammering on an empty vice that was mounted on a workbench. Bob came up to him and told him to keep up the good work. After that, Herb received the best ratings of his apprenticeship from Bob. Herb went from a having a shaky rating to being one of the best apprentices to come along in a long time. Bob was 100 percent behind Herb. Herb finished his apprenticeship with flying colors.

While I was assigned to the east plant, I listened to Herb and kept my hammer close by. Every time Bob came around, I started hammering away very intently on anything I could find. I got along just fine with Bob after that. He even let me work in the hydraulic repair area for a while. Not all of the apprentices got to spend time in the hydraulic repair area. I really enjoyed that. That machinist hammer worked wonders for me.

While there was a lot of work being done in the plant, there was always a time to play. Making work fun helped to pass the time and helped us to bond as a team.

Practical Jokes

We played a lot of practical jokes in the shop to help pass time. The die makers seemed to have the corner on this market. They knew how to set somebody up for a good laugh.

One of the more famous practical jokes they pulled was the watch trick. Someone would bring in an old, worthless watch and start talking to people about it. Then he would zoom in on his victim, usually a vulnerable apprentice. The time I witnessed it, the victim was a young woman, who was working die repair with her journeyman. He brought his old worthless watch into the plant and built up the story to her about how valuable the watch was to him. The story goes something like this:

> This watch belonged to my grandfather. He loved this watch. It is from the old country. My grandfather was an immigrant. My grandfather passed this watch down to my father. My father loves this watch. At the proper time, my father passed it down to me. It is very valuable to me, and I love this watch. It is now three generations old. You can't buy a watch like this anywhere in the world. I don't know what I would do if I lost this watch. I noticed that it has stopped working a couple of days ago. I can't trust someone I don't know to fix this watch. I know the die welder is also an excellent watch repairman. Do you think you could take my watch to him and see if he could repair it? I would appreciate it very much!

There was no hesitation on the part of the apprentice to take this precious family heirloom to the die welder for repair. Now the die welder involved worked in a partitioned booth so the rest of us didn't have to see the flashes of light from his welding work. Die welders worked in a secluded area.

On the day of this practical joke, the die maker notified the welder to be prepared for the apprentice. He also had the word passed around the entire department that at first break, he was going to pull his practical joke on his apprentice. At break time, over one hundred of us gathered around the welding booth area waiting for the show. The die maker was on the opposite side of us, so we went unnoticed.

The young woman enthusiastically took the watch into the welding booth. The die welder was waiting for her. She came in and interrupted his welding operation. He put his stuff down and listened as she told him the story behind the watch. I don't know how he kept a straight face through it all. After the woman finished her story, she gave the watch to the welder.

Now the die welder acted out his role in the practical joke to perfection. He acted very perturbed. He took the watch, looked at it, and growled something that the woman couldn't hear. Then he took his hammer and smashed the watch into a thousand tiny pieces. He gave the watch back to the woman and told her to leave his welding booth. He didn't have any spare time to be fixing old, worthless watches!

This stunned the apprentice girl. It broke her heart. She started crying, not just crying but sobbing. Then she exited the booth, and there were all of us standing there laughing at her. The joke was on her. Her journeyman started explaining to her the watch was worthless, that it was all a practical joke. The only problem was she didn't think it was very funny. Now the times, they were a-changing, because this practical joke had been standard practice for years in the shop. But now, the new apprentices didn't have to put up with this type of behavior. The die maker and the die welder were called to the office and chewed out. That was the last we saw of that practical joke.

Another practical joke that was frequently pulled was one where a person would try to guess your weight. A journeyman would find a willing victim and start talking about how he could guess the weight of anyone he came across that day. This was like what the guy does at the carnivals that pass through the towns. As the setup for this moved forward, the journeyman would correctly guess the weight of three or four other guys who were involved with the scheme. The journeyman would pick the person up from his backside. This left the person being weighed up in the air and off his feet with his backside exposed. After a few rounds of this where amazingly, the journeyman was getting all the weights correct, it was now the apprentice's turn to get weighed. Only now, the whole department knew what was going to happen and started milling around the area. When the journeyman lifted the apprentice off his feet, another journeyman whacked the apprentice across the buttocks with a two-by-four. Boy was the victim embarrassed after that, and that shot to the buttocks with a two-by-four hurt!

While the next item is not a practical joke, it was a bonding time in the shop. In line with the season, everyone was at peace and came together to celebrate.

Christmas Luncheon

One of the nicer rituals that we practiced in skilled trades was a Christmas luncheon every year. I don't remember having these while I was working production. Journeymen would take up a collection for food and organize all of the activities. Most everyone brought a dish to pass. The morning of the luncheon, the heat-treat area was cleared out and cleaned up. The ovens were set up to warm the food. Large tables were set up to hold all the goodies. Then around ten in the morning, people would start wandering into the area and sampling the food. Shortly thereafter, everyone would line up to get his or her plate of food. You see, this was a big deal because we typically got ten to twelve days off to celebrate the holidays. Christmas carols were played on a radio. Management even came down and ate with the guys. They allowed us an hour for the lunch. A lot of good camaraderie took place at these luncheons. It was the one time of year when we all put aside our differences and came together.

Car Heist

I had sold my 1973 Pontiac Firebird and purchased a brand-new 1975 Chevrolet Camaro. I had ordered a Z28 body style, but it was not available that year. I believe this was due to new air-quality emissions and gas regulations from the federal government. General Motors could not pass the new EPA air-quality emissions standards and did not put out a Z28 model that year. The Camaro was a very nice vehicle. I had this vehicle for eighteen months. I was selling it to purchase a brand-new 1976 Chevrolet Monte Carlo. I advertised the Camaro in the plant's newsletter. In those days, a small newsletter came out twice weekly in the shop. Employees were allowed to place advertisements in it. A couple came out to our house in Fenton and looked at the Camaro. They liked it quite well. They asked me if I would take it to their service station in downtown Flint so they could have it inspected by their mechanic. I agreed to do that.

Off I went to have the vehicle inspected. They did a very thorough job during the inspection. They lifted the vehicle up into the air and inspected the underside as well as the engine compartment. When they were done, they backed the vehicle out of the garage and gave it back to me.

For some reason—I really don't now remember why—my father drove the vehicle to work one morning. He pulled in and parked in the west salary parking lot. When he came out of the plant to go home, the car was missing. He went back into the plant and called me on the phone. He asked me if I had come and got the vehicle. I was surprised and told him I had not. He then called the police and reported the vehicle missing. When talking with the police while filing a stolen vehicle report, we found out that many vehicles had been stolen from the plant. This was a recent phenomenon. The plant was located adjacent to the I-75 expressway, and it made for a quick getaway once a vehicle was stolen. There was a treasure trove of new vehicles parked in these lots from which to choose. I never saw my Camaro again.

I received a check from the insurance company in settlement of my claim. For eighteen months of ownership, that car cost me three hundred dollars. Not a bad resale value in those days. Looking back though, I do believe that last couple who looked at the car was involved in the process of stealing it. I bet they either made a key impression or wrote down the key code and had another key made. Then, when it was convenient, they watched and waited to make their move. I believe someone on the inside of the plant watched the car so they could plot their course.

About this point in time, I was rotated to third shift for further training. I was on third shift for a short period of time. I think it was less than six months.

Third Shift

In the late 1970s, the plant had a thriving third shift. This is also known as midnight shift. It started at ten thirty at night and ended at seven in the morning. There was very little production on third shift. It was time spent on maintenance and preparation for the coming day-shift production operations.

The third shifters themselves were a motley crew. They were a different breed of men. Most of them had businesses that they ran on the outside. I believe they never slept. Their shift would end, and off they would go to repair their rental houses, farm their property, or whatever else they did on the outside. There was, however, a lot of sleeping that took place during the shift. Their culture was such that you gave the third shifters a job, got out of their way, and things would be ready for the day shift. Once their job was complete, however, you better leave them alone because then they rested.

I was placed on third shift for a short period of time near the end of my apprenticeship. Third shift came very hard for me. I've always been an early-to-bed-and-early-to-rise type of person. I have always preferred day shift. Day shift lends itself to a normal, traditional family lifestyle. But for my short time on third shift, I did see a lot.

The third-shift supervisor was a man named Jim. Jim ran a tight ship. If you didn't work Jim's way, he ran you right off the shift. The main core of journeymen respected Jim for this. But there were those who didn't conform. They didn't go along with Jim. So there was always some type of controversy going on. You see, to run you off the shift, Jim would continually write you up for violations of the shop rules. Jim spent most of his time in labor relations penalizing nonconformists. However, once the process was complete, Jim had a work crew he could trust and who conformed to his rules.

Now Jim wasn't perfect. He had worked his way up through the ranks. He had a sleeping problem. No matter where he went or how fast he traveled, once he stopped, he would fall asleep sitting on his scooter. He must've had some activities going on the outside as well. No one was allowed to touch Jim's scooter either. This presented a challenge to the guys every time they saw Jim sleeping.

One morning, we came in and there were pictures posted everywhere in the plant. They were the size of eight-and-a-half-by-eleven handbills. There was Jim sound asleep on his scooter. Boy was he pissed off. He spent most of the early morning running around pulling them down off of the column posts.

Another morning, when we came in, Jim's shoes had been painted fluorescent orange. This was another prank that had been pulled on him while he was sleeping. Jim didn't know his shoes were orange. He didn't see them, and his third shifters didn't tell him. Our supervisor, Louie, had to tell Jim his shoes had been painted. Man was he pissed!

One time, Jim had received a very good yearly performance evaluation. His boss told him he was outstanding in his field. Jim was very proud of this and told his guys. That probably was a big mistake. The next day, the third shifters had made eight-and-a-half-by-eleven handbills and plastered them up all over the shop again. The first picture in the cartoon showed Jim and his boss huddling up together. The boss had his arm around Jim telling him he was outstanding in his field. The next cartoon showed Jim all alone, isolated, and standing in a field somewhere lost. He had a dumb look on his face. The caption read, "Yeah, out standing in left field!" The third-shift guys got a lot of laughs out of this incident, especially as once again, Jim spent the next couple of nights ripping down all the handbills that were up. It seemed like the faster he pulled them down, the faster more of them went up. Everybody wanted a picture of Jim out standing in his field.

Things did take a turn for the worse. Jim was riding a few guys very hard. He had determined they were undesirable for third-shift maintenance work. He came to work one night pretty shaken up. Rumor had it that that morning, he had been in his house looking out the front picture window when a bullet was fired. The bullet narrowly missed him. It went right through his window. He was never the same after that.

Amos

There was a wonderful old guy on third shift named Amos. Amos was a big old country boy from down South. If Amos liked you, he would give you the shirt off his back. If he didn't, he could tear your head off. Amos loved to play the nightly gambling numbers that were run in the shop. He especially liked it after they started using the numbers that were pulled daily from the Michigan lotto. He felt this was a fairer system. Amos really started playing the nightly numbers then.

One night, on third shift, Amos hit the numbers for fifty thousand dollars! He couldn't believe his fortune. Amos came in the next night with a loaded pistol concealed in his pants. Plant security was very loose in those days. He went down into the plant basement and received a brown paper sack, a Hamady sack, stuffed full of money. Amos had a cab waiting for him outside the plant hourly entrance gate. He took his money, walked out of the plant, got into the cab, and went home. He had successfully received his tax-free winnings. When I congratulated Amos about this, he said he had one more goal to achieve before he retired. When I asked him what that was, he said, "To hit the numbers one more time for another fifty thousand dollars!" in his heavy Southern drawl. "A man can retire real nice on that kind of money." To my knowledge, Amos is still trying to achieve his last financial goal.

It was easy to gamble in the shop. The numbers runners were everywhere. In the fall, they would distribute the weekly football tickets that you could play for five dollars. Pick the right combinations of winning teams and you took home a nice payout. I played them on a few occasions, but I never won.

After a Monday night game, we almost had a suicide in the parking lot. One gentleman was deep in gambling debt. He had bet his next house payment against the Dallas Cowboys. In that game, the opposition was ahead the whole night. On the last play of the game, Dallas somehow scored a touchdown and pulled the game out. That guy lost a lot of money on that one play with no time left on the clock. His world came tumbling down around him. In an instant, his luck ran out.

Pussy Face

There was one other strange happening that went on while I was on third shift. The shift superintendent, a guy named Floyd, seemed to be quite the ladies' man. Floyd was a good-looking guy, and he kept himself in good physical shape. The story goes that one night, Floyd was out with the guys, and they were having a good time. Booze was flowing freely. Floyd was allegedly good at chasing women, and the guys were jealous. They were talking about Floyd's good looks at the table, and someone, maybe Floyd himself, said he had a "pussy face." Apparently, Floyd was very proud of this comment, and the nickname stuck to him like glue.

This is not hard to imagine because Floyd drove a full-size Chevrolet van. It was one of those customized versions with all the amenities included. Floyd loved the interior lighting system because they worked off of a dimmer switch. Floyd said these were his "mood lights."

Now, the problem was that word leaked out on the floor about Floyd's new nickname. The third-shift guys thought this was pretty funny. Whenever Floyd was walking the floor, everyone would start shouting his new nickname, "Hey, Pussy Face!" Floyd didn't like this very well. He had a couple of guys penalized for saying this about him. Well, that just fired the guys up even more. Now it became a game of hide-and-seek. As Floyd walked the floor, the guys would hide on top of presses, up on balconies, or wherever they could stay out of sight and shout out as loud as they could, "Hey, Pussy Face!" This made Floyd angry, and he would run around trying to find the culprits. He threatened to fire anyone he could find. Secretly though, I think Floyd was proud of his nickname.

However, I believe Floyd was all talk and no action. He played the playboy image often, but it was just a bunch of bullshit. I later got to know Floyd, and he wasn't a bad guy.

Plant Manager's New Television

One time on third shift, I went with my journeyman to the back of the plant to get some items out of general stores. The plant's general stores carried all kinds of goodies that we needed to conduct our business. The crib attendant there was a real nice old guy. He invited my journeyman and me into the back of the crib. This was a no-no. We were never supposed to go back there where we could grab supplies without turning in our crib requisition card that our supervisor had signed. Sitting there on a shipping pallet in a box was a brand-new color television. It was a real nice console -model, state-of-the-art television. It looked way out of my price range. The crib attendant said this was slated to go to the plant manager's house first thing in the morning. He said this was the second one that had come through the crib recently. An electrician who was there said that that was nothing and that there were electricians who had completely rewired his house on the lake. They said this took a couple of months to complete. They enjoyed the assignment.

***

After my short stay on third shift, I was rotated back into the machine room to finish the time needed to complete my machinist requirements. There is an interesting note here. After any machine repair apprentices completed their machine room training, they were never allowed to operate this machinery again. Only the die makers could work as machinists after their apprenticeships were completed.

Machine Room

I enjoyed the time I spent in the machine room. Once you had worked with a journeyman for a while, you were allowed to operate machinery on your own. At first, the journeyman was always nearby, and then after a while, you were left alone. Most times, you could start the machining ery process and complete the job without having to pass it on to others. It was good and fulfilling work. I especially enjoyed being a lathe operator. I enjoyed shaping round stock into usable and productive shapes. Usually, it turned into some type of shaft.

The time I spent in the machine room was probably the last highlight of my apprenticeship. The machine room was not actually a room; it was sprawled about throughout the plant.

The first machine I was assigned to was called a shaper. These machines do not exist anymore. They are outdated. A shaper would rough down steel blocks close to the finished size required for the job. It would also square up the steel block.

Next, I was sent to the small mills. Here, I cut keyways, slots, angles, and pockets into steel pieces as required for each job. After that, I went to the screw machine. You were required to set up the machine to make many of the same item. This work was very similar to working on a lathe. Once the machine was set up, you might make a hundred or two of the same item.

From the screw machine, I was transferred to the lathe. Basically, on the lathe, I made round objects smaller, cut screw threads, made machine shafts, and cleaned up scarred surfaces. I enjoyed my time on the lathe. What I did seemed to make sense to me. One of the negatives of working in a large factory was that there was so much going on you rarely got to complete anything. There were so many people involved in the various activities that rarely did anyone get full say on a job and then get to follow it through to completion. In the machine room, especially on the lathe, I could start a job, do all of the work required, and finish what I started. I enjoyed that feeling. I think the machine room was the easiest and best way to judge an apprentice's work because of this fact.

When I worked on the mills, we would sometimes have to machine brake lining. Often, the lining was too thick. We purchased brake lining material by the roll, and we would then cut it into the desired thickness. I remember looking down the aisle one time from the far end of the machine room and watching another apprentice who was milling brake lining. The machine room itself was pretty dark, and every machine had its own overhead light. These lights were attached to each machine so we could see better as we worked. I saw this guy's silhouette against the backdrop of the light. I didn't think much of it at the time, but I specifically recall seeing him surrounded by the particles of brake lining floating in the air. Years later, we realized how dangerous this was because the linings were made from asbestos. The government has mandated a health program for those of us who worked around asbestos. Each year now, we are all tested to watch for any signs of medical problems because of asbestos use in the factories. So far so good for me.

One morning, while I was working in the machine room, one of the female apprentices showed up in a dress. Man, did she look good compared to how she looked in coveralls! She was collecting her things as she had just quit the apprenticeship program. She said the job was making her lose her femininity.

***

Another guy I was friends with quit his die maker apprenticeship as well. Bill had been an eighth-grade math teacher in the Davison, Michigan, area. He said it was very difficult to teach eighth-graders mathematics, especially the boys. I asked him how he did it, and he said it took a bottle of aspirin a day to get by. Bill was contemplating going back into teaching. He said he didn't fit into the culture of the shop floor. I asked him why he felt that way. He said the best example of this had happened a couple of weekends earlier. While working on a Saturday, he was assigned to a die line out on the plant floor. He had to get in between an open die and grind overhead. His partner that day was another apprentice named Darcy. As they got situated and started to work, Darcy struck up a conversation with Bill. She asked him what his favorite subject was. Before he could answer, she told him what hers was. They were all the different forms of intercourse and foreplay. It seemed as though she just couldn't get enough of it. She was very promiscuous and was quite proud of herself. She described her encounters in stunning detail.

Bill was quite taken aback by this. He wasn't used to being around these types of people. Darcy told him her boyfriend had just kicked her out of his apartment because he couldn't have sexual relations with her as often as she needed. Bill told me he was flabbergasted and asked the supervisor to give him another job at lunchtime. This was one of Bill's last straws, and he ended up quitting his apprenticeship and going back to teaching.

While we were in the machine room, Darcy was quite the hit. She wore T-shirts with no bra underneath. Every once in a while, the machine room supervisor would come by and lift her shirt up to have a look at her goods. Darcy never objected. She got all the good jobs in the machine room.

One time, the machine room supervisor had a bag of popcorn that he was eating. He had the bright idea to throw a piece of it at Darcy. It went right down her coveralls. When Darcy wore her coveralls, she wore no bra and not many buttons were fastened. Well, this was a big hit. Soon all the guys were throwing popcorn down Darcy's coveralls. Darcy thought this was funny.

June

Another female apprentice named June was working in the machine room. June had exceptionally long hair. One time, when June was working on a lathe, her hair got caught in the spinning chuck. A large chunk of June's hair was pulled out of her scalp. This left a gaping wound. After that, people with longer hair had to start wearing their hair up off the top of their heads or they had to wear hats. A lot of people cut their hair short.

Keller

As I made my way through the various machines in the machine room, I finally got to operate the Keller machine. Not everyone got this opportunity. I was very pleased with myself. A Keller was a precision milling machine that traced a pattern of a die on one end and actually cut the die shoe on the other end. This is how we machined dies before we had computerized machines that could be programmed. It was quite an honor for me. My biggest accomplishment was to trace and cut the face of a quarter into a piece of aluminum. That was good stuff back then.

Grinders

On the grinders, I learned how to do very precise work. When grinding on hardened surfaces, I learned how to grind to tolerances within five ten-thousandths of an inch. That is thinner than the hair on your head, which is around ten thousandths of an inch thick (that's easy for me to say). Sometimes on the grinders, it seemed if I breathed too hard, it would take me out of the specified tolerance. I learned to grind smaller flat pieces of steel, round pieces, and also the inside holes on some pieces.

Gerstner Toolbox

One of the nicer items we received as we worked in the machine room was a Gerstner toolbox. This was a beautifully crafted wooden box that we kept all of our precision tools locked up in. This box was a source of great pride. We all saved the cardboard box that it came in and used it as a cover to keep the dust off of it. I still have my micrometers and precision measuring tools in my Gerstner toolbox at home.

***

After I finished up my hours in the machine room, I was once again placed back into the west plant bullpen. I was now approaching the latter stages of my apprenticeship. This was in late 1978. Whatever job I was on at the time came to a halt while we were waiting on something. We were waiting on the crane once again. I remember sitting on my toolbox waiting. We did a lot of waiting, for a lift from the crane, for other trades, for parts, or for further instructions. We were working in the bay where the cranes supplied the blanks for all of the production lines in the west plant. Nothing interfered with production. If we needed a lift, we would notify the crane operator. Then we would wait. I remember this case because it took three full days of waiting. I read the newspaper. General Motors was reporting very good news. It was earning record profit levels, and it had captured close to 50 percent of the United States automotive market. Man, things were looking very secure. I was almost done with my apprenticeship, and General Motors was rolling along just like it always had since World War II.

Tool Crib Assignment

One of the last assignments they gave to apprentices was to work in the tool crib for a couple of weeks. This was to show us how the crib system worked. As skilled tradesmen conducted their work, they were always going to the tool crib to get something, whether it was nuts and bolts, which were always kept locked, or precision measuring tools that were provided for loan on an as-needed basis. Working in the tool crib was great. You got to meet all kinds of people on a daily basis, as they all migrated to the crib for one thing or another. You also got to see all of the precious things that were carried in the crib. There were many desirable items.

The crib attendants also had a poorly kept secret. On the last day that an apprentice was assigned to the tool crib, he could take all of the tools he needed for free if he bought the attendants lunch. I must confess I partook in that tradition. On my last day, I went and purchased a feast from Kentucky Fried Chicken for the crib attendants. I purchased extra fixin's so it would take a lot of time to eat all of the food. While they were eating their lunch, I checked things out in the tool crib to make sure everything was okay! Wink, wink.

4
1979

Completions

The year 1979 was a very big one for me. After completing all of the required courses for my apprenticeship, I again returned to Mott College to complete my course requirements for an associate's degree. In May, I finished my last class at the college. I completed my degree in industrial supervision and achieved high sophomore honors, Pi Alpha. Man, was I proud of my degree. I was the first one in my family to earn a college degree. The next day, I took my degree up to salaried personnel. I was getting the itch to go on supervision. I had now completed my associate's degree and was heading toward the completion of my apprenticeship as well.

When I got to salaried personnel, I asked to see the salaried coordinator who was in charge of putting on new supervisors. His name was Bob. What a jerk he turned out to be! I entered his office feeling on top of the world. I told him about my new degree and that I would like to be considered as a candidate for supervision as soon as I completed my apprenticeship. This didn't go over very well with Bob. Looking back, I think I should have gotten down on my knees before I spoke to Mr. Bob. I didn't know my place. He began to let me know he was in charge there; I was not. His voice got very loud. His was a deep voice, and it resonated loud enough for the entire immediate office area to hear. He told me he didn't recognize any associate's degree. It wasn't a degree in his book. All he recognized were bachelor's degrees. He also let me know I wasn't finished with my apprenticeship, and it was a little early for him to consider someone like me as a candidate for supervisor. Then I believe he told me to leave his office. I was stunned to say the least. I felt like I had just been slugged in the stomach very hard. I turned and left his office. All the front office personnel were staring at me and smugly smiling. I was the hit of their day. I dribbled back to my work area. Man, was I crushed. I just kept hearing his words over and over in my mind. Then anger swept over me, followed by lingering doubt. Maybe I didn't know my place. Maybe General Motors didn't want someone like me. Maybe I wasn't smart enough, or maybe I was too raw and didn't have the necessary polish it took to be a salaried employee. Maybe, maybe, maybe …?

In August, my wife and I moved into our brand-new house that we had had built. It was a beautiful thirteen-hundred-square-foot ranch. We also had a beautiful eighteen-month-old baby girl. Then in November, I completed all the requirements of my apprenticeship and graduated to journeyman. It was a moment full of pride. I felt that I had made it. I was now going to take my place in the long line of machine repair personnel who had graced Chevrolet Flint Metal Fabricating. There were around 130 machine repair journeymen in the plant. Being that I was among the newest and had the least seniority, I was reassigned to the second shift. I still had a lot to learn. The journeyman's card in reality was a license to learn. There was still an entire plant full of machinery and equipment that I had never laid my hands on yet. I wanted to learn it all. I was extremely curious about how things worked and, more important, why they didn't work. Now I had the opportunity to continue honing my repair skills.

Second Shift

One of my first assignments on second shift was to "cover" production of the CK fender lines. CK was the Chevrolet designation for their pickup truck. These were the same lines I had worked on when I first hired into the plant and didn't yet have my ninety days in. Being the skilled tradesman on the line was quite different than being a production worker. Now, the culture was that as the production lines were running, we skilled tradesmen sat down. This was always justified by the fact that if we skilled tradesmen were sitting down, that meant the production line was running and if the production line was running, General Motors was making money! Now I didn't want to screw this assignment up. I knew it was coming because more than 50 percent of the machine repairmen were assigned to cover production lines. I wasn't looking forward to it. Really, to me, it was very boring sitting there all night long day after day. In those days, we traditionally were allowed to work Saturdays on our production lines for maintenance work. We were able to cobble together all the things that had broken or just worn out during the previous week. Really good tradesmen could make their repairs on Saturday and sit all the next week. The guys who had been at it a while we're very good at what they did. But to me, it was boring work. I wanted to work out of the bullpen on the major breakdowns, new equipment installations, and the hot jobs that always came up. I soon settled into my new assignment working anywhere between forty-eight and sixty hours a week. This was one of the benefits of being a skilled tradesman. You could always count on overtime pay even in a slow economy. Local banks would even loan you more money for a mortgage because you were a skilled tradesman and more likely to get overtime money than production employees. The pay was good, and it allowed me to enhance our new home. I did meet many a character covering the production lines.

Gerry

When I met Gerry, he was having marital problems. You see, Gerry was on his fourth marriage. His problem, as he explained it to me, was that although this was his fourth marriage, after a short while, the new wife became just like his first wife. He said he would look at his current wife, and his eyes would betray him, because physically, he saw his first wife. This was happening for the third time. Now, his first wife was never completely out of the picture because they had had two children together. Gerry was a responsible person and was a good father to his children. It was a wonder that Gerry didn't have a drinking problem.

The problem with his current wife had been going on for a couple of months. Gerry told me he was getting ready to file for yet another divorce. Then he told me he was having feelings for his first wife again. That turned a few heads. She was going through a nasty divorce herself. Gerry thought the feelings that were stirring up for his first wife were a little crazy at first. He told me he felt like an idiot and that he was going in circles. If this worked out, his fifth wife would also have been the first one. And that is exactly what happened. In time, he divorced his fourth wife and remarried his first wife. I thought that there might be a lesson in this for me. When I found myself in discussion with guys who were contemplating a divorce, I would always remind them of Gerry's story. As I went through a few bumps in my marriage, I thought of Gerry. *Go ahead,* I kept telling myself, *get a divorce, and get married again. Then everything will get better or maybe not! You'll just end up marrying the same woman over and over.* You see, the problem is with the person looking in the mirror and not necessarily the spouse.

Gerry also had a very brilliant mind. If I remember, Gerry had a bachelor's degree and was a schoolteacher. He often became very bored watching the production lines. One day, when he was very bored, he had the bright idea to try to trap a mouse that had invaded his work area. He brought in a mousetrap, and soon, he caught the mouse. The mice in the shop were very ugly. They were black, and they all looked sickly. There were many of them. Gerry reset the trap and caught yet another mouse. Then he saw a large-size rat travel through his area. This was too big for him to pass up. There was too much temptation there. Gerry graduated from mousetraps to setting up rattraps in his work area and all over his production line. Soon, Gerry was catching large, industrial rodents. Seeking further relief from his boredom, he started showing them to other people. Not everyone thought this was cool. Gerry kept catching and showing off his rats. One day, a woman complained to her supervisor about Gerry's activities, and that was the end of that. Gerry removed all of his rattraps.

Line Electrician

On these production lines, we had a full-time electrician assigned to us. I can't remember his name, but he was a blond-haired, blue-eyed good old boy from the Deep South. This guy was extremely intelligent as well. Too bad General Motors never tapped his brainpower for anything else. He could troubleshoot a production breakdown faster than anyone I have ever met. He was a fantastic cobbler. If you wanted the production line to run, he could use bailing wire and bubblegum to keep it going. But the guy liked to watch television. I mean, he really liked to watch television. He could watch television all night long. There was only one problem. Watching television on the shop floor was a violation of the stinking shop rules. Now we had a problem. This electrician who had a brilliant mind was bored out of his gourd. There was nowhere in the plant he could relieve his boredom. General Motors wasn't interested in his intelligence. They just wanted him to work when they told him and how they told him. What a sad case of wasted human resources. At the time, General Motors was the largest corporation in the world, and it wasted the vast majority of its human resources. I believe there were more than four hundred thousand hourly people working for them in the early 1980s. The GM management culture utilized less than 1 percent of the hourly brainpower that they fully bought and paid for, in many cases from cradle to grave.

This electrician brought in a small television and set it up in his work area. His supervisor, Percy, was right on him about it. The electrician put it away but soon set it up in a hidden area. Percy had been through this type of activity before. He camped out in the area. Every time he thought the television might be on, he would rush into the electrician's work area in an attempt to catch him watching television. This went on for a few weeks. Percy did catch the guy watching television and wrote him up for wasting time. This was a violation of the shop rules. The committeeman would get involved and get the write-up removed from the guy's record or would file a grievance. If Percy wouldn't remove the write-up, labor relations would remove the grievance as if it was never written.

Then one day, the electrician began to build a wooden cubicle-like structure from plywood in the middle of his work area. Percy came right over and demanded the electrician tear it down. The electrician called his committeeman, and he smoothed things over. The structure stayed, and the electrician agreed not to watch television anymore.

The electrician then built a set of shelves in his new enclosed work area to house the spare parts he needed to maintain the production line. On one of the shelves he enclosed, he made a trapdoor. He could flip the door open and hold it with an electrical magnet. At the entrance to his work area, he installed a photo eye. The photo eye worked like a tripwire that I had been trained on in the marines. If the trip wire was disturbed in any way, it activated some type of alarm. In the marines, this was highly desirable for use in ambushes. You wanted to know when the bad guys were coming. In the shop, you also needed to know when the bad guys were coming. The photo eye shot an invisible beam of light from the eye to a receiver. If the beam was broken, it would send an electrical signal to a controller. In this case, the controller, when tripped, would shut the TV off, turn the magnet off, and the trap door would close by the spring he had fastened to it. Now Percy would never catch the electrician watching TV again. This became quite a challenging game between the two men. Every time Percy came rushing up the aisle, he would trip the light beam, the TV would shut off, and the trapdoor would close. Percy never caught the electrician watching TV again. He and I watched many a night of TV while assigned to the truck fender lines. Years later, Percy finally had the millwrights tear down the electrician's plywood cubicle so he could not watch television anymore.

The same electrician was also a successful entrepreneur. He set up a popcorn stand just outside of his work area. Each night, he would pop popcorn, fill up brown lunch sacks, and sell them for fifty cents apiece. He would do this at the beginning of the shift and place the bags neatly into an old gutted-out electrical panel on the production line. He installed a light on the inside of the panel that kept the popcorn warm. He had very low expenses for his business. General Motors paid for his electricity, storage facility, and his time. This guy netted close to forty-five dollars every night. This was good money back then. There was nothing quite as good as the smell of popcorn permeating the oily shop floor atmosphere. Everyone in the entire shop enjoyed his popcorn. Superintendents, supervisors, and hourly employees all purchased popcorn from this electrician's stand. I had several bags of that popcorn myself over the years.

Oil Can Eddie

One line over from my production line was a machine repairman named Eddie. He was assigned to another truck fender production line as well. His nickname was Oil Can Eddie. Eddie had a large-sized oil can with a hand-operated lever. The first thing Eddie did at the beginning of each shift was to oil down his entire line. Any moving part that Eddie could get to received a shot of oil. He did this at lunchtime as well. Eddie had one of the best running lines on his side of the plant. At the first sign of trouble, he would grab his oil can and start firing. Most of the time, this didn't fix the problem, but Eddie was getting old and time and booze had taken its toll on him and it was about all he could do anymore. Usually, one of us younger guys would go over and give Eddie a hand to get his line running.

I remember one summer, we were doing some major upgrades to the presses on Eddie's line. Each night after our work was complete and we were cleaning up, many of the younger guys would have an after-shift drink with Eddie. This consisted of a sixteen-ounce Styrofoam cup half full of straight whiskey. Down the hatch it went, gulp, gulp, gulp. Eddie couldn't talk the rest of the night. It was as if a dentist had frozen his bottom lip with Novocain. It just wouldn't work. The younger guys would help get Eddie upstairs to change into his street clothes. This went on for the entire summer.

Shortly thereafter, our supervisor had to discipline Eddie. It seems

Eddie had a little problem. After he started drinking, he started pissing on the column posts that held the plant ceiling up. Some of the women in the area saw Eddie exposed, and they didn't like it. The supervisor put Eddie out on the street for a while. Eddie was in his late sixties at the time. I can't imagine what he told his wife as to why he wasn't working. The committeeman finally got Eddie back to work. It didn't take long and Eddie was drinking whiskey out of his Styrofoam cup. Then he must've started pissing in public again. This time, the committeeman talked Eddie into retiring. Eddie's defense was his legs couldn't walk down and back up from the bathroom stairs. No shit! Eddie was stoned.

Typical Journeyman: Bob

Bob was one of the typical second-shift journeymen. He was young and had served a tour of duty in Vietnam. Bob lived in Birch Run, Michigan, a rural community north of Flint. Bob fed his family on venison, a lot of venison. He hunted deer all year round. He processed all of his deer himself. Bob would shoot five to eight deer every year. His family ate every bit of it.

Bob wanted to build a new house. He decided to do it himself to save money. He found a doctor to place him on sick leave. There was nothing wrong with Bob, but it was very common in the Flint area in those days to find a doctor who would grant you a sick leave. You just had to pay the doctor a little money on the side. A lot of shop workers took the entire summer off this way. For a few dollars, these doctors would medically declare you too sick to work. General Motors had generous sick pay benefits. I believe you received your full pay for several weeks, and then it began to get reduced on a sliding scale. But it paid well until you could get back to work. Your medical benefits remained intact so you still had those. This practice has cost General Motors a great deal of money over the years. This was very prevalent in the Flint area. When Bob completed his house, he returned to work. I think he was off work for about four months.

Bob was also part of a group of guys who frequently smoked pot. These guys would go off into the basement and get stoned. If you are getting the impression that there was a lot of drinking and drug use on the plant floor, then I'm giving you the right impression. We made good money, and drugs and booze were readily available.

There were many guys who lived like Bob. I had a good friend named John. John's dad and uncle worked in the plant and were both machine repair journeymen. John was the guy who was able to get into the pre-apprenticeship classes that taught you to score a 100 percent on the apprenticeship test at the union hall. John verified for me that these classes did indeed exist. John realistically was already a journeyman when he started his apprenticeship. He merely had to complete his time to meet the graduation requirements. He already knew how to repair everything when he hired in. His father and uncle had prepared him all his life for this job. John had a different outlook on life than I did. I was fascinated by this perspective. John was what I would call a rugged individualist. He didn't think much of the federal government and thought it could collapse at any moment. There were many guys working in the shop who thought like John. John, like Bob, lived off the land. Venison and wild game were staples of their diets. They always had huge vegetable gardens each summer. They canned all the vegetables they couldn't eat and kept them in a safe place. John also processed all of his wild game himself. They all had plenty of guns. Hunting rifles were as good as gold. They were passed down for generations. They always had to be prepared for action at a moment's notice. If the government ever collapsed, they could live off the land. They rarely borrowed any money. They paid cash for everything. Credit was an evil, controlling system set up by the money people to control the little people. This was a very different perspective on life than what I was accustomed to.

Some of the guys, a lot of them, felt paying taxes was illegal. Some of them listened to different philosophies of men who would come along and tell them how not to pay taxes. These guys took action. They would claim they had 999 dependents, and therefore, they didn't have any federal taxes withheld from their paychecks. This went on for a few years. It was a big movement in the shop. One guy in the machine room spent time in federal prison because of it. I must say, their arguments were very persuasive. In the end, this line of thinking didn't hold up, and they all paid their taxes. Most of them paid a lot with penalties and interest. It seems as if the federal system is legal and has the ability to collect its due when necessary.

Wild Bill

Wild Bill was another of the older machine repairmen who stayed on second shift. Wild Bill was a mere shadow of what he was in his younger years. Rumor had it that Bill had had a stroke a few years back and that as long as he took his medication, he was all right. Wild Bill walked stiffly around with a glazed look on his face. Wild Bill had been quite the partier in his youth. He was a good guy and did the best he could, and the guys always took care of him. One night, Wild Bill was having difficulty on his production line. He went into his troubleshooting mode. He decided he needed to go up on top of the draw press to check things out. Up he went. But there were problems with this. For safety purposes, when you went on top of presses, you had to have the overhead crane locked out. Otherwise, if you were up there and the crane passed overhead, it could knock you down. General Motors had predetermined all the clearances and marked the areas where there wasn't sufficient clearance with a yellow line. This was a long-standing practice. If you were going above the yellow line, you had to disable the crane by shutting it off electrically and then placing your personal safety lock on the electrical disconnect. As you locked it out, no one could operate the crane. Now this wasn't a quick, routine thing to do. It took a long time. This was also in the work bay where the cranes lifted the stack of blanks onto the beginning of the production lines. They were always busy. Earlier, I had talked about waiting up to three full workdays before we could secure the crane. Nothing shut production down. But for whatever reason, that night, Wild Bill went up onto the top of his draw press. All of this area was above the yellow line. There was a huge safety concern. If the crane passed over Bill, it would surely knock him down to the floor. Luckily, the crane operator spotted Bill and stopped the crane to protect him. Wild Bill wasn't in his right mind, and seeing the crane stop agitated him further. He started pacing back and forth on top of the draw press. Now the tops of stamping presses are not places you want to be if you are not thinking straight. They are located twenty to twenty-five feet into the air; there is a safety railing around the entire top of the crown, but you could easily slide underneath it if you weren't careful. The top of a press is usually coated heavily in oil and grease. This is at least one-quarter of an inch thick. This coating is slipperier than any ice you can imagine. The crane operator was sounding his siren to alert anyone down on the floor. He was trying to get our attention. The noise of his siren sent Bill even further into a panic. People were gathering on the floor below trying to figure out what was going on. Wild Bill's partner ran over to the press. He started talking to Bill trying to calm him down. Wild Bill kept pacing back and forth. If he slipped and fell, it probably meant his death. The entire area was awash in industrial tooling and automation. There were no good areas to land. Some of the guys located a special yellow gondola. These gondolas had been modified for people to be lifted up by the crane to the top of the presses. I spent many an hour working out of the yellow gondolas. The guys pushed the gondola over to where the hook of the crane was located. They hooked up the gondola to the crane chains and prepped it for a lift. Wild Bill's partner, John, went up in the lift to the top of the press. John was able to talk Bill into the gondola. Thank God! It might not seem like much now, but it was a very emotional event for us machine repairmen. As far as I know, Wild Bill never went up on top of the press again.

Louie and Pete

Louie and Pete were the lead second shift machine repairmen in the east plant. They were quite a pair. They were the dynamic duo. They both drank like fish and got plastered every night. This went on for years. Yet, they were two of the nicest guys you could ever meet if they had been drinking. If they weren't drunk, man were they cranky! Especially Louie. Neither one of them was very big physically. Both were around five feet six inches tall and maybe weighed 150 pounds. But Louie could be a terror when he wanted to be. Most of the shop was afraid of Louie, and we went out of our way to avoid him when he wasn't drunk. Louie would have made a very good pirate—the kind that drank, fought, and ruled the seas. He could measure up with the best of them. I remember reading about one pirate who wore his boots on the opposite feet to be cranky. This was like Louie. Louie was always cranky.

One night, I was working with Louie and Pete. They took me under their wing. I was no threat to what they treasured. I was just a dumb-shit rookie. Whatever we were working on that night, the millwrights were watching us. One of them approached us and told us that we were doing their work. Well, this pissed Louie right off! It was early in the shift, and Louie was still fairly sober. He bunched up to make himself look bigger. It reminded me of the type of bird that a pirate always has on his shoulder, the kind that ruffles its feathers to appear larger than it really is and to also appear dominant to potential foes. Now, the millwrights were no small guys. They had sent over their enforcer crew. They had dealt with Louie and Pete before. So one of the millwrights reared up toward Louie. The millwrights in general were bigger guys. We in our machine repair arrogance always joked among ourselves that as the millwrights walked, their knuckles rubbed the ground. These guys were there for their muscle and not their brains. Louie and this millwright were standing toe-to-toe, chest-to-chest. The millwright was looking down on Louie. This didn't bother Louie at all. Now he had these millwrights right where he wanted them, under his control. Maybe it should be under his spell. All of a sudden, Louie took a deep breath of air, deep enough that it caused his shoulders to rise up into the air. Then his eyes started drilling holes into the millwright's face. He began to talk. As he talked, the tone of his voice sent shivers down my spine, and the hair stood up on the back of my neck. Louie, looking intently and never blinking, said to the millwright, "I'll go through you like a buzz saw!" That was it; his fists were doubled up, and he was ready to deliver his wrath all over this millwright's face. Folklore had it that when Louie got going on someone, his fists moved like pistons pumping in a car engine—fast and furious. Then, the millwright eased on back, one small step at a time. Louie never flinched. The millwrights left us alone the rest of the night, and we made our repairs.

Now I've got to say that Louie and Pete were some of the sharpest mechanics this side of heaven. There wasn't anything they couldn't repair, and they worked fast. This was why their drinking was tolerated like it was. They'd be assigned a job, and you could consider it done. They didn't need supervision. We always joked among ourselves about what Louie and Pete would be like as mechanics if they didn't drink. Common opinion was they wouldn't have made it. But, man, those guys were good in their alcoholic frame of mind.

One other time, Louie brought in his homemade hot peppers. He challenged anyone he could find to a hot pepper eating contest. This was the meanest batch of hot peppers he ever produced. I heard he did this once every year. There were few people left who would challenge Louie. I was not one of them. I was a hot pepper wussy! By lunchtime, Louie had found four new victims who dared try to out-hot-pepper the master. We all gathered near Louie's work area to watch the contest. All five of the contestants circled around Louie's masterpiece jar of hot peppers. One by one, they took a pepper and ate it. One guy instantaneously busted from the circle for the water fountain for relief. He guzzled water but found there was no quenching the hot, spicy pepper sauce that Louie made. This guy was doubled over in pain. Things looked grim. The four guys left ate a second hot pepper. A second guy's face turned red, and he made off toward the drinking fountain. He watered down his head but found no relief from the hot spices. The third guy simply turned around and left. He couldn't take it anymore. Louie and the fourth guy ate a third hot pepper. The fourth guy couldn't take it anymore and broke the circle. He too started drinking water. He was in a miserable state; apparently the hot spices stayed on your lips, gums, and the roof of your mouth and kept burning out of control for several minutes. There was nothing you could do to alleviate the pain. The water provided little relief. You simply had to wait it out. Now Louie was standing victoriously all by himself. Another year and once again champion! Louie was amazing. He took out one more hot pepper and devoured it in front of everyone. Maybe Louie was getting old because all of a sudden, his face and head got very red. Louie was trying hard not to show any weakness. Then tears started streaming down his face. He stood there before us with his eyes closed and his fists clenched until the moment passed. Louie didn't do much else the rest of that night. He didn't move from his chair. But we told no one because Louie was the man!

As time went on, both Louie and Pete quit drinking. I heard that after three days, Louie had a stroke. He made it back to work though. He was too mean and too tough. Pete did just fine after he quit. He became a leader, and everyone appreciated his help. He was like a father figure to us younger guys.

Mudrock

The supervisor on the west side of the plant in those days was a guy with the nickname of Mudrock. He was a hillbilly from West Virginia. He wasn't a bad guy, but Mudrock had a sleeping problem. He fell asleep everywhere and often. Maybe this was a common problem among machine repair supervisors. One time, my partner and I were working in the ram of a press. To get up to our work area, we used an extension ladder about fifteen feet tall. These types of ladders are outlawed for use in the shop today for safety reasons but were common back then. The tinsmiths would install sheet metal spikes on the feet of the ladder, and we would lift the ladder up and slam it down so the spikes would penetrate the wooden floor blocks. This wasn't a real safe work practice, as the ladders routinely would slip out of the blocks. Most of the time, the ladder would slide around on the floor until the spikes found some other deterrent to rest against. Once in a while, the ladders would fall to the floor. You had to be very careful when using these ladders.

My partner and I were up in the ram working away when Mudrock's face appeared at the top of the ram. He had climbed up the ladder and was peering over the top. As our supervisor, he needed to know what was going on. We started discussing what the job entailed, where we were on it, and the always burning question "How much longer?" My partner and I looked up, and there was Mudrock fast asleep on the top of the ladder. *Now what the hell do we do?* My partner and I looked at each other. If we startled him, he could move too fast and fall off the ladder or make the ladder shift and then fall. If we didn't do anything, he might just fall while he was sleeping. How the hell do you fall asleep while talking and standing on a ladder in the shop? We started calling out Mudrock's name, and he finally woke up. He just shook his head and picked up our conversation right where we left off. When he left, my partner and I just started laughing; we couldn't believe it.

Another time, Mudrock must have been very tired. He had lain down in the cylinder repair crib that was located in the back of our bullpen. There, Mudrock was lying down fast asleep. This was toward the end of our shift, and the third-shift guys were coming in to the bullpen area. They were not going to let this opportunity slip by. There was our supervisor, Mudrock, lying on his back fast asleep and snoring away. One guy came up with the bright idea of putting pepper in Mudrock's mouth in between his snores. He had his lunch bucket with him, and it contained a shaker of pepper. So they started doing this. This lasted for two or three snores, and then Mudrock started waking up. He finally sat up, spit out the pepper, and looked around at everybody laughing and watching him. He shook his head and said, "I don't even like pepper!" Then he got up and wrote his end-of-shift lineup and went home. We had a good laugh.

Keys: Hourly Resourcefulness

With all of the different people working in the plant, security locks were a hot commodity. Everything had to be locked up, or it would wander away. Our personal toolboxes were locked, and it remained taboo to take anyone's personal belongings. But anything that the company bought was fair game. It was kind of like what you see on TV with army property. Each bullpen area had several cabinets custom-made by tinsmiths to hold all their special gear. In the heyday of the Big Three, each shift had their own cabinets stocked full of tools and equipment for their specific use.

Keys for these cabinets were purposely made very hard to get. You needed a superintendent's signature on a key card to receive a key. These cards were kept by plant security. Security made all of the keys. There was an active black market for the purchase of these keys. Some security guards would sell keys, especially the master keys. Master keys would open several locks in the same series. One journeyman I knew became frustrated with the system and tried to have keys copied on the outside. These were special and unique keys, and the outside key makers would not copy them. The keys were stamped "Do not duplicate," so most of the time, the outside key makers would not touch them. The key blanks were not used on the outside, and they probably didn't have the blanks to begin with.

So this journeyman decided to make his own key-cutting machine. He studied the key-cutting machines on the outside. He drew up a blueprint for his machine. He gathered the necessary parts, and what he couldn't get, we helped him fabricate. This was good stuff. He built a fine key-cutting machine. There wasn't any key in that shop he couldn't duplicate. He made quite a bit of money making keys for others. I think this is a great example of the mind power that has always been available to General Motors on a daily basis. I shudder to think about the possibilities of what could've happened if General Motors had been willing to channel all of that power into making itself a world-class manufacturing competitor.

Richard

There is one other character on second shift who deserves mention. There was a production operator named Richard. Richard worked in the engine cradle department. Richard was a very religious individual. He always carried his Bible with him wherever he went. He always talked about Christ, as he belonged to a small cult-like Christian church that took it as their personal mission to save the world from itself. Richard was our resident shithouse preacher. Every plant seems to have one. Richard kept all the men's bathrooms supplied with trifold brochures damning you to hell if you didn't change your ways. I must confess, I always read these brochures when I used the restroom. I always felt like such a terrible creature after reading them. I had been raised in the Catholic religion, and they always taught us to be very private about it. They taught us to live our lives in God and that would do the talking for us. Now I was reading about a terrible damnation that was waiting for me if I didn't repent and follow the steps in the brochure—in the plant shithouse of all places!

One night after a Christmas dinner, I saw Richard, and he was extremely agitated. I asked him what was wrong. Richard stopped his preaching and told me he was very upset and was trying to save the guys who were laughing at him. They were sitting down on the area picnic table. While talking, Richard became even more agitated. I asked the other production people what was going on. It seems the guys at the picnic table had told Richard that they didn't believe in his God and his Bible was nothing but a pack of lies. Well, this sent Richard right off the deep end.

The committeeman showed up and calmed Richard down. He found out that Richard had not been taking his medication again. Richard was on an early type of Prozac. The committeeman said he was a good guy when he took his medication. They took Richard up to medical.

Later on, the pastor of Richard's church passed away. The small congregation prepared the pastor's body to meet his maker. They believed that the pastor would be resurrected in three days just like Jesus. They locked and barricaded themselves in their church with the pastor's body. After three days, nothing happened. The police had to finally break down the doors to get the pastor's body out of the church. His remaining flock was very disappointed.

Union Contractual Issues

There were some UAW contract rules that were near and dear to our hearts as hourly union members. I especially remember two of them. I spent many an hour discussing and debating these rules. I remember being worried, anxious, and just plain scared about them. The lines of demarcation were constantly changing. We were very afraid that our trade would lose all of its work and therefore its value to the company. If we lost our value, we could lose our way of life and may not be able to provide for our families and do all of the things in life we wanted to do.

The hours list, called paragraph 71, was a checks-and-balances system to ensure the supervisor didn't play favorites among the employees. There had evolved very strict rules around which person received overtime and which person did not.

Lines of Demarcation

Lines of demarcation are a very emotional issue to a skilled tradesman. These are the rules of engagement we had to work by. They can be likened to the rules we abide by when driving our vehicles. We stay on the right side of the road. We stop at traffic lights, and we travel the posted speed limits. These lines defined who got to do what work. In other words, pipefitters worked on pipes and air lines; die makers owned the dies; and electricians had all the wiring and machine controls. This seems to be real simple, but there are many, many gray areas. These rules grew to a high degree of complexity.

For instance, as a machine repairman, it was my job to repair air cylinders that provided movement for automation. However, if I needed the air lines removed from the cylinder, I had to call for a pipefitter. Pipefitters were responsible for all of the air lines in the plant, be they big or small. If all of the available pipefitters were busy on other jobs, it could take a long time for them to get to it. I spent many an hour waiting on other trades to do their work. They spent many an hour waiting on machine repair as well. If I removed the air lines—and we're talking two small air fittings—I was seen as a scab. I wasn't a good union brother if I did other trades' work. If I was working on removing an air valve, I had to wait for the electrician to undo the two small electrical wires. All electrical power had already been turned off to the valve, so it was safe to remove the wires. If all the electricians were busy, this could take all shift. We wasted a lot of time in the shop with these rules. It is a major contributor to our uncompetitiveness in the skilled trades.

Some trades would have designated crews walking out and about overseeing what everyone else was doing. They would confront anyone they saw "doing their work" and call for the committeeman. The committeeman usually would file a grievance looking for a monetary payoff for the violation of the lines of demarcation. Now, don't get me wrong, some lines of demarcation are necessary for orderliness and safety, but in the shop, it had been taken to the far extreme. This was done to protect jobs. General Motors probably had too many skilled tradesmen because of this, so ultimately, it helped to lead toward uncompetitiveness.

One time, I was working with a crew of machine repairmen installing a new stamping press. It came time for us to install the tie rods. These rods hold the body of the press together. They are very large. We lifted the tie rod nuts to the top of the press with the area crane. The millwrights were watching—they were always watching—and confronted us about using the crane. They claimed any use of the crane was "their work." We said that that wasn't written in the contractual language, and we were not violating any shop rules. They got pissed off at us. They enticed the crane operator to leave the job, as he was their buddy. The committeeman then got involved. He tried to calm everybody down. Even the two different skilled trade supervisors were verbally going after each other. This was big stuff! This was a new press, and we had never seen tie rod nuts like these. Normally, we placed the nuts on the threaded end of the tie rod and had the welders heat a section of the rod until it was cherry red. This caused the tie rod to expand. We then very quickly tightened the tie rod nut as tight as we could get it. Then when the tie rod cooled down and the length of the tie rod shortened, we had a nice, tight, pressed fit that would hold the press together.

The tie rod nut on this new press was hydraulic. We were to place it on to the tie rod, screw it down, and then pump up the hydraulic cylinder that was located in the nut. The press company had provided metal shims about one-quarter of an inch thick, which we would then place under the inside perimeter of the nut. As we released the hydraulic pressure and the nut settled down onto the shims, we had our nice, tight, pressed fit. This new technology was not covered under our existing lines of demarcation. We didn't stop working on the job as the millwrights protested. The committeeman and the millwrights left.

The next day, when we got to the job, one of our journeymen's toolboxes was missing. Normally when this happened, you'd find it a couple days later in a remote location or maybe hidden down in the plant basement. In this instance, the journeyman never did recover his personal tools or his toolbox. There was a strong rumor going around that it ended up in a railroad boxcar and had been shipped out of the plant. This was unheard of. No matter how strong our conflicts were, nobody ever messed with a journeyman's personal tools.

The plant's policy was there were no replacements for missing tools. If you broke one, say a socket, you could take it to the tool crib and they would replace it one for one. But for missing tools, the plant would do nothing. For all the plant knew, this guy could be making the entire story up, looking for free tools. This guy was out quite a bit of his own money.

The committeeman then settled his grievance with our foreman. They agreed that all of us would be involved with the job. It used to be that two people would secure a tie rod nut. Under the new agreement, we now had to have two millwrights lift the nut to the top of the press, two machine repairmen turn the nut onto the threads of the tie rod, and then two pipefitters operate the hydraulic pump. The committeeman had secured work for everyone involved. He was very popular and was regularly reelected every three years. Although not as bad now, these types of uncompetitive practices still go on today.

Paragraph 71

Another very cherished contractual item is titled paragraph 71. The company and the UAW have agreed that the company will track all of the overtime hours each person works and keep the list posted for all to see. We did this by workgroup. So all of the machine repairmen, my group, were listed and tracked together. These hours lists were tracked to the tenth of an hour. General Motors' standard work hour was broken down into ten six-minute segments. So we hourly would get paid for every tenth of an hour worked. There must have been severe violations of paragraph 71 in the past, because it was one of the most sacred contractual rights earned by the UAW. These lists were scrutinized with a fine-tooth comb every week when they were published. It was a violation of the union contract not to publish the list each week in a timely fashion. Too many hours were spent on publishing the list. A lot of grievance money has been paid because of violations of paragraph 71. If a guy was somehow missed for overtime and he complained, the supervisor would make it right by paying the guy for his missed opportunity. Sometimes, guys would purposely hide so the supervisor couldn't find them, and then they would get passed over. They would then call the committeeman and file a grievance, and they would get paid for doing nothing. Most of the time, it was easier for a supervisor to pay an employee than process a grievance. These lists also had to be balanced by shift and by trade. If either got out of whack, grievances would be written and corrections made. I don't remember even talking about these lists while I worked on production. But I also became caught up in the 71 lists when I was on skilled trades. One time, I remember a guy getting ahead of us by over four hundred hours. That is a lot of money. This was supervisor favoritism. The supervisor claimed the employee was the only person who could do the job he was on, and therefore, he was technically in a group all by himself. That didn't go over very well with us, and we got the committeeman involved. One day, they settled the grievance by putting everyone in the group back to even hours. This meant that everybody went back to zero hours. What the hell was that? The only thing we could figure out was the committeeman got something he really needed. This usually occurred when they brought back someone who had been fired for legitimate reasons. The shop committee always got the fired people back, but they had to do very heavy horse-trading with management. It would cost them dearly.

More Economics

Sometime in early 1980, the economic downturn began to affect the auto industry. In the fall of 1979, we had had the Iranian hostage crisis, which in turn led to a spike in gasoline prices. General Motors was not yet positioned to sell smaller, more fuel-efficient vehicles. At this time, the Japanese auto manufacturers really began to penetrate the United States market.

While this was happening in the larger automotive market, my plant was feeling the effects on a smaller level. In the early part of 1980, I was once again placed on layoff. There were several of us machine repair journeymen who were laid off. I had not been on layoff since I had gone on skilled trades. This was a stressful time for me. As I indicated earlier, my wife and I had just moved into a brand-new home and we had an eighteen-month-old toddler. I was able to live comfortably on my journeyman's wages, especially with overtime pay. We bought a lot of nice things with our overtime money. At the time, we lived for overtime money. Being skilled tradesmen, we typically based our "bills" on forty hours' pay and paid for the extras with overtime money. Even the local banks took overtime money into account for skilled tradesmen when considering loans. It was a given way of life in the Flint area.

The unemployment compensation I received wasn't close to my weekly wages. General Motors and the UAW had contractually agreed to SUB benefits. I believe that stands for supplemental unemployment benefits. These benefits supplemented the unemployment compensation benefits we received from the state of Michigan. I believe I received about 85 percent of my regular take-home pay. Without the additional money from these sub benefits, I would have been in financial difficulty. As it was, I was able to get by on the unemployment money I received.

This time, I didn't run into the difficulties I had the first time I was laid off in 1973. Now in Michigan and in the auto industry, we were all getting quite accustomed to massive, long-term layoffs. This time, we were able to sign up for unemployment at our local union hall instead of the unemployment office in downtown Flint. At the union hall, they treated us like men instead of lowlife trash. That made things a little nicer.

It looked like I was going to be off work for a while. The way these SUB benefits worked was you received a fixed number of credits depending on your General Motors seniority. Ten years of service earned you a fixed amount of credits. At twenty years, you'd earned enough credits that you'd never run out of them. I believe this was the first of what was considered a lifetime employment security agreement.

I had now accumulated seven years of service. I didn't have many earned SUB credits. I had maybe enough to last through twelve weeks of layoff. Every time I received SUB benefits, a deduction was made from my running total. It looked like I was going to be off longer than twelve weeks.

I was bored being on layoff. I started up a daily jogging routine that I had done on and off since I left the service. While I was in the service, I developed a liking for running. We used to run five miles at a time three times a week. Sometimes, we ran with most of our gear on; most times, it was full utilities and boots. Near the end of my enlistment, I took a physical fitness test. Part of the test included running three miles within a required time frame. I ran the three miles in eighteen minutes and twenty seconds. That's not too shabby. I regularly jogged after I got out of the service the first year, after that, not so much. It felt good to jog again. It was winter in Michigan, so I had to bundle up. But it got me out of the house.

I think I was laid off for about four weeks. It was a relief to get back to work. When I got back to work, I was two pounds lighter than before layoff. Most of the other guys had gained between five and ten pounds while they were off.

As we got back, we worked a strict forty hours a week. This lasted quite a while. It took a long time for the auto industry to shake off the effects of the unstable gasoline prices. When gasoline prices went up, sales of General Motors trucks went down. Now consumers were really looking at cars that got high gasoline mileage. This was something new and different than in the past. This gave the Japanese brands an advantage because that was what they specialized in. The Japanese were very competitive at making small cars that got great gasoline mileage.

General Motors had come out with the Chevrolet Chevette by then. I had a stripped-down two-door version. It had a four-speed manual transmission and a hatchback. I had never had a hatchback before. I thought I was pretty cool! For the time, it got pretty good gas mileage. I remember bombing down the US-23 Expressway going seventy miles an hour and shouting to my passenger because it didn't have any noise reduction built-in. I had to sell that car to meet the mortgage requirements for our new home. But we had a four-door, fully loaded Chevette for our family car. This version had an automatic transmission, custom interior, and chrome spoke wheels. What the hell was I thinking?

The country as a whole was waking up to the realization that we had a finite amount of reserves of fossil fuels and then they would be gone. The era of cheap energy appeared to be over. President Jimmy Carter had given a speech on television with a sweater on. His message was that we had to learn how to conserve energy. Well, that was all it took for us skilled tradesmen to begin thinking about energy efficiency. It seemed like that was all we talked about.

Windmills were a hot topic. We could reduce energy consumption, and with a personal windmill, we could even end up selling energy back to the local power company. Now that was something to get excited about. I remember drooling over geothermal furnaces that didn't use natural gas. All you needed was a water source that you had year-round access to. Groundwater remained at a constant temperature of fifty-five degrees, and these furnaces could squeeze heat out of the water. Man, what I would have done to get one of those furnaces. We talked about that style of furnace for hours on end. They were cost prohibitive at the time. I would've never gotten my money back.

One of our guys went into the photovoltaic business. This is where you convert solar power into electricity. He had a system set up to power his sump pump. The only problem was that in Michigan, we routinely have cloudy days. Photovoltaics do not work real well in the shade. Besides, they were too costly and weren't real efficient at the time.

So I settled down like the rest of the guys and worked on making my house more energy efficient. I put an insulated jacket on my hot-water tank. I placed plastic over my windows in the winter, and I wrapped my hot-water pipes in insulation. I installed Styrofoam insulation in all of my electrical outlets. I built a plastic insert for my fireplace to stop the cold air from coming in from the chimney. I insulated every square inch of my house to stop drafts. It seemed like everyone was working hard to improve their personal energy efficiency any way they could.

***

During this time frame, the itch to go on supervision, which is a salaried position, continued to grow in me. Long-term, that was where I envisioned myself. I was enjoying myself on skilled trades, working with my hands, but I didn't see myself doing this type of work for the rest of my working career. And actually, I saw myself as a skilled trades superintendent, except I couldn't tell anybody about it. It seemed so far away. When I had let some of the guys know my desire to go on salary, quite a few of them would have nothing more to do with me. The division between hourly and salaried was that great. The rivalry and hatred was felt on both sides. There was no opportunity at this time to even try to go on supervision. Things were too slow.

After my run-in with the salaried personnel coordinator, I knew I had to complete my bachelor's degree. After I completed my associate's degree from Mott Community College, I transferred to the University of Michigan Flint. They had just opened their new campus in downtown Flint. They had a program set up for students like me who had earned an associate's degree in applied science. Their bachelor's degree was called a two-plus-two program. I took two classes at Michigan in the fall of 1979. I passed them both. I was still on a roll from completing Mott Community College earlier in the year. I followed those two classes up with two more in the winter term of 1980. I withdrew from both of them. College just wasn't as easy as it was when I still lived at home with my parents. I had a lot more responsibilities now.

I enrolled again at Michigan in the fall of 1980 for two more classes. But the same thing happened. I didn't complete either one of them. I knew I needed to complete my bachelor's degree, but the traditional method of going to college wasn't working for me. I stopped going to the University of Michigan and wasn't sure how my education would be completed. I felt uneasy about this.

B-15 Draw Press Installation

Around this time, I received one of my favorite job assignments as a journeyman. I was assigned to work on the installation of a brand-new Danly draw press located in the plant at column B-15. The Danly Press Company in Chicago, Illinois, had built this leadoff press. This baby was state of the art. It could develop up to fifteen hundred tons of pressure on the outer dimensions of the sheet metal blank to hold it tight. This allowed the inner die to form the sheet metal into its desired configuration. I hit it off real well with the Danly representative who came in from Chicago to lead the installation process. After a time, the Danly representative had convinced the other shifts to let him and me take the lead on the project. Man, what great fun that was. It seemed like there were a million pieces of the press lying about and stored in baskets. Piece by piece and bit by bit, the press was being fully assembled. When it came time to install the crown of the press, the plant hired outside contractors to perform this delicate task, as we didn't have the equipment or knowledge to do so. The contractors set up a gantry crane system to lift the crown up in the air and then move it along the tracks that they had set up. They then lifted the crown up into the air and placed it on top of the press columns already installed in the bed of the press. I found that to be an awesome sight. Those contractors, called "riggers," knew what they were doing. It was like a symphony in motion. They arrived on site, completed their work, and were gone in no time.

On this press, instead of bolting the die to the press ram by manually placing die bolts and die nuts in place, it had built-in die clamps. These clamps were automatic. When you lowered the ram down to the bottom of the stroke, the clamps would all unlock at once. Then the ram would move up out of the way, and the die cars would move—one in and one out. What a novel concept! We had never seen this before. That was one of my better job assignments, as it fully held my interest all the way through the project.

We finished installing the press and placed it into production after that. This press had a quick die change system that was built in. The side columns were open-ended, and this allowed the two die cars to move in and out of the press quickly during line changes. This also allowed us to pre-stage the next die before the line change. This would have allowed us to greatly speed up the die change process except on this truck fender line, we never changed the dies.

***

New technology was beginning to filter into the plant. Around this time, the plant received the production work for the S-10 pickup truck fenders. This was General Motors' small pickup truck. Part of the project funding included a brand-new Cincinnati Milacron hydraulic robot. It installed five screws in the wheelhouse area helping to secure the inner panel to the outer. It also performed a couple of spot welds. Boy, did this piece of equipment garner a lot of excitement and anxiety at the same time. In years past, production workers would have performed those jobs. Also, the skilled trades were licking their chops for all of the new work possibilities these robots brought with them. There were lines of demarcation fights everywhere. They were not physical fights but mental ones. Everybody assumed this was all their work and not anyone else's. I was right in the middle of the fight. When it was all settled, the union and management assigned some of the work to each of the trades. Peace was maintained in the short-term, but uncompetitiveness was once again creeping up into the long-term. We couldn't see it then. The union always felt each trade should have a little piece of the action. In the long run, this led to highly uncompetitive practices. It cost General Motors a lot of money. But in the short-term, these agreements kept the peace. This mainly benefited the elected union officials.

The robot itself did not perform very well. It was very difficult to

135

program the computer, and the robot wasn't nearly as precise as it needed to be. The hydraulics were a pain in the rear end. If you were to look at the latest version of robots today, you would laugh at the rawness and lack of sophistication of the robotics back then. But it was a start, and now the plant could continue to refine the process as technology advanced.

5

Per-Diem Supervisor Training

The overall economy of the country must have begun to pick up toward the end of 1980. Management was coming around asking people if they were interested in going on temporary supervision during the 1981 calendar year. I think the managers on second shift knew that I was interested. They approached me, and I told them I was interested. In the late fall of 1980, management set things up for a supervisor orientation and training program in January 1981. I was accepted as one of the candidates.

The pre-supervisory training class lasted a total of eight weeks. The first two were classroom training, and the next six were spent out on the plant floor. The salaried training supervisor I had dealt with in the past coordinated the training. I think there were about a dozen of us students in the class. (This eight-week program was the first training that I received at General Motors. I had worked for the company for seven years as an hourly employee. They had never provided any training for my co-workers or me during this time. It is true that I received training on my apprenticeship, but to me, that was different than this supervisor's class. That was technical training on how to do my job. The training was not about how the company worked, its expectations, or its current direction. Think about that for a moment: seven years of working for a company and not one hour of training on the business aspects of the company. Is it any wonder that the hourly workforce wasn't in tune with management?)

The class was held in one of the plants' larger conference rooms. We had a full agenda. They had representatives from every department in the plant present to us what they did and how they fit into the overall scheme of things. There were some very good presentations. I learned a lot, but I also sat a lot. I sat for eight hours a day, five days a week. One of the first skills

I had to learn was how not to fall asleep when in meetings. Throughout the rest of my career, I used this skill well. Everyone was falling asleep all of the time. We had all come from the floor, and we were used to moving around a lot and having control over our time. Here, we were subjected to the class coordinator's whims, and I'm sure he was watching us even when he wasn't present in the room.

In one of the more interesting presentations, we learned how the plant had to bid on all new work coming in. We had to bid it by piece cost, and we had to be the lowest bidder to win the work. We went up against outside companies like Dana and Bud who also built components, such as vehicle frames, like we did. At the time, we were competitive with the outside on high-volume work, and we made most of the Chevrolet front-end sheet metal. The plant had always specialized in these high-volume jobs, but these were beginning to deteriorate as overall competition in the domestic auto market was heating up. General Motors was beginning to see a decline in its domestic market share. There was a great deal of arm-twisting going on to win new work for the plants. This was shared with us and helped us to better understand this process.

We spent a great deal of time with the labor relations representatives. They went over all of the shop rules, the grievance procedure, the local and international union contracts, and how to conduct employee discipline. Some of my classmates memorized the shop rules by heart. Good supervisors did a lot of employee discipline back then. The more discipline a supervisor completed on the shop floor, the more highly thought of he was by executive management. He was seen as doing his job. That was the main purpose of a floor supervisor, to maintain employee discipline. The thinking was: Do not let the hourly employees get out of line. They cannot be trusted. They must be watched at all times. If you leave them alone, they will just screw off and waste the entire day doing nothing constructive.

It seemed to me that the shop floor existed around labor relations and violations of the shop rules. General Motors spent and wasted a lot of time on these violations.

The materials department explained how they did things, and the timekeeping office had a lengthy session. In those days, we kept time manually. Computers had yet to arrive on the scene. Each day, the supervisor had to list employees' in and out rings so they could get paid properly. As supervisors, we spent a lot of time in the time office straightening out employees' pay.

***

The plant metallurgist explained to us what his function was. The quality and safety departments made presentations as well.

It was a very long two weeks. I learned more about the plant than I had in the previous seven or eight years. There was a lot of interworking between departments in the plant to make it go. After the two weeks in the conference room, we were assigned to our own departments for further training.

My department was called master mechanics. This was compromised of the die maker, machine repair, and welder repair trades. The department was ruled by the die makers. The department's upper managers were all die makers. There were about three hundred hourly skilled die makers in their group. There were about one hundred and thirty from machine repair and one hundred from welder repair in our group. The die maker voting block ruled the UAW politics in the skilled trade section.

I was assigned to the day-shift general supervisor of machine repair and welder repair. His name was John. John was a great technician. He knew his stuff. He was forever drawing diagrams of how machinery went together and pinpointing what wasn't working properly. John placed me with the west plant machine repair supervisor for further training. My job now consisted of following the supervisor around the plant all shift to learn what he did. John and I were walking the plant floor together, and he was getting ready to turn me over to the supervisor when he stopped by some of the journeymen who had pretty much taught me all I knew about machine repair. We stopped in the main aisle, and he told me to find out what the hell they were doing and to get them to work. He stayed in the aisle as I approached the guys.

As I was walking, I realized I was being tested. It is very tough to move from being people's apprentice to being their boss. I was very nervous as I was walking up to them. The traditional management style used in the plant was a benevolent-dictator type. There was a strict chain of command, and everyone from the superintendent on down followed his or her orders precisely. The first-line supervisor really didn't have a whole lot of authority, nor did the general supervisors. In General Motors, orders came down to us from headquarters in Detroit into the plant, to the department heads, and then to the superintendents. Then the general supervisors and the supervisors carried out their orders and plans. They didn't have a great deal of latitude.

***

Flashback: Marine Corps Leadership Training

I learned my personal style of leadership while I was in the Marine Corps. I had risen to the rank of E-5, which is a buck sergeant. I had attended the Marine Corps noncommissioned officers training while I was at Camp Lejeune, North Carolina. While I don't have any of the material that was presented in the class, I went to the Marine Corps Web site and looked up what they have posted on leadership. This brought back a lot of memories from my leadership training in the marines. In the school, the instructors taught us how to lead our men in Marine Corps style. They taught us to always place our mission and marines first. Our men would eat before us; they would sleep before us; and they would get cleaned up before us. Everything the marines prepared us for was a combat situation. They taught us to take care of our men and put ourselves second. The marines are a highly disciplined organization. It was expected that everyone followed orders from their superiors without delay every time. This was necessary in combat to achieve our objectives and to complete our mission.

Here are a few of the listed leadership principles from the Web site with my thoughts thrown in after them. They are not listed in any particular order:

Set the example.
As a Marine progresses through the ranks by promotion, all too often he takes on the attitude of "do as I say, not as I do." Nothing turns Marines off faster! As a marine leader, your duty is to set the standards for your Marines by personal example. Your appearance, attitude, physical fitness, and personal example are all watched by the Marines in your unit. If your personal standards are high, then you can rightfully demand the same of your Marines. If your personal standards are not high, you are setting a double standard for your Marines, and you will rapidly lose their respect and confidence. Remember your marines reflect your image! Leadership is taught by example.

I can remember the instructors drilling into us that as sergeants, we must always be "squared away." In the marines, we called this personal military bearing, this being how we presented ourselves to the world and to our marines. We were always to have spit-shined boots and shoes; our uniforms were to be cleaned and pressed at all times. Our belt buckles were to be polished and precisely lined up to our blouses (shirt). We were never to wear our covers inside, and we were to ensure our salutes were crisp and precise. On and on, it went. To gain the respect of our men, we had to set the example.

Another leadership principle from the Web site is:

Be technically and tactically proficient.
Before you can lead, you must be able to do the job. The first principle is to know your job. As a Marine, you must demonstrate your ability to accomplish the mission, and to do this you must be capable of answering questions and demonstrating competence in your military occupational specialty (MOS). Respect is the reward of the marine who shows competence. Tactical and technical competence can be learned from books and from on the job training.

I remember starting out my enlistment as a private. This level is the lowest of the low. After a set time at a given level, we became eligible for promotion to the next level if we demonstrated competence where we were. The next two levels, private first class and lance corporal, came rapidly as these levels didn't require leadership. They were preparatory levels where we could learn our MOS. The next two levels, corporal and sergeant, demanded leadership, as we began to lead small squads of marines. This is where I first focused on leadership.

I made sergeant early in my career. To do this, I had to go in front of four different review boards to determine my readiness. The members of these boards drilled me on my technical and tactical knowledge. Remember my year of duty on Okinawa deprived me of time in an infantry unit, and I had to play catch-up to get to this point. Once I made sergeant, my unit sent me to Marine Corps noncommissioned officer (NCO) school for more training.

I can remember answering a lot of questions from the privates who rotated into our platoon about our MOS. These were the new guys, and they were hungry for knowledge. When we would go to the firing range to shoot our weapons, in my case the 3.5 rocket launcher, I would always go first to show them what to do.

Another leadership principle from the marines is:

Train your Marines as a team.

Every waking hour, your Marines should be trained and schooled, challenged and tested, corrected and encouraged with perfection and teamwork as a goal. When not at war, Marines are judged in peacetime roles: perfection in drill, dress, bearing and demeanor; shooting; self-improvement; and most importantly, performance. No excuse can be made for the failure of leaders to train their Marines to the highest state of physical conditioning and to instruct them to be the very best in the profession of arms. Train with a purpose and emphasize the essential element of teamwork.

The sharing of hardships, dangers, and hard work strengthens a unit and reduces problems, it develops teamwork, improves morale and esprit, and molds a feeling of unbound loyalty and this is the basis for what makes men fight in combat; it is the foundation for bravery, for advancing under fire. Troops don't complain about tough training; they seek it and brag about it.

Teamwork is the key to successful operations. Teamwork is essential from the smallest unit to the entire Marine Corps. As a Marine leader, you must insist on teamwork from your Marines. Train, play, and operate as a team. Be sure that each Marine knows his position and responsibilities within the team framework.

When team spirit is in evidence, the most difficult tasks become much easier to accomplish. Teamwork is a two-way street; individual Marines give their best, and in return the team provides the Marine with security, recognition, and a sense of accomplishment.

Once I had gotten into an infantry outfit, it seemed as if all we did was train. We would always break down into small squads and train together as a team.

We frequently went out into the field to conduct compass marches, work with tanks, work in large formations, and spend the night out in the boondocks. There was always a large variety of training in the infantry units.

When not out in the field, we always did physical exercise together. We ran frequently as a unit to stay in shape. Occasionally, we would go on twenty-five-mile forced marches. Those would kick your tail, but when the march was completed, you felt proud of the accomplishment.

I remember hearing somewhere in the corps that a very famous marine general, Chesty Puller, was quoted as saying, "A training officer who sends his men out into combat battalions soft of body and ignorant of their weapons ought to be court-martialed. He is guilty of manslaughter."

On the other hand, I can recall a few instances when we had been training hard, and at the end of the training, the company leaders would throw a big barbeque to celebrate our accomplishments with us. They would haul out barbeque grills and bring along cooks, who prepared steaks for all of us. They would bring out fifty-five-gallon drums of iced-down beer for all of us to drink. We would all drink together. One time, on the godforsaken island of Viegas, Puerto Rico, our leaders threw a huge barbeque on one of the most beautiful beaches I had ever been on. We drank and ate until we passed out. This didn't take too much, because we had been hard at training for a week. Many fistfights broke out in that melee, but there was much camaraderie between all of us during these occasions.

Performance is listed in this principle. The marines were always about performance. No matter what rank or MOS, each of us as an individual had a job to do and were expected to do it precisely each and every time. Performance was the key to the success of the corps. It was the absolute execution of all of our collective training to accomplish our mission. If any individual parts failed to do their jobs, marines could be placed in jeopardy or could die. This was a high price to pay for failure or lukewarm mission attainment.

In contrast to the marines' focus on performance, I found it quite different at General Motors. General Motors practices performance by what I've come to call the "If we like ya" philosophy. If the executives in GM like you as an individual, if you strive to become just like them, then they'll shower you with money and privileges. Performance to reality, such as the marketplace, be dammed.

***

Another of the leadership principles is:

Make sound and timely decisions.
The leader must be able to rapidly estimate a situation and make a sound decision based on that estimation. Hesitation or a reluctance to make a decision leads subordinates to lose confidence in your abilities as a leader. Loss of confidence creates confusion and hesitation within the unit.

Once you make a decision and discover it is the wrong one, don't hesitate to revise your decision. Marines respect the leader who corrects mistakes immediately instead of trying to bluff through a poor decision.

Could you imagine if we revised our decisions as we discovered they were the wrong ones? I don't recall any events around this principle while I was in the marines, but I couldn't pass up listing it here. There must be some cultural attributes from this that I picked up along the way. Certainly, General Motors' management could use a heavy dose of this, as I never saw them admit they were in error. It seems to me they always tried to bluff their way through it.

***

Another leadership principle listed is:

Keep your Marines informed.

Marines by nature are inquisitive. To promote efficiency and morale, a leader should inform the Marines in his unit of all happenings and give reasons why things are to be done. This, of course, is done when time and security permit. Informing your marines of the situation makes them feel that they are part of the team and not just a cog in the wheel. Informed Marines perform better and, if knowledgeable of the situation, can carry on without your personal supervision. The key to giving out information is to be sure that the Marines have enough information to do their job intelligently and to inspire their initiative, enthusiasm, loyalty, and convictions.

I don't recall being that informed while I was in the marines. I remember a lot of complaining among the troops about being kept in the dark. Yet, we were always looking for information, and I do think we got it; we just didn't recognize it. There is a common expression in the marines: "What's the word?" I can remember hearing this a lot. I can remember hearing information and being told to "pass it on." It probably wasn't information on how to win the war, so to speak, but it was always relevant to what was going on that day or week. Most of the time, we didn't like what we had heard, but hear it, we did.

In combat, we wouldn't have time for discussion or group decision making. They taught us that combat was like leaving a burning house; there wasn't time for nice discussions. It was time to do it or die.

If I compared the communications in the marines to that of being an hourly shop worker, it would be like night and day. In the marines, they told us as much as they could, when they could, out of respect for us. In the shop, we hourly workers were considered as disposable employees and not worth the effort to communicate with.

***

For the first time, the question of *why* comes up in the book. I've always been a why person. I can remember driving my parents nuts asking, "Why? Why? Why?" I think I tried their patience on many occasions with this question. It wasn't until I went to the optometrist the first time that I realized I did have a problem with this. I remember asking him about all of the items in his office often followed up with the question, "Why?" My mother tried to hush me up, but the optometrist overruled her and answered all of my questions that day. He encouraged me to continue with my overwhelming, inquisitive nature. This was an eye-opener for me. After that, my parents were a little more tolerant of me and the why questions.

I don't remember asking why a lot in the corps, but I remember having most things explained to me, especially in training. We didn't need to ask why as much, because it was all laid out for us. Information was readily provided to us.

The Japanese have developed a problem-solving technique called "the five whys." They discovered that by asking why five times about a problem, they could usually get to the root of it and then work to put it to rest. This method wasn't effective just because they asked why five times, but because they listened to the people who knew the most about the problem and then worked with them to solve it. It might take up to five repetitions of the question *why* before they really had the problem solved. I am a natural why person. There are thousands of us down on the shop floor who are considered too dumb to participate. Once again, I feel the need to point out all of the lost opportunities the GM executives gave away simply because they held us shop rats in such low esteem. It seems we were too stupid to think.

The last leadership principle I want to write about is:

Ensure the task is understood, supervised, and accomplished.
This principle is necessary in the exercise of command. Before you can expect your Marines to perform, they must know what is expected of them. You must communicate your instructions in a clear, concise manner. Talk at a level that your Marines are sure to understand, but not at a level so low that would insult

their intelligence. Before your Marines start a task, allow them a chance to ask questions or seek advice. Supervision is essential. Without supervision, you cannot know if the assigned task is being properly accomplished. Over supervision is viewed by subordinates as harassment and effectively stops initiative. Allow subordinates to use their own techniques, and then periodically check up on them.

Here again, individual initiative comes into play. How can a strict, disciplined organization like the marines depend on the lowest levels within it to use personal initiative to accomplish its missions? Everything in the marines was geared toward placing the marines into combat with the enemy.

Everything about the marines focused on supporting the marine infantrymen in combat. This philosophy was followed from the commandant of the corps right down to every private in the service. First of all, every marine was trained as an infantryman right out of boot camp before entering his specialty occupation. The marines were very dictatorial in everything they did until it came down to the infantrymen engaging the enemy in combat. The infantrymen are the golden jewels of the corps. Once in combat, small squads are free to carry out their objectives to the best of their training. At this point then, the leadership style became somewhat participative. This is better known as our American ingenuity. The infantry would figure out the tactics of the enemy and annihilate them. So we always had strict discipline to follow orders. These were never questioned, but once in combat, the entire corps switched to the support of the men fighting, and the small teams used all their training and know-how to overcome the enemy. That was how I first learned leadership, and that's how I've always conducted myself.

One time, when I was stationed in Camp Lejeune, North Carolina, I overheard some of the guys in the barracks breaking in a new kid. I was most proud when I heard one of them say, "Watch out for Sergeant Gall. He'll kick you in the butt if you step out of line, but if you go along with the program, he's all right." That summed up just how I saw myself as a leader. I believe the marines said it like this: 'If they do all right pat 'em on the back, and if they're out of line, kick them in the ass, but when you kick them in the ass, do it in private." What's always amazed me about the marines is how as a sergeant, there were times when I needed to get in some people's faces to motivate them to do the right thing. Now back then, we marines weren't the sharpest tacks in the bunch and most of our elevators didn't go to the top floor. We were lean and mean fighting machines. Some of these boys were big. I mean physically really big, like six foot two or three, 220 to 230 pounds. They were in good physical condition. I am five feet eight inches tall and was 150 pounds back then. What amazed me was never once did any of these big brutes attack me or swing at me. The discipline of the marines was absolute. The corps is a shining example of how an organization can utilize all of its human resources—every bit of it!

I had a year and a half of the best management training I could get in the Marine Corps.

***

Back to the present ... As I continued the short walk to the journeymen, I wasn't sure what I was going to say or do once I reached them. I was a little nervous. When I got there, I asked them what they were doing. They harassed me a little bit, and I vaguely remember them pulling on my necktie some. Back then, salaried managers wore ties. They told me what their assignment was and what they were waiting on. They knew John was out in the aisle watching every move I made. I asked them what the next steps were. They explained what was going on, and then they went to work. I've always found this to be most helpful. I've always tried to ask the journeymen what they saw and how they would do things. I'd say 90 percent of the time, that is the correct way of doing it anyway. It usually doesn't take a genius to figure it out. In this fashion, I facilitated a participative style of management as opposed to a dictatorial one. If you can earn the cooperation of the guys, it's a hell of a lot easier than being a dictator. Being a dictator takes a lot of time and takes a lot bigger effort from the supervisor. It is hard work, and it'll wear you right out. You must make every decision, and you must be everywhere at all times. The guys will sit and wait until Mr. Genius shows up and tells them the next steps. This is nothing but waste!

This point in the story leads me into the supervisors' primary mode of operations in the plant. They were pretty much all the same ...

Flashback: Benevolent Dictators

One time, I was working with a guy making repairs in the ram of a press. This was a hot job. The supervisor stayed with us all night, or I should probably say stayed *on* us. This guy was a very poor leader. It seemed the

147

shop was full of them. We weren't allowed any input into the repair. This guy dictated our every move. Now we were quite used to this leadership style, and to fight back, all we did was do whatever we were told 150 percent of the time. Nine times out of ten, the job would take longer, cost more, and you would end up with a piss-poor result. But that was the way it was when I was a journeyman. My partner on this night was getting upset with the supervisor, Chad. We had completed our interim task and were waiting for Chad to show back up so we could continue. All we had to do was tighten down some nuts that held the ram's screw housing in place. Finally, Chad got back to the job; he had attended a meeting while we were waiting. My partner, who was more experienced than I, wanted to complete the job a different way than Chad wanted, but he was denied input. Chad had his way, and so we continued working as instructed. Finally, we put the nuts on and were tightening them down. Chad insisted that we tighten to a specific torque value. He waited while we went and got a torque wrench. Then we tightened the nuts to Chad's specifications. Now this struck me as funny. Here we were, both journeymen. We had completed over seven thousand hours of training. We had practiced our trade after our apprenticeship for several years. Yet, because of the prevailing leadership style used on the plant floor, we were not free to utilize our skills. There were around twenty journeymen to every one supervisor. There was no way one guy could efficiently tell all twenty how to do their jobs every night. What a waste. What a case of micromanaging.

This job stands out in my mind because Chad won that night. We made sure that we tightened those nuts to Chad's exact specifications. We left that night frustrated because we knew this job had been done wrong. We were justified the next night when we came in to work. The press ran for a short time on day shift and broke again. It was still down and production was scrambling to ship parts to meet schedule. Chad's way was incorrect. What a waste of human brainpower and effort!

Millwrights Build a Monorail to Blueprint Specifications

One other job sticks out in my mind to illustrate my point about no participation from the hourly workers. One time, the millwrights were reworking a major monorail system in the west plant. It was changeover time. This work had to be completed so that as production came back to work from layoff, the lines were ready to run. I don't remember what machine repair was doing on the job. But I remember the millwrights studying the blueprints of the reworked monorail system. They discovered that the two ends that had to come together were off by one bay. I believe one bay is about forty feet. If the millwrights reworked the job as specified, the two ends of the monorail would end up forty feet apart rather than married together. There was a serious error on the blueprints. The millwrights brought this up to the engineer on the job. The engineer on the job didn't even bother to look at the prints. He told the millwrights he was the engineer and they were to do as they were told. If they had a college degree like he did, then they could be the engineer on the job. Well that's all it took to piss the millwrights off. They got together with all the other millwrights on all shifts associated with the job and formulated a plan. They would work their asses off as quickly as they could to rework the monorail to the blueprint. And away they went. The rest of us trades were cheering them on. They worked night and day completing that monorail; nothing—and I mean nothing—got in their way. Time passed quickly, and we had to complete our jobs and prepare for production start-up. Nothing stopped production from running, and I mean nothing! Suddenly, the engineer realized his error. In fact, I think he was crapping his pants. All of the millwrights were standing around him laughing. This was very funny, if you think about it. This all could have been avoided in the very beginning if they had been willing to talk about the blueprints. But it highlights the mentality of supervision at that time: We are the gifted class of people. We are the college graduates, and you are the stupid asses who must do everything we say because you are so incredibly stupid. Without us, you are unable to complete your work. You are untrustworthy; you are incapable of managing your own work! (This social stigma even carried over outside the shop. Recall the early incident in the book where the hostess at the house-warming party called me a "shop rat" for the first time. I believe her attitude represented that of society's. We blue-collar workers were all stereotyped into a very poor and underwhelming picture. And I now ask why? Why does the American manufacturing culture completely dismiss its blue-collar workers' contributions? It doesn't make sense to me. There'll be more on this at the end of the book.) The millwrights worked night and day to rework the monorail system so it connected together correctly. They were placed on maximum overtime—a just reward for management's failure to listen to the hourly peons. It was not ready in time for production start-up. I believe the millwrights won that battle of "Who's the smartest?" But I believe General Motors lost the war in the long run.

***

Once again, back into the present ... These were the thoughts that were going through my mind as I confronted my old teachers while my new boss was watching from the aisle.

The journeymen I was talking with fully expected me to be like most of the others before me and dictate to them how to make their repairs. I felt pressured to be decisive and to look good in front of the general supervisor. I felt pressure to fit into the existing management culture and become like most of the other supervisors in the plant, but I remembered my leadership training from my Marine Corps experience and I also remembered the people who raised me, the working men and women of my family. I remembered the journeymen who taught me my machine repair trade. They were standing right in front of me. I was obviously confused and didn't know what to do. I didn't want to betray those who had in some way helped me in the past, and yet I wanted to make a good impression on the general supervisor who was impatiently waiting in the aisle. There were several currents of thoughts running through my mind simultaneously.

Then all of a sudden, in a flash, it hit me as to what to do. I pretended I had told them to do exactly what they told me they were going to do anyway. Then I walked back to the general supervisor who was anxiously waiting in the aisle. I told him what I told the journeymen, and he was satisfied with my response. Off we went to find the supervisor.

Charlie

My idol at this time was a machine repair supervisor named Charlie. Charlie was one of the best supervisors I have ever come across. You would always find Charlie with his hands in the grease and with the guys making repairs. He was the smartest and most technically competent supervisor we had in the plant. Charlie knew it all, and there wasn't anything he couldn't fix. Charlie got along great with his crew and knew when to pat guys on the back and went to kick them in the butt. All the hourly guys respected Charlie. I got to spend a lot of time around him.

I did have a small difference with Charlie though. I was taught in the marines to never complete the work of the men below me. That was drilled into us often as noncommissioned officers. It was our responsibility to get the work done by the men, not do the work for them. I never did get my hands into the work like Charlie did while I was a supervisor. That training always stuck with me.

It was okay for Charlie though. He had a good knack to work as a straw boss or working boss. Even upper management respected Charlie. For the longest time, I always tried to emulate Charlie, even though I couldn't hold a candle to him.

Ed

I met some interesting characters while I was on temporary salary. One guy was a welder repair supervisor named Ed. He had flaming red hair. Ed was older when I met him. I don't think Ed really cared much for being a supervisor. He didn't follow all of the unwritten rules that supervisors were supposed to live by. Ed was sloppy in his dress and most often fell asleep in every meeting he attended. His guys all liked him, and that was a sure sign he wasn't doing his job like he should. Ed liked to hunt and fish in his spare time with the guys. I worked with Ed for a couple of weeks. I hadn't worked around welder repair before, so I enjoyed the opportunity to explore what their welders were all about. Ed wasn't the cleanest guy in the shop. As supervisors, we carried six-inch precision measuring scales in our pockets so we could take measurements as needed. We would often wipe our scales off and use them to stir our coffee. Ed never bothered to wipe his scale off; he just used it as it was. One time, I saw Ed use his necktie to stir his coffee. He couldn't find his scale. It had been lost.

Per-Diem Supervisor—Finally on My Own

After my eight weeks of training were completed, I was kept on as a per-diem supervisor. I would spend the next seven months on per diem. I was sent to second shift to be used as a vacation replacement supervisor. I felt good that I had completed my training and I would finally be out on my own. Not all of my classmates were put on per diem. Most of them went back to their tools. I was anxious to see how I would do. I found out that being a supervisor is no easy task. It should be and could be, but for various reasons, it seems that your hands are always tied behind your back whenever you want to do anything or accomplish something. I found the job challenging and exciting and yet very frustrating. There was a mountain of rules to learn and follow. We had the UAW contractual work rules, GM policy rules, and federal regulations that all governed our way of doing business. I soon learned that a good supervisor was doing well if he could make his work area just a smidgen better than when he first took it over.

I really didn't fit in well with the current second-shift machine repair managers of the day. They were all rough-and-tumble relics from the past. They were pretty much all theory X oriented—theory X being "I am the boss. You are my slave, and you do everything exactly as I tell you. You, as an employee of General Motors, are not worthy or capable of anything. I am superior to you in all aspects of life and employment."

I dreamed of being different. Matter of fact, I think I was born very different. I think if we went back and talked with the managers of that day, they would readily admit I was very different than the traditional manager. They would probably say it was a mistake to keep me on supervision, and yet, I had the ability to get things done through people. I desired more of a participating style of management. I desired to utilize the full resources each employee brought to the table and was willing to use for the good of General Motors. This was in direct contrast with 90 percent of the managers on second shift. I didn't hit it off well with the second-shift general supervisor, George. I didn't realize my differences at the beginning. I didn't realize how different I really was. George pulled me into his office one night early on and let me know I wasn't cutting the mustard, so to speak. He didn't speak very highly of me. After that, I was confused for a while, but I soon realized I had to be more like them. I realized that to continue on temporary supervision, I had to learn to cover up my internal feelings and externally become like them. I had to morph into a theory X supervisor just to stay in the program. I called this my M&M theory of management. On the outside, I was hard and crusty, or at least appeared to be, while on the inside, I desired to manage in new and different ways to get the most out of my human resources. So I learned to speak in their terms, and I conducted myself like them. But on the inside, I wasn't comfortable with my adaptive style of management. I pretended to be like them. I had to fit in. I had to be like them because they were in control of my destiny.

One night, at the end of the shift, I went to George's office to turn in my nightly lineup. These lineups were a recap of all the events that had happened or were accomplished during our shifts. They were written down so when the next shift came in, they could read them and get up to speed on where we were on all of the jobs. George took my lineup from my hand and started reading my report. He began to challenge me on where we were on various jobs on the lineup. He insinuated that I was falsifying my records. He said I couldn't possibly be as far along on these jobs as I had written in my report. He said no one could get that much work done in one shift. I didn't see this coming, and I was stunned. He jumped up from behind his desk and told me to take him to each of the job sites so he could review for himself exactly where each job was at. We went out of the office, and I drove him to each job site on my three-wheeled electric scooter. He reviewed each site, and I saw a touch of anger come over him. He couldn't find any falsifications in my report. Each job was exactly as I had stated in my end-of-shift report. In fact, some of the jobs were even a little further along than I had written.

Looking back at this now, I realize I never had any intention of falsifying records. I just simply put down where we were on each job and what we had accomplished that night just as I was trained to do. I think it was like taking candy from a baby getting the guys to work with their semi-participation. It didn't take much, and they were working harder and faster than they had worked in a long time. Once they realized I was genuine in the fact I wanted their participation, it was hard to hold them back. They were not making me look good; they were making themselves look good while utilizing all the training and skills that they had learned along the way. It was like opening the floodgates. What I didn't realize was I was showing up the old theory X–style supervisors. They would plod along and get so much done each night, but they had to push and pull and discipline to accomplish anything. Everything they did distracted from the act of getting the task completed.

After we reviewed each job, I took George back to the office. He never said a word to me. I wasn't sure what to do. I knew he didn't like it, but I was clean. There was really nothing he could do. It then further dawned on me that I was somehow different than George and the others. I was different, but to me, it was a very good difference. I felt very good even if it meant I would never make it as a supervisor at General Motors. I realized that by pretending to be a dictator on the outside to cover my tracks but really utilizing a participative management style whenever or wherever I could, I could work circles around everybody else. I could build a trust and rapport with my crew and watch them to go to work. Most of the hourly guys really liked the style. I was taking baby steps with this approach. After a short time, I left George's office and went home. He didn't like it, but he never questioned my lineups after that.

Now I have to tell you, the guys on the floor didn't care for George.

They never spoke very highly of him when he was a journeyman working on his tools. Rumor had it he had a severe drinking problem and was drunk quite often. The guys always said George made general supervisor because he mowed the lawn of one of the superintendents all summer long. That same guy took George to Indianapolis stamping later on to help him out, but George left after a while because he didn't like being away from his home. George and I never really saw eye to eye.

George's favorite supervisor was the one I talked about earlier in this book, Chad. Chad was a clone of George. They covered each other's back. They ran a tight but wasteful ship. From Chad, I learned about what I came to call smoke screens. In the marines, one of the tactics we used in training was smoke bombs. We would throw these forward to screen us from the enemy as we moved toward them. It was an effective tool of deception. Chad too was an expert at the art of deception. Chad was also a tattletale, just like a small child on a playground. The higher-ups tolerated this, and it was seen as being a good supervisor. (I believe the executive managers thought of the supervisors and general supervisors like the supervisors and general supervisors thought of the hourly personnel. They were incompetent and untrustworthy; therefore, snitching was good business to keep people honest and on their toes.)

To create his smoke screens for what really was ineffective supervision, Chad would always poke his nose in everybody else's business to find things wrong, and then he would run and tattle to George. He didn't discriminate in his use of this tactic; he did it to everyone. He did it more when the heat was on him. Being a rookie and the new kid on the block, I seemed to fall victim to his ways often.

One of the things Chad was notorious for was finding all the people he assumed were coming back late from their breaks or lunch. You would often find Chad right by the escalator writing down the names of those who were perceived as late. Then he would run to George to give him the list of names. George would then demand we, the rest of the supervisors and especially those on per diem, write up and penalize these people for wasting time.

Writing somebody up was no easy task. There was a strict contractual procedure you had to follow. You had to first address the employee to determine if there might be a problem. If you determined that there might be a problem, you had to place the employee on notice of a possible violation of the shop rules. This was a verbal declaration. Then you had to formally interview the employee along with his committeeman. Now it was explained to me that the committeeman was likened to a shit-house lawyer. You know the kind. They chase the ambulance to the hospital; they represent the known criminal offenders and get them off on technicalities. Their sole purpose was to free their represented brothers of the terrible atrocities that management accused them of so they could be continually reelected to office.

These interviews could last for hours at a time, as the committeeman tied you up in knots. It was a brutal, wasteful, and time-consuming game. There really wasn't much training you could have to prepare you for these situations. Half the time, we didn't want to be there, but we couldn't admit this because we were trainees. These interviews took up valuable time during the shift. At the end of the formal interview, as a supervisor, you had to make the determination of guilt or innocence. If you determined guilt, you had to fill out the necessary paperwork and present it to both the committeeman and the convicted offender. If you determined innocence, then the person just left the office; the exercise was over.

If you let the employee off by determining that there wasn't a violation of the shop rules or that the punishment wouldn't correct the behavior, you had to incur the wrath of George and of course Chad. George was always watching this process. It was how he made a name for himself. He was ruthless in the punishment of those damn employees who were always screwing up. Well, you know what? It takes one to know one. George also felt it was a severe sign of weakness if you didn't write everyone up, especially when Chad had done the reporting of the violations.

When you were in conferences, you could lose control of your ongoing jobs on the floor. This was exactly what Chad wanted. Now he could rule in his theory X manner and be the king of the hill because he got more work done than anybody else. When Chad performed a shop violation interview, it took him less than three minutes to declare the victim guilty. Against the agreed-upon process in the contract, he would have already completed all of the paperwork. He would leave the hearing room, usually George's office, for about thirty seconds, pretend he had just written up the paperwork, and then return to the meeting. He would get the required signatures from the committeeman and then leave. He was so seasoned at this it took him less than twenty minutes to complete the entire process.

However, if your guys were working on their own, with some input as to how the job should be done, you didn't have to be there every single minute. They still accomplished a fair day's work. This is what I now see that I was doing, but I didn't know it at the time. No wonder George and

Chad did not care for me. (I am by no means advocating that employee discipline doesn't have its place. There are times when it is necessary to correct performance difficulties. However, while I was on per diem on second shift, it was used to further the career ambitions of some managers, make rookie supervisors jump through hoops, and keep the management-union conflict alive.)

This process went on every night. It didn't take long to figure out that Chad never reported any of his own people's violations. It seemed like he only found other supervisors' employees violating the shop rules. His people could do no wrong. Thus, my use of the term *smoke screens*—Chad kept George and the other supervisors tied up with the things he tattled on so that there was never enough time to look at Chad's employees' violations. This repetitive, nightly activity was stupid, and I don't like to use the word *stupid*. We wasted so much precious time disciplining employees for no good reason. If we had reversed this practice and spent the majority of time training our employees and utilizing their experience through participation, we could have accomplished so much more with way less.

Once I caught on to Chad's game, I learned how to beat him to the punch. I would look for violations in Chad's area. I would run into George's office and tattle about what I had found. George didn't like this very much, but what could he do? This tactic would keep Chad out of my area for a while. I hated doing it, but it was about survival. I apologized more than once to the hourly guys who were penalized by Chad because of me. But this was the only effective way I could keep Chad at bay.

One night, late in the summer, George took me to the superintendent's office in the quality department. He introduced me to Ron, who ran the quality department on second shift. Apparently, George had heard that they were looking for inspection supervisor candidates. Ron was a good guy. He had served time as an hourly employee, fought in Vietnam, and now was working his way up into executive management. I respected Ron. He asked me to place my hands on my butt. I must have had a dumb look on my face. He encouraged me again to place my hands on my butt. I went ahead and did this. I placed my hands on my butt. Ron smiled and said, okay, he just needed to know if I knew my butt from a hole in the ground. He asked me if I was interested in working in the quality department, and I said that I was. He told me if he had any openings, he'd keep me in mind. I thanked him, and then George and I left his office. Later, it dawned on me what George was up to. I wasn't cutting the grade as one of his supervisors. I didn't see it then, but I see it clearly now.

As summer ended, the need for temporary supervisors was reduced. The regular salaried supervisors had taken most of their vacation time, and the economy still wasn't in the best of shape. Car sales were sluggish nationwide. At the end of September, I was placed back on hourly. But there was a problem with this. According to the union contract, when people like me were placed on temporary supervision, we could only serve for fifteen weeks. After fifteen weeks, we lost seniority in our work group day for day. In the past, per diems had been placed on temporary assignment for years at a time. When they were no longer needed as supervisors, they were then cut back to hourly. During this time, they had not only maintained their seniority; it had increased day for day while they were on management. To stop this practice, the union had negotiated with management to only allow fifteen weeks of being placed on per diem per calendar year. If a per diem stayed on longer than the allowed time, he would then stop accumulating seniority in his work group on a day-by-day basis. I had been on per diem for nine months. Most everybody else had been put back on hourly when his or her fifteen weeks were up. I took a chance that I could make permanent supervisor. I chose to stay on after my fifteen weeks were used up. I lost around six months of seniority while I stayed on. Now, as I was going back to hourly, the plant was laying people off again. If I had gone off of per diem after fifteen weeks, I wouldn't have been in danger of being laid off.

Before I was cut back, the second shift die room assistant superintendent called me into his office. He had been watching me throughout the summer. He told me that there were two openings for permanent supervisors. He said that I was his recommended candidate and he would do what he could to get me one of the open spots. I didn't realize it then, but Bill and I thought a lot alike. He had been an hourly die maker and had completed his college degree after he hired into the plant. He had worked up in engineering and out on the plant floor. He didn't tow the die room line that only die makers could be supervisors in the master mechanics department. This was a radical shift in thinking. Bill believed that the best management candidate should be taken on, not just the ones with die maker skills alone. Bill believed in me!

After the plant had formally made their selections for permanent supervisors, he called me back into his office to let me know the results. The hierarchy of the die room had chosen two die makers to fill the open positions. A guy who was a third-generation die maker filled one of them. His grandfather and father had both been general supervisors in the die room before him. His way had been prepared for him. It's too bad, because he could have been a very successful home builder. He had a good knack for it. He built his first house himself and exhibited superior carpentry skills. But duty called, and he took the place that had been prepared for him. The second guy was a minority candidate. That was it. I was all done. The traditional way of thinking, the cemented culture of the plant remained intact. No outsiders were allowed in! Bill apologized to me and said he would like to keep me in mind as things opened up later. I thanked him and walked out of his office.

I didn't handle myself very well. In fact, I lost it. I went into a minor depression. My hopes and dreams were shattered. It felt like all I'd ever wanted had been taken away and denied me. I developed a very negative attitude. I wasn't any good to anyone, not even myself. I don't know why I reacted this way, but this incident shook me to the core. It just felt so unfair. I felt pathetically sorry for myself. This funk I put myself in lasted for the better part of two years.

In February 1982, I was laid off.

Real Estate License

Now that I was once again back on layoff, I didn't know what to do. It felt like all my options were closed. There was no work available in the auto industry at that time. Everything was shut down. I felt too young to give up trying to better myself, but I had lost my sense of direction. I didn't seem to fit in as a traditional machine repair supervisor at Flint Metal, and I didn't fit in with the hierarchy of the die makers that existed in my department. I just didn't seem to fit in anywhere. I was devastated. I looked around for something else to do. Maybe I should resign myself to just being a skilled tradesman in the shop and start my own business on the outside as a secondary venture, one where I could call the shots and feel included in running the business, where I could use my brains to assist my company toward success.

I answered an advertisement to sell real estate. The owner of the local franchise and I hit it off right away. He encouraged me to get my real estate license. I was all for that! I had to try something. A lot of guys in the shop sold real estate part-time. Maybe this was the answer for me.

I enrolled in a class through Real Estate One that prepared students to successfully pass the required written exam. Passing this exam qualified you for your license to sell real estate in the state of Michigan. The course lasted several weeks. I threw myself into my studies. I passed the test with ease. I had kept in touch with the real estate broker during this time. As I was waiting for the test results, feeling confident that I had passed (the test was not rocket science), I visited all of the property listings the office had. After I received my license, I was ready to go to work! General Motors' sales were still down, and it looked like I was going to be off work quite a while. The broker had thrown me a bone and had assigned a couple to me who were house hunting. I mapped out the available homes that were of interest to them and created a plan to take them around for showings. I then received my license, and I was ready to rock and roll. I put all the things in place to drive this couple around the next morning. Everything was ready.

When I woke up that morning, I discovered we had had an overnight snowstorm. We had received over ten inches of snow. All the roads were shut down. I wasn't going anywhere. I think this was a sign from God that this wasn't meant to be. The couple called and passed on that day's showings. I never heard from them again.

One of the activities I had to do as a real estate agent was spend time in the broker's office answering phones and prospecting for new customers. It was being pounded into me that the successful real estate agent was the one who achieved the most listings. This is where you have home sellers sign a contract with you to be their representing agent. As the house sells, you receive 50 percent of the commission just by being the real estate agency that lists the property. It is much tougher to work with buyers because they have no legal requirement to work only with you. They are free to move about from one agency to the next.

They had warned us in our training about going after FSBOs (fizz-bo). FSBO stands for "for sale by owner." These people were rough and tough and didn't want to be bothered by real estate agents. They were the hands-on, do-it-yourself people, who were looking to avoid paying commissions. I should have known; I had sold my first house myself. I was a FSBO experienced seller. But after them I went. I called all of them I could find. I was thoroughly beaten up by them, and it felt as if my body had been tossed high upon the pile of those who so boldly had gone before me. I didn't get one of their listings.

I did catch a break and found a couple interested in listing their home with me. It was a doctor and his wife. They were not very nice to lower class people. They treated me like dirt. I sat at their kitchen table and took all the duff they could dish out. In the end, I boldly asked them for their listing and they gave it to me. Looking back, I listed the house way too high price-wise. It wasn't in a great location, and the sellers were extremely difficult to work with.

We didn't receive many inquiries on the property, and when we did, the higher price scared prospective buyers away. The sellers called me it seemed like every hour badgering me on why their house hadn't yet sold. I might have painted the wrong picture, too rosy for the economic times in the greater Flint area, as I gave them my sales pitch as to why I was the right guy for this job. The contract they had signed expired in thirty days, and they did not extend their listing with me. Thank God for small favors. This real estate career might not be the right one for me.

Shortly after this experience, I found myself back in the real estate office once again on standby phone duty. Now though, things were different. Something had changed. When the phone rang, I was reluctant to answer it. When I would go to pick the receiver up, it felt like it weighed one hundred pounds. I realized that there were a lot of mean-spirited people out there in the world. I was beginning to realize I wasn't cut out to be in sales. I found it very hard to talk with strangers and to be a salesperson. I began to shy away from my real estate duties. I did come across a young couple looking for a house. We hit it off right away. We had grown up in the same part of Flint and had briefly known each other. We looked at quite a few houses together. They ended up purchasing one in a suburb of Flint called Flushing. For all my work, I received a check for seven hundred dollars. This paid back all the money I had invested in getting my license and all the expenses I had incurred. I left the real estate business after that sale. I was beginning to understand myself more as a person. I realized I had an introverted, not extroverted, personality type. Deep down inside, I knew that if I had to sell for a living, my family and I would go hungry. I was very good at maintaining machinery and equipment in the shop but not at being a salesman. I liked and missed being a skilled trades supervisor. That was what I really wanted, but I couldn't get it. I felt it had been unfairly taken from me.

As I was working with the young couple, I was unexpectedly called back to work at Flint Metal. I reported back to the plant in May of 1982. I was not a very good employee. I had a chip on my shoulder that was eating up my insides. I really had a thing for fairness, for a level playing field, and in my eyes, this situation was just unfair. The playing field wasn't level.

I didn't know what to do. I barely completed my work assignments. My supervisor had to stay close by me to ensure I completed my assignments and stayed on the job. I became what the marines called a "shit bird."

I was continuously searching for a career change. The overall economics of the United States were quite slow, and as I inquired about jobs with other companies, I learned their compensation policies were drastically lower than what I received as a General Motors skilled tradesmen. This is around the time that a lot of people in Michigan left for Texas. Texas nicknamed these folks the "black plague," because our license plates were black in color and there were a lot of us. The typical joke of the day was the last one out of Michigan turns the lights off.

There is one interesting tidbit of information that I received during my real estate adventure that is worth mentioning. The day I was sworn in as a real estate professional by the Flint Board of Realtors, I was given a preferred reading list. The books on the list mostly dealt with self-image psychology. I began to read these books one by one. As I finished the list, I was hooked on the theory that "what you constantly think about will happen." In other words, we do have control over our lives through our thoughts. This will come to further fruition a little later.

Around this time, I remember sitting on my toolbox and reading a series of lengthy newspaper articles from the Detroit papers about the wages of hourly autoworkers. This article compared and contrasted a person who went to college for four years versus a person who completed an apprenticeship with the Big Three. This article concluded that the apprenticeship was the better way to go economically. After paying four years of tuition, fees, room and board, and interest on student loans, that person was way behind the earnings of the apprentice. The apprentice had all expenses paid, so to speak. When the apprentice graduated, he had no accumulation of student loans; he was free and clear of that kind of debt. The college graduate would have to outearn the journeyman by a large margin the rest of his career to overcome the cost differential that occurred in the beginning of their young lives. Journeymen normally got good-paying jobs with substantial overtime. That overtime pay was very hard to overcome by college graduates. So I concluded, based on that series of articles, that my apprenticeship had been the right way for me to go. But now I felt forced into giving up what I had earned in order to achieve a new start. What a mess! Did I mention I was in a mild depression?

Not knowing what to do, I concluded that maybe I was supposed to become an active union member. My father had very early on in his career been active in union politics, and I was getting the urge to explore that avenue for myself.

***

Flashback: United Autoworkers' Family History

Back in the 1940s, the UAW was still fairly new. As they moved forward, there was unrest within their membership. My father was part of that unrest. The way the story was told to me was that in the beginning of the implementation of hard-won union contracts, skilled tradesmen's wages were double what production workers earned. If a production operator earned fifty cents per hour, skilled tradesmen earned one dollar per hour. As the UAW moved forward and gained strength, that gap began to deteriorate. The union's strength came from the number of members it had. There were many more non-skilled trades employees than skilled trades workers. Therefore, the union began to cater to the largest group of their membership. In the late 1940s and early 1950s, the skilled tradesmen began to become restless. They either formed or connected with an organization that only represented skilled trades. This was the International Society of Skilled Trades (ISST). My father, having completed his die maker apprenticeship after taking time off to fight in World War II, was caught up in the movement.

This ISST movement was attempting to split off from the UAW and represent the skilled tradesmen separately. One night, as the movement was gaining momentum, they filled the IMA Auditorium to capacity (IMA stands for Industrial Mutual Association). It had a five-thousand-seat auditorium in downtown Flint. This would become the site of the ill-fated Auto World that the governmental leaders used in an attempt at a comeback in the city of Flint in the 1980s. My father was one of the men up on the stage that evening. He may have even spoken to the assembly. After this event, the UAW came down hard on these guys and kept the UAW together. My father and many others were blackballed from being UAW members. Apparently, this was a common event in those days; the union kept a list of employees not favorable to their cause. They would extract union dues from these employees' wages but would not really represent them in the plants. My father wasn't a big fan of the UAW after that. He left General Motors and worked several years as a die designer in the local job shops. This was a common occurrence back then. That type of work was plentiful.

My grandfather had retired as an hourly skilled tradesman from the Buick complex in the 1960s. He had worked at Buick before the UAW won its right to represent the hourly workers at General Motors in 1936. When the infamous sit-down strikers were striking in the Flint area plants and the UAW was winning the battle for recognition, many hourly General Motors employees did not come to work in protest at plants that were not on strike. This was encouraged as an act of solidarity with the sit-down strikers. My grandfather chose to continue working. He came to work every day, and he told me he was later ostracized when the UAW took over their factory. My grandfather had had a rough time during the Depression years. He had had a nervous breakdown. He probably wasn't mentally strong enough to resist all of the conflicting social challenges that were swirling around him.

***

So as I contemplated getting active in the UAW, as my potential destiny, I didn't have a strong UAW background, unlike some of the guys I worked around. One guy, a pipefitter, firmly believed that because he was a third-generation UAW brother, General Motors owed him lifetime employment and a healthy retirement. His belief system also allowed him to produce nothing in return for his wages and benefits. I specifically asked him one time if he really believed this. His reply was direct and stunning. He told me General Motors owed him a living simply because he was alive and living in Genesee County. He didn't have to do anything in return for it, and he went out of his way to prove it. His connections within the UAW got him to where he was and would always protect him. This guy wasn't well liked by his peers. Even though we had our differences with management, most guys would put out the work. Whatever the supervisors required, they always managed to complete.

I started hanging around with the union guys in the shop. In 1983, I began attending some union meetings. Afterward, we would go over to the Wooden Keg bar and watch football games. I became more like the UAW in my thinking and my approach to life in the shop. But I found in the long run, it wasn't for me. I wouldn't have put up with the guff the elected committeemen had to take from their constituents. I would have told them where to go! This was a very small but vocal minority. This seemed to be what dominated the internal UAW politics: a very small but vocal and dominant minority. The union meetings were sparsely attended. Most represented people weren't interested in union participation, they just needed the protection it provided. They really didn't have a choice. I also would have had a difficult time representing people who were in fact guilty. I would have felt management was justified in their discipline. Not everyone was guilty, but there was that very small percentage of people who were. So I let my active UAW days go. It wasn't meant for me.

Speaking of my friend, the pipefitter, and his attitude about GM leads me into some thoughts that I have had throughout my career in the shop. GM was required to hire everyone who sought employment in the factory. It seemed as though it did become a God-given right for some people to simply show up for work, do nothing, and receive the generous wages and benefits GM provided. I know during this period of my employment, I wasn't the best employee. Yet, I did enough to get by. I have often wondered what GM would be like if it had a fair filtering system where it could have gotten rid of some of the people who didn't fit.

Bell Curve

In my opinion, the vast majority of employees working at General Motors were hardworking men and women. There was a small percentage of people who didn't fit. There were some on both sides. There were two distinct sides: management and the hourly. We were at war with each other. (Percentage-wise there were just as many poor managers as there were poor blue-collar workers. A poor manager was more devastating to the company though, because managers have more authority within the organization.) I always felt that if we could have somehow filtered out around 5 percent of the total workforce, 2.5 percent per side, we would have been a much better and stronger organization. All good sports organizations each season "cut" people who didn't make the team. For many, many reasons, General Motors was never able to make any cuts. It wasted a high degree of resources dealing with the 5 percent. Management is just as guilty as the UAW in this. The federal government and some of its policies didn't help. The government always seemed to be breathing down both General Motors' and the UAW's necks. If there could have been some type of filtering system available where a very small number of employees who just didn't fit could have been removed, General Motors would have been a better and stronger organization. The UAW would have been better and stronger as well. They spent a lot of their resources defending their actions in court against their own brothers, and they spent a lot of time dealing with managers who shouldn't have been there. I know this sounds harsh, and I could have been one of those who were let go, but I challenge you to look around you. I'll bet you'll find this is a common occurrence in most other companies. There are some people who just don't fit.

Here again, the Marine Corps training comes back into play. The marines always taught us that there was the 10 percent of the corps that would just not go along with the program. Think about that for a moment. One of the oldest and largest institutions in America operated on a philosophy that a small percentage of its people, employees if you will, could not or would not fit into the mainstream of the organization. They had the articles of the military code of justice, the shop rules, they used to punish and attempt to move people toward conformance, but if these tools failed, they reserved the right to discharge these individuals. They had a mechanism by which to maintain the integrity of the corps. This activity occurred with both the enlisted men and the officers. It leads me to wonder why GM never attempted to operate in this manner. One of the conclusions I keep coming back to is that the executives considered all hourly employees as mostly useless, not adding any value to the company, and therefore not worth the time. I think they thought that all of us hourly employees were just like the worst of the misfits.

Quality of Work Life Seminar

In October of 1982, I attended a quality of work life seminar (this focused on one's personal work life). If I remember correctly, it was a forty-hour program, and we were taken to an off-site location. Up to this point, I had never spent a working hour out of the plant. This was all new to me. Union and management facilitators conducted this seminar jointly. It was the first time I remember hearing about "jointness." This was the first of many attempts both parties would make to become globally competitive.

I enjoyed the class. One exercise we did taught us about the fragility of communications. The instructor selected several people from the audience and had them stand in a row at the front of the class. The instructor then pulled the first person in line aside and privately read him a one-paragraph story. The story purposely had too many details in it. That person in turn had to pull the next person in line aside and whisper the story to him or her. No one but the instructor had the sheet with the proper story. This continued up until the last person in line had heard the story. There were about ten people in all. That person, a good old country boy from Virginia, really embellished his personal vision of what he had heard. His role was to tell the story out loud to the entire class just as he had heard it. He had us rolling in the aisles with laughter as he told his tall tale. Our laughter and delight encouraged him all the more. The instructor then read the original story out loud. The differences were night and day. They taught us that each person hears things from his or her own personal point of view and as the story gets passed along, it becomes quite different from the original version. They compared this to rampant rumors that occur out on the plant floor. These rumors, most of which are destructive in nature, very seldom represent the original message that started the rumor in the first place.

I can remember participating in many of the rumors that flowed savagely throughout the shop. We had a very effective and active grapevine of communications in the plant. Messages from the plant leadership would fly around the shop in no time. Usually, these messages were from the UAW leadership, as management didn't communicate to the hourly employees in those days. Either I was repeating something I had heard or a few of us would get together and start a completely new and wild rumor to see how it would come back to us. Our most common rumor that we started was that they were going to sell the plant and turn it into a chicken farm. I remember having a lot of fun doing this.

We did another exercise where we pretended we were stranded in the desert and had a few small items left for survival. We had to work as a team, both management and hourly, sitting at the same table to determine the most important items needed for survival. We listed the items from the most necessary down to the least necessary. The rankings weren't that important. The exercise had us working in teams together, management and hourly. That was the first time I can ever remember doing that. Man, was that uncomfortable. We didn't do so well. In a dictatorial, theory X environment, participation and teamwork were from a completely different world.

Another exercise we did left a lasting impression on me. The instructors provided each table with a multidimensional object. The object was a pre-folded piece of cardboard that had many sides. Each table had a different one. We had to write down our description of the object utilizing all the people at the table. We didn't do a very good job. We couldn't come close to an objective description. When the exercise was over, we found that most tables had had the same problem. The instructor told us during the debriefing that this was very common. It seems that when working in teams, each person sees things a little differently than the next person. This person is probably looking at a different side of the object than you are at the time. They stressed that all input is important, valuable, and necessary.

If, as a leader, you eliminate someone's input just because the person is different from you, you are probably throwing away valuable resources. Different perspectives may help to eliminate potential difficulties down the road. I've always taken that lesson learned with me since that time. Whenever I start a new project, I always keep this in mind. It can get pretty frustrating at times with everyone's input coming so very differently. But as we move forward in the project, we'll encounter about 90 percent of what the team members are bringing up in the beginning. They are just seeing a different side of the object than we are at the moment. I found this very interesting!

Jointness (Participation?)

In the early 1980s, General Motors still had command of the North American market. Their market share was over 40 percent. They employed over four hundred thousand hourly employees. I often think of the opportunities General Motors had back then to solidify their market share by capturing the full use of the hourly workforce. Instead, they kept enforcing the same strategies toward the hourly workforce that they always had done. These strategies had helped to make it the largest and most successful corporation in the world. Or did they? Were the operating principles of General Motors a facade? Were they able to cover up the financial excesses built into their system because of the lack of meaningful competition? A slogan we heard in this class may have said it all: "If you always do what you've always done, you'll always get what you've always got." General Motors had plenty of excessive cost and very poor quality. Like I said before, their mentality was to use the cheapest parts they could, build the vehicle, and then fix it later at the dealerships. Maybe! Maybe they would get the defects fixed or maybe they wouldn't, or couldn't. Some inherent designed-in flaws could never be repaired. Their cars became very cheap. The customers were growing uneasy and would soon be able to vote with their feet as the foreign competitors were gaining popularity. Lots of customers were beginning to be able to overcome the stigma of not buying a vehicle made in the United States. Voting with your feet occurs when you, as a customer, choose never to step foot in another General Motors dealership or never come back to General Motors' products.

Having attended this forty-hour seminar, we went back to the plant the following Monday. I reported to second shift. I was full of excitement at the possibility that maybe, just maybe, things were going to change.

I had a rude awakening upon my return. Nothing changed! Theory X was still the predominant management style throughout the plant: "Do what I say, when I say, and how I say, and you'll survive just fine. Know your place, hourly boy!" Funny, I've always likened this to the Bible verse of the gnawing and gnashing of teeth, or in other words, the description of being in hell. Yes, that was it! Working on the plant floor was exactly as the Bible described. For our eight-hour shift, we were in hell! Maybe this helps to explain the mad dash that occurs in the parking lot at shift change. We weren't trying to get the hell out of there; we were trying to get out of hell!

There is one other point on this repetitive theme in my book. From the day I walked into Chevrolet Frame and Stamping in September 1973 right up until now, I have seen a slogan written everywhere. This slogan was written on most presses, electrical panels, tooling, and equipment. The slogan says, "It's not the humidity; it's the stupidity." Everybody who has ever walked the floor in this plant has walked past that slogan at one point or another. It was like the Kilroy phenomenon that occurred in World War II. The GIs were always drawing Kilroy everywhere they went. He followed them everywhere throughout Europe. Looking back on the plant slogan, I now see it as a desperate cry for help. It was a message from the hourly people asking the managers to allow them participation in the manufacturing process. They were begging for the opportunity to help make things better, more efficient, quicker, faster, and more reliable. Right through 1982, the hourly were still allowed little to no input in the running of their areas, whereas our Japanese counterparts had built a philosophy of employee participation. I believe they had utilized a system of employee participation taught by Renis Likert, who was a professor at the University of Michigan located in Ann Arbor, Michigan, right under the noses of the General Motors executives located in nearby Detroit.

I often wonder what that plant could have been like if we were able to pull off employee involvement. On a scale of one to ten, with ten being the highest form of participation, what would the plant have looked like if we had achieved a six or a seven rating? In my opinion, the place would have gone crazy. The managerial scorecard would have busted through the roof. Genuinely working together, side by side, there would have been nothing we couldn't have accomplished back then. Instead, we all chose to continue down the same path—management not utilizing all of its available resources, the union fighting management tooth and nail, people milking the system, and we hourly workers just putting in our time. After all, what could we do? We hourly were just small fries in a very large pond. We got by, paid our bills, raised our families, and retired early so we could finally control our lives and find something meaningful to do. Too bad we all didn't come to the table back then to secure our collective futures. A picture they showed near the end of the quality of work life class summed up our situation well. The picture showed three people in a small rowboat that was out in the water. The boat had developed quite a water leak. One of the parties in the boat was bailing water out of the boat as fast as he could. The others were all just sitting there watching that one person. The boat was sinking fast. The point was we were all in our collective situation together. The ship of General Motors was beginning to sink, and we all were watching the water coming in and saying, "It's not my job to bail it out!"

Lou Tice Seminar: New-Age Thinking

In January of 1983, I was selected to take a seminar called New Age Thinking. This was a forty-hour class that came prepackaged with videotapes by a man named Lou Tice. There were two management co-facilitators provided for the class. We were set up at the local 659 union hall. The plant had purchased the right to show this program to its employees. The union was involved with the selection of the class participants. We were all hourly employees.

I had never seen anything like this material in my life up until this class. This material paralleled very nicely the books I had read as I received my real estate license. This is the line of thinking: where your thoughts control an awful lot of what happens to you in your life. They determine long-term where you head in life.

Mr. Tice very nicely laid out how your brain works positively or negatively toward achieving what you as an individual and collectively as a company are striving toward. I couldn't begin to describe these concepts as well as he does. All I know is that I was mesmerized for those forty hours of the seminar. I needed something positive in my work life, and here it was all laid out for me. The entire basis of the class moves toward the value of affirmations. Every day, whether you realize it or not, you are constantly affirming thoughts about yourself and where you see yourself going in your life. Mr. Tice submitted to us that we could take control of what we wanted by utilizing positive affirmations and achieve all of our goals. Man, was I in need of a shot of positive thinking! I really took to this line of thinking.

Twenty-six years later, I still visualize each of my affirmations daily and then effortlessly work them out into my life. I was very excited about the endless possibilities this presented to me.

One subject that Mr. Tice spent a lot of time on is called the Pygmalion effect. He showed us a video summary of the movie *My Fair Lady*. In the movie, Professor Henry Higgins, an elite society member, agrees to a challenge to pass a lower class flower girl off as a lady. The movie goes through several scenes where the professor is reprogramming the flower girl. Magically, in a short time, the girl is able to overcome her lack of education and training and is able to be passed off as a lady in London high society.

Mr. Tice referred to this as the "self-fulfilling prophecy." His point was that this self-fulfilling prophecy is a powerful tool held by leadership. Mainly, his point was that how you saw your subordinates determined how they came to be over time as employees. Think about this for a minute. If you value your employees and continuously reinforce that value to them, then the employees will react to your expectations positively. They will become like you see them to be.

In General Motors, for recruited college graduates and GMI students, this happened automatically. They were showered by the company's continuous positive Pygmalion expectations. They were each provided a senior member of management as a mentor to privately counsel them. This also reinforced the positive self-fulfilling prophecy. The more the graduates reacted to the positive reinforcements, the further up the management ladder they traveled. Soon, you had an entire management culture that had the highest expectations for their members, and the members were living up to the expectations! How cool is that?

For the hourly employees, there was the negative self-fulfilling prophecy, which happened to me for instance. As I was hired into General Motors as an hourly employee, I was given a couple of hours of orientation on my first day and then shuffled off to begin my work. The constant barrage of negative expectations never stopped. I had to be watched all shift because I probably would screw off on my own. I had to live by the shop rules because I couldn't be trusted without them. I had to be herded back and forth from production line to production line because I wasn't worthy of decision-making responsibility.

I had no mentors to help shape my opinions and attitudes. If you recall, I was late punching in the second day of my employment because I couldn't figure out how to find my department in the two-million-square-foot facility. If I had been a salary employee, I would have been escorted each time until I learned my way around. Hell, as a salary employee, I wouldn't even be required to punch in. I was automatically trustworthy.

To this day, I firmly believe that the General Motors' hourly workforce behaves as it does because of the very negative self-fulfilling prophecy they encounter day after day. How else would you expect them to act when their managers constantly tell them how unworthy they are? This is ongoing as this book is being written. General Motors' management as a whole still doesn't get it.

As the class was unfolding, my classmates and I were beginning to detect something wasn't right between the union and management. As usual, there were problems between management's thinking of how things should be and the union's thinking. Unbeknownst to us participants, when we started the seminar, the union and management were not on the same page. We had been recruited by the union to take the class and then facilitate future seminars for all the hourly personnel in the plant. This was such a cool and radical idea, who could say no? As the week progressed, the differences between union and management began to surface. Management clarified its position. In no way were they going to allow each hourly person in the plant a week off of work to go through the class. If and when the seminars were to be conducted, it was going to be on nights after work and on weekends. If the hourly were to receive the benefits from the class, it would be on their own time, damn it! What we, the current class participants, didn't know was that the entire salaried workforce had already taken the class. Theirs was held off-site in Flushing, Michigan. Some salaried members had included their spouses. They were provided breakfast, lunch, coffee, and snacks each day—quite a nice setup and atmosphere to facilitate change. Good for them!

Now, here we were nearing the end of the program, and we were asked to develop a plan to facilitate training for all of the hourly folks in the plant. At that time, there were around four thousand of us hourly personnel. Well, right away, the union jumped all over this concept of the training being held on your own time. It didn't seem right to them that their members had to supply their own food and coffee, provide a place to hold the seminar, and then do it on their own time. The union was not happy about this. Everything fell apart after that encounter. This was a recurring theme in this plant. Management would make plans, finalize the details, and then include the union asking for their cooperation in the new activity. The union always desired to be included up front, before the plans were finalized, not after the fact.

We finished the class and presented our plan to the managers who came for the presentation. I was talking to one of them, and she told me she had the heebie-jeebies from simply being in the union hall. She had never been in one before. In our presentation, we laid out how we would offer the training to the hourly personnel in the plant. We had started by donating money to a coffee fund so at least we had coffee available for the participants. Management stuck to its guns and didn't allow us any time off the job for the class and didn't provide any resources for it.

When we went back to the plant, the union held a sign-up period for the training. It took a while, but they finally got enough participants to sign up for one class. They started one class. I don't remember it going through to the end. I wasn't chosen as an instructor. I wouldn't have felt qualified if I had been. The salaried facilitators of the class had been flown out to the Seattle, Washington, area where Mr. Tice was located. They went through the seminar out there and received some facilitator training as well. Back at the plant, we simply saw the material one time and were not provided any facilitator training. We were then supposedly qualified to conduct this seminar.

After this one attempt to provide this wonderful training to the hourly folks at the plant, the effort evaporated. I felt the prevailing attitude was that the hourly workforce wasn't worth the cost of the program. In business terms, the benefits would not outweigh the expenses in the eyes of management. How tragic!

In the proper atmosphere, what if we could have developed four thousand hourly personnel into problem solvers? What if each day, week, and month, we hourly workers went to work solving the plant's productivity, cost, and quality issues? What if we were allowed to participate in the obtaining of the plant's scorecard goals? What if we had up-front, genuine participation with a legitimate chance to implement our solutions? The problems I'm talking about are the ones that affected our jobs daily down in our little areas of the plant, not the gigantic, systemic problems that the executives faced every day. In my opinion, with many small teams chipping away at their tiny, specific problems, all of a sudden, the larger problems wouldn't be so huge. Isn't this what Toyota has been doing since the 1960s? They are continuously working to improve and solve problems utilizing their entire workforce. They didn't just empower the managers.

They expected the managers to create an atmosphere of participation and then to execute this strategy.

You see, I think there is a dirty little secret inside General Motors. The executives reached an agreement with Toyota in the 1980s for them to take over the closed assembly plant in Fremont, California. This joint venture is called NUMMI; it stands for New United Motors Manufacturing Inc. As Toyota took over the factory, they installed their production system. They screened the laid-off General Motors workforce, and from their ranks, they populated the Toyota workforce. They didn't bring back any of the old managers.

This old plant thrived under Toyota's production system. It became the best within General Motors. Now how could this be with the same hourly workforce? Could the dirty little secret be that the upper echelon of General Motors' executives did not know how to run their factories? Or is that they just didn't care?

NUMMI is still one of the top producing plants in General Motors. I know for a while they produced the Chevy Nova. I purchased one. It was a fine car. It met my expectations as a consumer. However, on the same production line, they also produced a sister car. It was the same as the Nova, but it had the Toyota logo on it and the Toyota dealer network sold it. The Toyota was seen as a superior vehicle in customer surveys. The Toyota received better quality scores from consumers and had a higher retail value than the Chevy clone.

You would have thought that the chairman, the board of directors, and the rest of the many presidents and vice presidents would have demanded the entire corporation employ this production method used at NUMMI, ASAP! Maybe they should have contracted with Toyota to manage all of their plant operations. Maybe they tried, and Toyota told them to go fly a kite.

But instead, the corporate leaders kept plodding along down the same road of poor quality, poor productivity, and very poor meeting of customer expectations.

As you see from this example, it doesn't appear to be the hourly workers' fault! They have borne the brunt of the criticism leveled at General Motors and the blame for its productivity problems. I see this as yet another smoke screen by General Motors' executives covering their inept management system.

A popular television program these days is ABC's *The Nanny*. Weekly, the nanny shows up at the house of parents who are having trouble with their unruly children. She quickly solves the behavioral problems and then teaches the parents how to raise their children properly. Maybe the board of directors of the corporation should hire the nanny to solve their managerial problems with the hourly workforce for them. The only problem is she would have to teach them how to manage as she teaches parents how to raise their children. She would have to teach them how to manage *people*!

There is a footnote that needs to be included here. During GM's bankruptcy reorganization, they decided to pull out of the NUMMI joint venture. Since then, Toyota has announced plans to close the factory and move its work to other existing factories. It was too expensive for the Japanese to run by themselves, as they could incorporate the production into other factories and increase their overall utilization percentages, which means they could lower their costs.

Bachelor's Degree

In early 1983, I found out about an alternative education method leading to an accredited bachelor's degree. Some people I knew were already in the program. They were enjoying the benefits of a nontraditional program aimed at adults in the business world. I made an inquiry into the program. I found out that I qualified. If I was brave enough to sign up for the program, I could finally complete my bachelor's degree in one year's time. After discussing this with my wife, I decided to take the plunge. First, I needed to attain a student loan to cover the cost of the program that was in excess of what General Motors' tuition plan covered. Once I got the loan, I completed the paperwork for the program. I started my classes in May of 1983. I soon found that this program was overwhelming. The workload was almost unbearable.

At this point in time, I received quite a shock. I was called into the second-shift superintendent's office one night. He informed me that there were a couple of openings in the master mechanics engineering department and wanted to know if I was interested in one of these openings. I didn't know what to say. He had to know that my current job performance wasn't the greatest, but he still had confidence in me. I responded that I was highly interested in an engineering position. He told me he'd see what he could do. I thanked him and left the office. I felt like a shithead for the way I had been acting. I remember the day the decisions were made on who would fill the positions. I couldn't sleep. I was up all night thinking about all of the possibilities this new position could open up for me. I did not get one of the jobs in engineering, but the reaching out by the superintendent helped to get me back on track. It helped me come back to my senses.

My job assignment at the time was still covering a production line. Each night, I would show up for work, open my toolbox, and crack the books to complete my school assignments. Most nights, production ran fairly well, and I was allowed to study most of the shift. Looking back, I'm not real proud of this effort, but never once did I get in trouble with my supervisor. I was always on the job and keeping my eye on production. If it stopped for any reason, I was right on top of it. I'm not proud of being allowed to study all night, because it isn't a competitive way to run a business. But rationalizing this thought, I wasn't the only one reading all night, and at least it was schoolwork I was doing.

Sometime around the end of 1983, I was given a new job assignment. I was assigned to be the second-shift hydraulics crib attendant. My job was to follow the lead of the first-shift journeyman. I was to complete the overhauls and repairs that he had left for me. Also, if I was needed on the floor to assist other machine repair personnel, I was to be readily available. This proved to be a perfect opportunity for me. Day shift had just relocated the hydraulics crib down in the plant's basement. Out of sight, out of mind. I was left alone quite a bit. I'd see my supervisor most weeks on payday and when he had to ask me for overtime. Other than that, I was on my own as long as I kept the day-shift lead guy happy. This wasn't too difficult because there wasn't a lot going on. My main focus was repairing the hydrostatic drives located throughout the plant. These drives consisted of an electric motor, a hydraulic pump, a couple of valves, and a few controls. There was a lot to learn with these systems. I threw myself into learning all that I could about hydraulics. I remember my instructor at Mott College saying you could lift the world with hydraulic pressure if you wanted to. After a short time, I was able to get all my work done and still have plenty of time to complete my studies. This became helpful as my studies became brutal.

In the late fall of 1983, this college program became unbearable. I really should have gone on an educational leave for six months to complete my degree. But there was no way I could do that. Not only was I married and my wife wasn't working, I now had two children and a house. In other words, I had bills! A lot of bills. I couldn't afford to take a leave from General Motors, and I couldn't afford not to complete my degree. When I signed up for the program, I had been told it was very demanding and there would be a lot of work. It took all of my available time. The yard work and chores around the house all took a back seat to completing the program. There were too many benefits from its completion, and they far outweighed the negatives. Unfortunately, my wife and children did not receive the attention from me that they deserved during this time.

I had been into the program for about five months. I felt like I was at a crossroads. I wasn't sure deep down inside if I could finish the program. I had to make a critical choice. I could either finish or not finish school. If I didn't finish, I could remain a skilled trades journeyman for the remainder of my time at General Motors. If I remained a journeyman, I was adamant I would have something going on the outside. It was not fulfilling enough to be just a journeyman for me. A lot of guys had small businesses on the side. This seemed to fit the electricians best. There was a high demand for their electrical skills on the outside. But the mechanical trades had a variety of work as well. Most guys bought rental homes and successfully ran their rental businesses. It seemed like a lot of guys put their time in at General Motors and received the benefits but concentrated on their secondary work. This work became their passion.

At this point, I was in my early thirties. Already, the physical demands of the work were taking their toll on my body. My knees hurt from always kneeling down. Climbing all those ladders wasn't as fun as it was in the beginning. I often thought what this work would be like as I aged into my fifties. So far, the physical demands had not affected my work performance, but I knew they would as I went along in my life.

The other choice was to continue this educational program and complete my degree. By completing my degree, I should be able to compete with the others who were desirous of getting on permanent salary from the hourly ranks. Matter of fact, it might even give me a leg up, so to speak, over the other candidates who had not earned a bachelor's degree. Going on supervision seemed like the next logical step for me. I enjoyed the shop. I enjoyed working in the metal stamping arena. I had enjoyed the time I had put in as a temporary supervisor.

My problem now though was that I did not have enough time in the day. I still had seven months to go in the nontraditional college program, and I felt like I was drowning in the workload.

I really didn't have a choice, and I decided to continue on with my education. Education to me is very important. I let everything else go. I didn't do anything around the house. All I did was study. While my wife wasn't very happy about this, she tolerated the situation and supported me. No one in her or my immediate family had graduated from college. There wasn't a lot of understanding from families on either side. Also, it began to impact my work. I began to slip in my nightly work completion. Thank God I was out of sight down in the plant basement. There were many nights I studied the entire shift. I bought a small portable typewriter and would carry it in to work each night. My day-shift counterparts were somewhat understanding of my situation.

I made it like this through Christmas of 1983. I mainly studied all day and all night. We had to attend class one night a week. I had made arrangements with the second-shift superintendent to let me off work for four hours one night a week to attend the class session. I did not receive any pay for these four hours off unless I used vacation time. I never in my hourly career received pay for time when I wasn't there. I was always there. I continued to feel guilty for all of the schoolwork I did on company time. I can rationalize this by saying I was never once written up while doing my homework on the job, but this is truly rationalizing the facts. I could also say I probably would have read the newspaper and paperback novels if I wasn't doing schoolwork, but those are excuses as well.

One night toward the end of my studies, I did have one incident. I was downstairs typing away on a paper that was due when one of my friends came down to see me. He told me he had overheard a temporary supervisor telling the general supervisor, George, that I was down in the basement doing schoolwork. George said he would look into it. George couldn't tolerate the situation because one of his employees wasn't working; I also might represent potential competition down the road if I completed my college degree. (I am proud to say that later in my General Motors salaried career, I would have been George's boss.) My buddy advised me to put away the typewriter and schoolwork for the time being. I quickly put everything away and locked it up in my personal cabinet. Sure enough, about fifteen minutes later, here came George and his faithful sidekick, Chad. They entered the hydraulics crib and looked all around. There I was working away on a hydrostatic drive. They made some small talk, and then they left the hydraulics crib. Whew! That was a close call. I felt guilty about this. But again, looking at the whole picture of what was going on, you can see there was a whole shop full of second-shift machine repair personnel just waiting for further orders from George and Chad. They were waiting and waiting and waiting, wasting large amounts of precious time. I keep harping on this, but it was just so blatant. With their dictatorial management styles, everyone had to wait until they received their personal instructions from one of them. That waiting is an extremely wasteful and expensive way to run a business.

I still had until the end of May, about four months, left to complete my degree. I once again did a self-assessment of where I was going in life. Was this educational program worth the risk of losing my job? I did what we called in the marines a "gut check." This is when you stop, take inventory of your situation, and then proceed to move forward toward the adjusted goal. I paused and thought about what I was doing and decided to continue. For once in my life, I had a white-hot focus. That focus was on completing my degree come hell or high water.

Into the early part of 1984, things started to improve. The overall economy began to get back on track, and car sales must have improved. There was a need for temporary supervision once again. Things had been bleak since Christmas of 1981. During the down period, General Motors had begun further contracting in size. This reduction would never cease. It is still ongoing today.

The corporation had decided to close the engine plant located in downtown Flint. This entire complex was lovingly known as "Chevy in the Hole." This was a large manufacturing complex. It was located across the street from General Motors Institute. GMI is now known as Kettering University. In its heyday, this complex employed close to eight thousand people. It was quite a blow to the community. The engine plant wasn't the only manufacturing site on this complex, but it was the largest. The site had seen quite a bit of activity during the sit-down strike in the 1930s. This was the strike where the UAW won recognition from General Motors to represent the hourly employees. The local unit that represents the hourly people at this location is local 659. Their motto is "home of the sit-down strike." This local also represented my plant. I believe it was the largest amalgamated local within the UAW's General Motors division.

As the company was going about shutting down the engine plant, they did a good job taking care of their salaried employees. In those days, the common saying was that General Motors always took care of their salaried employees. Generally, whatever they gave to the union-represented employees, they gave to their salaried employees plus a little more. Those days were almost over, but we didn't know that then.

As supervisors became available from the Chevy in the Hole complex, upper management would place them in other area plants. My plant took in several of these supervisors. It was another personal blow to me in my two-year period of feeling sorry for myself. These supervisors were taking all of the available openings I thought I was qualified for and felt I deserved. There was nothing I could do, and I had to wait this delay out. Looking back on this from the company's point of view, it was entirely the right thing to do.

Anyway, into the early part of 1984, the supervisors from the engine plant must have all been placed, because this source began to dry up. Around this time, I started coming out of my two-year funk. I believe the Lou Tice training was beginning to take a personal effect on me. I had written down my goals and reviewed my affirmations daily. I reviewed them one at a time, and I always saw them in their completed form. This method of semi-programming my mind was having wonderful effects on my overall psyche. I began to feel good about myself again, and I began to believe that somehow, someway, I would have a good future for my family and me. I could see it in my mind's eye even if it hadn't worked its way out to the surface just yet. I used these positive affirmations in every facet of my life, not just work. However, at the time, work wasn't going well, so it was the highest priority. Somewhere, I read that ulcers are not from what you are eating, but from what's eating at you. I soon realized that the biggest effect of the monstrous chip on my shoulder was on my family and me. I learned that when things like this happened in life, they happened for a very good reason. My role in all of this was to continue along until I discovered what that reason was. In this case, I discovered the reason I didn't make permanent supervisor the first time around was because I was meant to finish my bachelor's degree. If I had made permanent supervisor right away, I would never have finished my degree. I would have remained a supervisor for the rest of my career at General Motors. I would have become stuck in a terrible rat race. I didn't know that then, but I know it now. I learned that when life throws me lemons, my job is to make lemonade. I was to grin and bear the unfairness that was to come at me. I was to smile on the outside and not let anyone know what was going on on the inside. I carried this learning for the rest of my General Motors career.

As we moved into the second quarter of 1984, the second-shift die room superintendent called me back into his office. He asked me if I was still interested in going back on supervision. I told him that I was. He let me know he still thought highly of me and was willing to put me back on temporary supervision when openings occurred.

So here I was about to finish my bachelor's degree and my mind-set had come out of its two-year funk. The overall national economy was picking up from its downturn, and the plant was beginning to crank back up to full capacity once again.

My classmates and I completed our class work in May 1984. We didn't officially graduate until December. That was all a paperwork thing. The brutal section of the one-year accelerated program was over. While those of us in the class weren't home free, we could see the light at the end of tunnel. We had the end in sight! The homework was reduced significantly.

Somewhere around March or April, I once again went on temporary supervision. The second-shift superintendent allowed me time off work to attend class once a week. I was working as a skilled trade supervisor in the engine cradle area of the plant. This area had always been good to me. Back from my first layoff to now, the good old cradle area always seemed to seek me out. This area operated a little differently than the east or west areas of the plant. The cradle area supervision had evolved into what was called multi-trade supervision. Supervisors here managed machine repair, welder repair, and die makers as one unit. It was an early attempt to change things up. The traditionalists were skeptical. Thus, they let the new guy do it. This was all right with me! I was looking to be different and very willing to try new ways of doing things. I really liked improving the efficiency of operations. In fact, I have always considered myself an efficiency expert, and of course, I was always utilizing all of the human resources at my disposal to make improvements.

Permanent Supervisor

The race was now on to make permanent supervisor. At this point in time, I had two main competitors. They were both die makers by trade. They had the upper hand because of the prevalent culture in the die room. Die makers ruled! Come hell or high water, die makers always ruled. It didn't matter what other resources were available. The first-shift superintendent who was the department head shut down all other possibilities when die maker candidates were available. After all, it was his die room. The only exception was when upper management sprinkled in college graduates. Then he had no choice. He went along with the program.

One of the other temporary supervisors was a man named Josh. Josh had a strong Croatian background, and he was proud of it. He had been married several times. He was now the proud father of what he termed the "Mercedes twins." You see, Josh was a frequent womanizer. This was okay because he wasn't married. But sometimes, there is a heavy price to pay. Josh was like the cartoon character in the newspaper comic *The Born Loser*. Whatever could go wrong for Josh did. Just ask him, and he'll tell you so.

This one time, Josh met a woman at a bar. He struck up a conversation with her. They hit it off real well. That night, they ended up at Josh's house. Things didn't go real well at first because one of Josh's ex-wives was waiting for him at his house. She hid herself in a closet until he got into the house. Then she came running out of the closet. According to Josh, there was quite a scene. Somehow, Josh got his ex-wife out of the house. The woman from the bar stayed at the house, and they continued to get to know each other a little better. According to Josh's memory, nothing more happened that night, just friendly conversation. So he thought! Shortly thereafter, this woman ended up pregnant. She told Josh it was his baby. But Josh, having no recollection of having intercourse with this woman, flatly denied being the father of this child. Josh thought this woman was trying to pull a fast one on him. He thought she was just out for his money. Now here comes an example of Josh's luck. The woman soon discovered that she wasn't carrying just one baby. She was having twins!

All throughout the pregnancy, Josh continued to deny being the babies' father. After the twins were born, the mother brought a lawsuit against Josh. Josh obtained a lawyer. He told his lawyer his side of the story. His lawyer was ready to fight this unjustified claim against Josh. There was just one thing Josh had to do. He had to submit to a paternity test to determine if he was the father or not. Josh was more than willing to participate in this test. After all, having had no intercourse with this woman, there was no way he could be the babies' father. Josh took the test. The test results came back showing that Josh was indeed the father of the twin girls. Josh denied these test results and said there must be some mistake. Josh took the test for a second time. The test results came back with the same results as the first time; it clearly showed Josh as the father of the children. Josh was still in denial. His attorney was getting a little goosey about his story. Josh fired that attorney and hired a new one.

Apparently, the judge was getting impatient with Josh as well. Josh refused to budge. He did not have sex with that woman. He always said if he had had sex with her, he should at least have some vague recollection of it. After all, wasn't sex supposed to be an enjoyable adventure? How could one become a father without any recollection of the act? Josh and his new attorney talked the judge into one more test. Something just had to be wrong with the previous two results.

Josh took the parental test for the third time. For the third time, it was proven that he was the father of the twins. This time, the judge didn't allow any more denials or testing. He ruled in the woman's favor. Now Josh had a stack of expenses to pay from the birth of the twins plus eighteen full years of child support to come. Josh sat down and added up all of the money he had spent in legal fees, medical tests, and all of the future support costs yet to come. He figured he could have gone out and purchased a brand-new, top-of-the-line Mercedes-Benz for all the money he was to put out for his babies; thus, he coined the term the "Mercedes twins." To this day, he doesn't remember having had intercourse with the woman.

I've always used this story as a lesson learned for me. Later in my General Motors assignments, I did quite a bit of traveling. A lot of the guys I traveled with couldn't wait to hit the bars at night after work—strange town, new faces, new prospects. But for me, after meeting Josh, I always found a way to eat dinner and get right back to my hotel room. I took no chances on a possible Mercedes twins situation.

While we were temporary supervisors, Josh and I would go out each night for lunch. There was a Coney Island restaurant about a mile from the plant to which quite a few of the salaried guys went. The restaurant was quick with the food, and service was good. Service was good for everybody but Josh. It seemed like there was always something wrong with Josh's order. It was never quite right. Either it was cold or not done or not quite what he had ordered. Somehow, Josh always found an issue with his food. Because he always had issues with his food, Josh never left the waitress a tip. Because he never left a tip, he continued to receive poorer and poorer service. It was definitely a downward spiral. I enjoyed the nightly show. Josh always made me laugh. He frequently got quite angry, but he never got angry with me. It was very easy to laugh with Josh through all of his misfortunes.

One night, Josh ordered a bowl of chili for dinner. He didn't care much for our waitress, as he was always sparring with her, and he specifically told her he wanted his chili *hot*! That night, when he received his order, his chili was not to his liking. He immediately, without hesitation, called the waitress over and let her know about his dissatisfaction. The waitress wasn't very happy with Josh. The next night, we went back to the Coney Island for lunch. Once again, Josh ordered a bowl of chili. We had the same waitress as the night before, and he told her it better be *hot*! When the waitress showed up with our food, she served Josh last. His bowl of chili was piping hot. As Josh started to eat the chili, he began coughing and choking. His face was as red as a beet. Josh couldn't breathe for a few seconds. There was no water on the table to drink, and he had ordered coffee. He indicated to us that he needed water, and he needed it now! He thought he might be having a heart attack. (Josh wasn't in the best condition, and he wasn't a spring chicken.) Slowly, the waitress brought over a small glass of water and placed it down by Josh. She looked down at him and with a slight smirk on her face asked him if his chili was hot enough for him tonight. Josh couldn't even talk. The rest of us were laughing so hard we couldn't finish our lunch. Josh never went back to that place to eat again. We found out later that the waitress had doctored up the chili just as Josh had demanded. She told one of our guys that she had poured an entire red chili pepper shaker into Josh's chili. Once again, poetic justice served Josh.

As part of the prevailing management culture in the die room, some of the supervisors would squeal on other supervisors in an attempt to get ahead and to keep up with the smoke screens so nobody would look into their areas to find waste or shop rule violations. Most nights, near the end of the shift, some supervisors would huddle up inside the heat-treat area preparing to leave the plant. We were always after the hourly to stay on the job right up until the end-of-shift whistle blew, so this wasn't a good practice to participate in. Another supervisor and I have reason to believe it was good old Chad who complained to the superintendent about the supervisors in the heat-treat booth. I know my name was included in this, because later, my general supervisor, Jerry, told me about it. The squealer said I was in the heat-treat booth at the end of the shift every night. In reality, however, I never once spent time in heat treat prior to the end of the shift. I was always writing my lineups and double-checking all of the work we had completed that shift as well as lining up my third-shift counterpart.

True to form though, a sting operation was set up. They were going to catch violators of the policy. After Chad had tattled, a couple of general supervisors had it out in the superintendent's office. The two of them agreed to a surprise raid of the heat-treat booth at the end of the shift. They put their plans in place and waited.

Just before the shift ended, the two general supervisors made their move. One went in the front entrance, and one went in the back entrance of the heat-treat booth. There was only one person in the heat-treat booth. Yup, you guessed it; it was Josh. There he was sitting in a chair reading the newspaper. He had not only taken his boots off, he had removed his socks as well. He had his feet propped up on the heat-treat table. Josh was busted. He got pissed off. He put his socks and boots back on. The last I saw of Josh while he was on per-diem supervision, he was walking through the die room playing golf. He had a golf club and a wadded-up piece of aluminum foil used in heat treat shaped into the size of a golf ball. Josh was swinging the club and hitting the aluminum ball a few feet at a time. He was muttering to himself. He went off per-diem supervision right after this incident and never went back on again.

Once again, Josh's bad luck had caught up with him. I'm sure this is one more of his born loser stories that he has stored up over the years. Man, was he in the wrong place at the wrong time.

There was one other per-diem supervisor still ahead of me. His name was Harvey. Harvey, like Josh, was also a die maker journeyman. Harvey was a very rough individual, and he didn't have a great track record. But there he was ahead of me simply because he was a die maker by trade. Harvey had one problem though. His toolbox was the flip-top style. With this type of toolbox, the top lid was lifted up exposing the first row of tools. The inside of the top provided a nice place to post things. Most of the guys who had this style of toolbox decorated the top. They would post pictures of their families, calendars, and other such items.

Harvey went down a different road. He decorated his toolbox lid with a collage. His collage was of female genitalia. There were hundreds of female genitalia on Harvey's box. He didn't leave out any nationality or creed. He showed no discretion. He had all of the possible angles of shots covered. Harvey was very proud of his artwork.

Some of the female die makers protested about Harvey's display. This encouraged Harvey to make sure he rushed to his toolbox at the beginning of each shift and flipped open his top so all the world could enjoy his artwork all shift long. This was before the current sexual harassment laws were on the books. Today, Harvey would be fired under the zero-tolerance policy on sexual harassment. Back then, this was only seen as a minor inconvenience. A lot of guys had some form of girlie pinups posted in a lot of places. Most of the vendor calendars passed out at Christmas time were of girlie pinups. But the world was a-changin'. Harvey didn't get it though. He refused to remove his collage. I believe his supervisor was going to discipline him for this. The committeeman then got involved. They struck a deal. Harvey agreed to keep the top of his toolbox closed at all times. In a trade-off, he could keep his collage. This seemed to settle the issue. I believe this must have hurt Harvey's chances at making permanent supervisor. I don't think he was asked to go back on after that.

There is one other thing about Harvey. He didn't and wouldn't buy General Motors products. He drove a Subaru Outback. This was one of the first all-wheel-drive non-SUV vehicles. He owned two of them. Everyone knew it in the die room. It wasn't as acceptable or popular then as it is now for GM employees to not drive GM products.

All of that didn't matter. The man who ran the die room with an iron fist had a policy that all his supervisors were to be die makers, period. There were no if, ands, or buts about it. He had control, and that was the way it was, even if his second-shift assistant superintendent had other ideas; they didn't count.

So there had been three of us vying for the one open supervisor's position. The two die makers, Josh and Harvey, and me. However, both Josh and Harvey took themselves out of the competition by their own actions. That left me as the only one still standing.

May of 1984 was a huge month for me. I finally completed all of the requirements for my bachelor's degree. I was now a college graduate! The first in my family. Granted, it wasn't a pristine degree from MIT or GMI, but it was an accredited bachelor's degree. I had made it. I had achieved one of my life's goals.

Also, that month, the second-shift superintendent, Bill, let me know he was recommending me for a permanent supervisor's position to the HRM committee. (The plant had what was called an HRM committee. HRM stands for human resources meeting. Typically, these meetings were held once a month. This was where all the lower salary positions were filled. These hirings had to be approved by this committee.) There was an opening in the cradle area. Upper management approved my promotion. I'm sure the lead superintendent of the die room was in that meeting. I'm sure there was quite a lively debate with him against me. Somehow, I prevailed.

It was a very proud moment for me. I was surprised at the overwhelming emotion I felt when Bill informed me of my promotion. In my mind, I kept hearing the theme song from a very popular sitcom of the time, *The Jeffersons*. The song was about moving on up. That was what kept playing in my head. I was moving on up to the east side. I had finally gotten a piece of the pie!

I had been an hourly employee for eleven years. It was eleven years of layoffs and learning. Now I was in a better place.

I would go on to work for General Motors another twenty-four years. In 1991, I am proud to say that I earned a master of science degree in administration from Central Michigan University. I am very proud of this accomplishment. Not too shabby for a guy who had to go back and take the high school equivalency test to earn more points for his apprenticeship application.

I worked my way up to superintendent level. I ran a maintenance department. I accepted an early retirement offer from the company in December 2008. I, in essence, jumped a sinking ship. Shortly thereafter, I was at home watching the congressional hearings for the Big Three automakers who were in trouble. They were on Capitol Hill begging for low-interest loans to bail them out of their financial catastrophe. I found it sad and painful to watch the proceedings. Looking back on my thirty-five years with General Motors, I can see we had had plenty of opportunity to right the ship. We could have emulated our stoutest competitor: Toyota. We could have adopted their methods and techniques. I strongly believe the General Motors way of doing things, mainly the Alfred Sloan managing and accounting methods, both made General Motors the largest corporation in the world and worked against it to destroy it from within. This self-destruction took the most powerful corporation in the world down into the depths of despair. Its leaders found themselves on bended knee, asking Congress for a lifeline. Congress didn't act. It turned its back.

I liken this to a drug and alcohol addict who has hit bottom. He cannot proceed further unless he changes his ways. One of these changes must be hourly employee participation. In today's competitive world, no corporation can compete while not fully utilizing all of its resources. It simply cannot win the battle with its competitors while also battling with its own internal labor force. I realize there are many issues involved with bringing General Motors down, as I am now part of the legacy cost and added burden the company has to bear. There is also the price of the yen that gives the Japanese an unfair competitive edge. But I firmly believe step one is to fully utilize all of the human resources available within General Motors today, not just the chosen few. The chosen ones mainly come out of highly ranked academic facilities. These employees are recruited and then moved up through the Sloan system. Very rarely, if ever, do floor-smart employees like myself ever make it too far up the executive ranks. There are a few, but they are rare.

I would think a major corporation would desire a mix of their human resources, a blend of floor-smart personnel and those who have never worked as hourly employees in their careers. This diversity would strengthen the corporation's competitive position. Floor-smart people know how to run the floor. They know what works and what makes common sense. They also know bullshit when they see it and are not afraid to call it such. In GM's later years, they always squashed this feedback by claiming that that salaried person wasn't a team player. That was the kiss of death. In my opinion, General Motors has always kept these resources muzzled. It didn't fit their entrenched system.

And yes, I'm talking about myself, guys like me who made it to the managerial ranks from hourly. There were many of us available, but we were never fully let in. There were so many more of them that were more qualified than I ever was.

Who's to Blame?

The way I see it, there are three parties directly responsible for the demise of General Motors. These three are: management, the UAW, and the hourly employees. Nobody else is directly responsible. The three of us are locked in a death grip, and no one is willing to let go. There are many indirect influences on the company, but a divided house is weak and will fall, as did General Motors.

Management

The first and most responsible is the management of General Motors, mainly the executive class. These were the highest educated resources the company could recruit. They were the best and the brightest. Yet, in all of their arrogant splendor, they ran the company into the ground. With their self-righteousness, they made the company bankrupt. Like a beggar, they asked on bended knee for government loans to see them through their bankrupt world. Yet, like the banking executives before them, they still expected all of their executive perks. This included very high salaries, bonuses, private jets, the best hotels, and expensive dinners. They still expect to be treated like the kings of industry. You see, in my eyes, that was more important to them than manufacturing great cars and trucks that customers desired to buy. They paid lip service to becoming competitive in their manufacturing practices, and they never seemed to be able to execute their manufacturing strategy. They continue to operate the company just as Alfred Sloan had set it up many years before. However, current reality continues to show the vast number of major flaws in Mr. Sloan's business model. My complaint is that executive management, mainly the CEOs, presidents, and vice presidents, continued to run the company the same way well after it became painfully apparent that something was wrong. They continued their ways, in my opinion, to continue earning their large salaries and bonuses, continue receiving their arrogant executive privileges, and to continue activities that provided their large egos with very flattering feedback on just how good they were. The person who always comes to mind is Roger B. Smith. He is the epitome of executive management arrogance and waste. Under Roger, they designed the look-alike vehicles. The worst of them was the Cadillac Cimarron. The Cimarron was a Chevrolet Cavalier dressed up as a Cadillac. The customers didn't go for this. They resisted paying for a premium vehicle while receiving an entry-level Chevrolet. Ford had a field day with its advertisements about General Motors' look-alike vehicles.

Mr. Smith purchased EDS to help move the company into the computer age. However, I believe Mr. Smith had more in mind. He set it up so that EDS received exorbitant payment for its services. This doesn't make sense, because they could have gotten the services provided cheaper by two-thirds on the outside. No, I believe Mr. Smith did this to siphon off profit from the manufacturing division of General Motors into other parts of the corporation. In this manner, he didn't have to pay the UAW-represented employees profit sharing. Mr. Smith was a shrewd business operator. Why not pay four to five times the going rate for a desktop computer system and funnel the profit out of manufacturing and into EDS. EDS was all white-collar employees. They didn't have that dirty little commodity called blue-collar workers. Under the Sloan system, we blue-collar workers, *shop rats*, were nothing more than an evil necessity.

Mr. Smith also drove the Saturn project in Tennessee. This was his attempt at an end run around the UAW, down South, in a right-to-work-law state. In addition, in the mid-1980s, Mr. Smith also spent a large amount of money on new technology. This too was an attempt to get rid of the hourly employees through automation. This strategy failed as well.

Mr. Smith was really a banker at heart. He came up through the financial organization. Most of the long line of top executives came up through finance. They lost their way in manufacturing. Manufacturing was a means for them to fund their banking business. GMAC was their favorite division.

Shortly after the end of World War II, General Motors became the largest and most profitable corporation the world had ever witnessed. It became a powerful juggernaut. The top executives cemented in the culture of the corporation at this time to continue its success. General Motors' operations were bigger than most of the smaller economies around the globe. At one point in time, GM was comparable to the tenth largest economy in the world.

In the late 1940s and throughout the 1950s, the domestic auto industry was growing by leaps and bounds. Most of the other world competition was in recovery mode from the devastation brought on by World War II. General Motors was able to cover up its major weaknesses with the rapidly expanding growth in vehicle sales. It locked in forever very poor manufacturing techniques. It became extremely arrogant in its unparalleled success.

In the domestic marketplace, there was very little competition for General Motors. Ford and Chrysler were much smaller and weaker than General Motors and followed its lead. General Motors began to fall away from manufacturing excellence as the financially minded executives took control of the company. Whatever actions they took, whichever strategies they chose, General Motors always made money—lots of money. The executives of that era couldn't see how their practices were setting up the company for failure down the road. Who dared to question General Motors? They scoffed at any outward signs of criticism. They scoffed at any internal criticism, if there was any, as well. Nobody could tell them what to do! "Look how successful we are," they said. "How dare you suggest to us that we change our ways?"

This culture that was cemented into the company after World War II was a facade. By always looking after the short-term cost issues, the executives consistently managed to post record profit levels. In turn, they paid themselves handsomely with bonuses and stock options. They were the best and the brightest and could do no wrong. However, looming in the far distance were two big issues: One was the finite resource of oil that provided cheap gasoline prices. The second one was that the rest of the manufacturing world was recovering rapidly from the ill effects of World War II.

General Motors had an ongoing love affair with gas-guzzlers. They refused to build a small car that achieved high gas mileage. They made a few attempts with the Corvair, Vega, and Cavalier but never really put their heart into it. They always claimed they couldn't make a profit from smaller vehicles. When the first oil embargo hit in 1973 and American consumers began to desire smaller, more fuel-efficient vehicles, they didn't attempt to learn how to build them profitably. Soon after the embargo went away, the company went right back to building larger vehicles. This to me is summed up nicely with the purchase of the Hummer brand and the production of its vehicles, especially the large Hummer H2.

The executives never would face the reality that fossil fuel resources were limited and would become very expensive. In the beginning, they refused to acknowledge the fact that air pollution was also caused by their vehicles. This refusal to accept and address reality would come back to haunt the company in the years to come.

On the second front, the executives failed to realize the threat of competition from foreign manufacturers. As we eased into the 1960s, other parts of the world had recovered from the economic devastation of World War II—mainly Japan. Their domestic auto industry was beginning to thrive. From their internal competitiveness, the surviving auto companies became excellent manufacturers. Japan has very few natural resources. They must purchase the vast majority of the material needed to build things. They had no choice but to figure out how to become the most efficient manufacturers that they could become. Once they learned how to do this, they desired to become bigger than they were. They desired growth.

The first oil embargo provided them that opportunity. They were excellent at building small, fuel-efficient vehicles, while making a profit. They ate the American automobile manufacturers' lunch. They looked at Henry Ford's River Rouge manufacturing complex as their model of excellence. They copied his techniques. At this stage of his career, Henry Ford was the premier manufacturing specialist in the world. Henry Ford didn't come from a prestigious university, nor did he come up through finance. He was a true floor-smart person. The Japanese called his technique "just-in-time manufacturing." They figured out that it was cheaper to build the vehicle right the first time rather than continually passing along defective parts to the next operation. They generated tremendous cost savings by not having to do in-house repair work.

Inside of General Motors manufacturing, all we had were repair stations. There were repair booths on every major line in the stamping plants. These repairmen worked round the clock on product defects. Then these parts arrived at the assembly plants. Here, there were more repairs to do. The standards were higher at the assembly plants. Then, as the parts were assembled onto the vehicles, even more repairs had to be made. There were repair stations after final assembly. General Motors was very good at making repairs. It added tremendous cost to its vehicles. Then to top it all off, after the customers purchased their vehicles, there were several trips required to the dealership for warranty work. General Motors, for the longest time, was among the leaders in warranty repair cost. Yet, the executive class never really addressed its poor manufacturing. It gave lip service to it, but God forbid it might cost them their short-term bonuses and stock prices for that year.

The older General Motors got, the more entrenched its executive management's culture became. To make it big in the company, you had to become just like them. They didn't tolerate different people. This is where I believe they locked out the factory floor-smart managers. They were different and had to be kept at bay. As a matter of fact, the top executives became just like the characters in the Hans Christian Andersen fairy tale about the emperor's new suit. You remember the story from when we were children? The story goes like this:

There once lived an emperor who spent all of his money on new clothes. He loved to be well dressed. One day, two swindlers came to town and made the people believe they were weavers. They declared that they could manufacture the finest cloth that could possibly be imagined and that it was so lightweight you could not feel it touching your skin. Their clothes possessed the wonderful quality of being invisible to any man who was unfit for his office in the empire or who was unpardonably stupid. The emperor himself bought into this idea. He thought he could determine which men in his empire were unfit for their places and could determine the clever from the stupid. The emperor agreed to allow the swindlers to make him a new suit of clothes. Off the swindlers went to manufacture the new suit for the emperor.

After a short while, the emperor sent one of his old ministers to check on the weavers. He desired to know how they were coming along. When the old minister got there, he could see nothing at all. He thought to himself he might be either unfit for his office or unpardonably stupid. When the swindlers asked him what he thought of the material they had created, he responded to them, telling them how beautiful the fabric was. The swindlers were very pleased. The old minister went back to the emperor and told him how beautiful the new material was.

The emperor soon sent another honest courier to the weavers to see how they were doing. He too looked at the looms but saw nothing, as there was nothing to be seen. The thought that he was stupid and might not be fit for office crossed his mind. He was not going to let anyone know that he could not see the fabric. He praised the cloth. When he returned, he told the emperor what an excellent material it was.

Shortly thereafter, the emperor himself went to see the fabric being made at the weavers'. The emperor did not see anything but an empty loom. He felt terrible. He asked himself if he was stupid and unfit for his office. The emperor told himself he must not let anybody know that he could not see anything. He then told the weavers they were doing a fine job. He told them how beautiful the cloth was. All of the attendants who were with the emperor looked and looked but could see nothing. Yet they too told the weavers the cloth was very beautiful. The attendants suggested to the emperor that he wear his new suit of clothes at the great procession that was soon to take place in the empire. The emperor agreed.

The swindlers went into overtime to finish the emperor's new suit. It was completed in time for the great procession that was taking place.

The emperor tried on his new suit the morning of the great procession. He declared to the weavers how beautiful it was and how well it fit him. In fact, it felt as if he had nothing on at all. The emperor then marched in the procession under a canopy. Everyone who saw him proclaimed the beauty of the new suit of clothes. Nobody wished to let others know that he saw nothing, for then he would be seen as not fit for his office or very stupid.

Finally, an innocent child, who was watching the procession, proclaimed, "But he has nothing on at all." All of the people watching the procession cried out that the emperor had nothing on at all. They realized it was all a hoax.

The emperor kept walking in the great procession right to the end. His attendants held his imaginary cape all the way.

Though this story is meant to be lighthearted, the executive ranks of General Motors parallels this fairy tale. Yes-men surround them. They are all alike. In the 1980s, they broke their affiliation with General Motors Institute to help stop this practice. It didn't work, as they are still all clones today. They are all afraid to rock the boat, afraid to damage the price of stock, while watching it fall to seventy-five cents a share and be removed from the Dow Jones Industrial. They are afraid to lessen their executive compensation packages, afraid to lessen their perks. God forbid they take on the UAW to eliminate uncompetitive practices. No, instead, they keep right at it, doing what they've always done.

The swindler in this story is the Sloan manufacturing techniques. There are much better ways to manufacture than those from the 1920s. General Motors' executives never continuously improved their manufacturing methods. Even today, they are lax in implementing their vaunted global manufacturing system.

But they have discovered an out. They could farm out all the manufacturing to third-world countries! Now they could remain in the good old days with the good old ways. The third-world countries treated General Motors' executives like they were kings once again. The hourly workers were hungry and humble. This was more like it. This was the way it was supposed to be! It is my opinion that is why General Motors leans toward third world countries for its manufacturing base. It is not because of the wages of the hourly employees, as they so often claimed. It is because in a country of growing markets, General Motors can produce their vehicles utilizing the Sloan methods and still make a profit. Rather than face reality and change their ways, they just pack up and leave.

It is also my opinion that the executive class at General Motors is a full 80 percent accountable for the problems with the company. They hold the keys to the kingdom. They are the leaders charged with maintaining a strong and profitable enterprise. They have failed miserably and have hurt many innocent people and communities in the process.

The UAW

The UAW was born out of necessity. Under the Sloan system of management, the hourly workforce was a commodity that was a necessary evil for manufacturing. General Motors and all manufacturing of that era treated its blue-collar workers like slaves. This appears to have evolved during the Industrial Revolution of the 1800s. Receiving their cue from England, our industrial giants treated hourly employees like slaves. I'm not sure why. Maybe it's a leftover remnant of the serf era. But treat them poorly they did. General Motors pounced on this practice. The details we hear about life inside the plants before the UAW are almost unbelievable.

My father-in-law had one of those stories. He was born and raised in the South. I believe his father was a sharecropper in Mississippi. As a young man, my father-in-law was full of piss and vinegar. He became restless and moved north to find work in the factories. This was during the Great Depression and sometime before the UAW was recognized by the company as the representative of the hourly workforce. My father-in-law hired into the Fisher body plant on South Saginaw Street in Flint, Michigan. It was called Fisher One. He told me the conditions in the factory were intolerable. In order for an hourly person to make it, he had to have his foreman over for Sunday dinners. During the Depression years, the men had a hard time feeding their own families let alone the foremen's. You also had to buy the foreman his booze. If you didn't go along, they would put you out on the street with all of the other unemployed workers who were going hungry. There were long lines of men begging for the opportunity to work in the factory.

I'm not exactly sure what Freck (his nickname, because of all of his freckles) did that day, but I know he dared to back-talk his foreman. He said that was all it took. The next thing he knew, he was physically thrown out of the plant. He found himself lying on Saginaw Street, bloody but still alive. He always remembered that Saginaw Street wasn't paved in those days. He had to pick stones out of his hair.

So the union was born out of necessity. It gave a voice and some dignity to the blue-collar worker. Every contract the union agreed to from 1936 all the way through to 2007 had more gains for the workers in it. They have become the highest paid and receive the best benefits of any workers in the world. Everyone, so it seems, started focusing on the UAW as the major problem of General Motors. It was a great smoke screen used by management. They would always say if they didn't have all of the provisions of the union contract and if they didn't have the burden of the legacy costs, then they would be competitive. Or would they? Looking back, if the executives didn't have these costs to bear, they would have taken larger bonuses and bigger stock options. That money would have gone right into their collective pockets. The executives didn't know how to design, manufacture, and sell vehicles the public desired. They weren't interested in becoming a premier, world-class manufacturing company (I'm still not convinced they desire to be one). This was General Motors' downfall. As General Motors' demise slowly continued, the UAW did come to the table and make concessions to the company. It did little good. The executives still didn't know what they were doing.

In my opinion, the UAW is 15 percent at fault for the demise of General Motors. This number comes up mainly due to the strike at the Flint stamping plant in 1998. That plant had some terrible uncompetitive practices that needed correcting. Instead, the union took the corporation head-on. It provided needless negative PR for both sides. In the end, the union quietly agreed to end the uncompetitive practices.

The union is also well aware of the incompetence of the executive ranks. It took full advantage of this. They knew the executives would do anything to avoid short-term losses. So they bear their portion of blame for the problem. But they do not hold the keys to the kingdom as the executives do.

The biggest problem I see with the way the UAW runs itself is the election process at the plant level. Inside the plants, most of the union officials are elected. These elections occur around every three years. Most of the elected union officials are very good people. They work hard and do their best to represent their constituents. However, with election time coming at them every three years, it is very hard for them to address uncompetitive work practices and survive the next election. I witnessed this event at the Grand Blanc stamping plant in the early 2000s. The plant had been under threat of closure for a long time. The shop committee collectively chose to enter into a long-term collective bargaining agreement with management. The committee stood by their agreement and supported work rule changes. It helped to discontinue uncompetitive work practices. At the next election cycle, most of the shop committee was not reelected. Some chose not to run again. It is much easier to run a negative, doomsday election campaign than it is to defend all of the changes that were brought to bear. The selection helped the company to close down the plant and discontinue its production operations.

The UAW went from over four hundred thousand hourly workers at General Motors to under sixty thousand by the end of 2008. They have to bear their piece of the responsibility for this downturn. I don't know much about their business, but this negative election cycle internal to the plants wreaked havoc on their membership. They should have done something sooner that may have saved more jobs at the local level.

In the early 2000s, I was lucky enough to attend a national PEL program conducted jointly by the UAW and General Motors. PEL stands for paid educational leave. This program was a one-hundred-and-twenty-hour course that lasted three weeks. The first week we spent in Boston, Massachusetts. The theme that week was mainly the high cost of health care. The next week of the class we were in Washington DC going over legislation and lobbying at the federal level. The last week of class we spent in Detroit going over current events and the competitiveness of the auto industry.

I know from these UAW presentations that at the national level, they got it. They understood the entire situation and the many threats to their membership. Yet, they stood by, frozen to major action. They lost hundreds of thousands of members. I heard their economist talk; I heard their lobbyist talk; and I heard their leaders talk. Even though they heard all of the facts, the UAW leadership still allowed the ongoing fight between the floor worker and management to continue, right up until bankruptcy. They finally ended their hold on the jobs bank program. The jobs bank had so many negative repercussions for the union. It allowed the company executives to bang away at the UAW on this uncompetitive practice. Long after the rest of the country began sharing the price of medical benefits, the UAW clung to its privilege of no cost to its union members. They lost the PR fight on this issue. The UAW received a black eye, and this allowed the executives to continue their uncompetitive ways. This allowed them to blame the union for its ills. In the end, we all lost.

There is one other subject that deserves mentioning. These are the transplant factories that have been located in the United States. These factories have been very successful. I do not recall any of them closing down. The Japanese opened the early transplants, mainly Toyota and Nissan. Not one of these plants has chosen to be represented by the union. They have tried on multiple occasions but have always been turned back. The union has cried foul on this. They feel the transplant managers will not hire anyone who is favorable to union representation. I don't see how they could screen prospective employees thoroughly enough to discover this favorability aspect of their thinking. Maybe, under a management that utilizes the vast human resources of their hourly employees, they feel that they do not need to be represented.

The cost of union representation is very high for the Big Three. If you look at the entire labor relations department inside of General Motors, the financial number has to be staggering. Maybe the executives should ask themselves, "You mean to tell me that if I treated my shop rats as a valuable commodity, I could reduce my costs?" What a shock this could be! "It could also reduce the costs from all of the elected officials in each plant and the shop committee as well? Hmm, now we're talking. But wait, how many full-time appointed UAW representatives are there in each plant? There could be upwards of twenty to thirty. Maybe we could even reduce these numbers down to zero or a small handful. Cost-wise, we could say, 'Holy cow! Now we're getting somewhere!'"

The transplants, by not having all of the structure built into their costs, have a tremendous advantage over those of us who do. This could easily run into the millions of dollars per plant. Yet what about the cost of the joint ventures at the national level in quality, safety, and human resources?

Back to the upper executives for a minute—Could you imagine a General Motors where at one time, they employed over four hundred thousand hourly employees who were treated as value added to the manufacturing process? What if they created four hundred thousand screaming Mimi's enthusiastically carrying out the company plan, working all of their shifts to reach the company goals? Okay, that's impossible, you say, but what if they could have gotten three hundred thousand? Or maybe just two hundred and fifty thousand? That is an astronomical amount of brainpower to channel toward your objectives. Instead, the executives chose to throw away all of these resources. They didn't allow these employees to contribute to the success of the enterprise. Instead, they fought them all the way, tooth and nail.

When I hired in and was still an hourly employee, I shuddered to think about General Motors' Southern strategy. The executives were looking to move down south with their manufacturing plants. This was to take advantage of their right-to-work laws. This strategy was maintained right up through the start-up of the Saturn experience in Tennessee. The company's top executives were looking to dump the UAW and the problems they brought. But the UAW successfully blocked the strategy and ended up representing these plants without a unionization vote. If the company didn't go along, the UAW would strike, and we couldn't have that, now could we? The short-term losses would mean no bonuses that year and the price of their stock options would take a nosedive. Nope, we couldn't have that!

The transplants have done a good job in keeping their costs down. In the stamping plants, the union always pushed the line that the material cost was 90 percent of the total cost of a stamped part. I witnessed this when we would put on dog and pony shows for the bigwigs who were paraded throughout the factory. On the stamping lines, the plant would put up poster boards with the costs broken down for each product run on that line. No one has a cost advantage in material cost anymore. The foreign manufacturers used too for a long time, but the domestic Big Three have caught up with them. The transplants do a better job using their human resources, all of them. General Motors, to this day, still doesn't! They talk a good game. They have their global manufacturing system, copied from Toyota, but they continually fail to execute their plan. To this day, they do not allow true input from their hourly employees. They still treat them as Mr. Sloan directed so long ago. They are merely a bought and sold commodity! They bring no value whatsoever to the company. They must be driven into submission. They must be continually watched because they'll just screw off and waste the company's true resources: *money!*

The Hourly Employees

These are my fellow *shop rats!* I will always be one of you. However, we too are responsible for the state of the company. There are two main reasons why I say this. First, we have always humbly accepted our fate as General Motors blue-collar workers. We accept the fact that the company doesn't value us very much. We tolerate being pushed and prodded along by our superiors. We tolerate all of the rules and regulations that guide us through our careers. We have morphed into a serf-type of lifestyle while being on the clock for General Motors.

We have become like the example of the jar of fleas I first heard about in a motivational seminar. The speaker used this analogy to talk about human behavior and performance. I in no way mean that hourly people are like fleas. The way the story, as I remember it, goes, is like this: Fleas have the ability to jump very high. If you collect fleas and put them in a jar with a lid on it, they will continue to jump while bumping up against the top of the lid. After a while, the fleas become trained and will only jump so high to avoid hitting the top of the lid. If you remove the lid, the fleas will never jump out of the jar. Fleas, having been trained, will only jump so high forevermore.

The hourly workers inside of General Motors have become conditioned like the example of the jumping fleas. If management removes the lid to our jar—and they have on occasions tried this—we seem to fail to jump out of it. We merrily continue to jump only to the top and not outside of the jar. In this crazy environment we find ourselves in now, it is time to make the leap. You must put down your old, conditioned ways and take control of your manufacturing lives. You see, you really don't need all of those white shirts in your area. You collectively can run your area better by yourselves! You need a good team leader to show you the way. You must leave the era of "it's not my job" behind, step up to the plate, and take charge of your teams. I know this is hard. Most of you have many years in the plants. How can you suddenly trust management now? Why should you trust them? The answer is simply because you have no other choice! Or you stand the chance of losing the rest of your jobs. You must embrace the team concept and run your areas to accomplish the company's goals and objectives. You see, you do not need supervisors anymore. You never did in the first place, but it took a long time to figure this out. Your team leader can take better care of you than management ever could. All you need management for is to make sure you get the correct pay and on rare occasions conduct discipline. Other than that, you should not need them around you, reminding you of how you used to be treated. This is how modern manufacturing must work. It is really the only way manufacturing works, but it took until now for the reality to bear fruit. Put down your lines of demarcation. Make sure your wages and benefits are competitive in the world market. Most of all, pray that new managers come into the factories who truly understand how to run them. Pray that new executive managers come in who know how to run the company.

But the bottom line is this: if you're allowed to participate in the manufacturing process in your area, you must put aside your past practices and step up to the plate! If you do not accept this new role when and if it is provided to you, your numbers will continue to dwindle. Good luck to you!

The second reason you share in the demise of General Motors is your participation in the local union elections. You have a mixed track record in these elections. You cannot listen to the Pied Piper anymore. Those days are over! If you elect local leaders who have vowed to fight against management, seek plentiful overtime pay, and follow the no-concessions path, you'll continue to lose your jobs. You'll lose your members in droves. There are not that many of you left. Fighting has lost its value. If you have a local UAW official who dares to stand up to poor work practices, you must support him or her. If you find local leaders who dare to address members who are obsessively uncompetitive, you must support them. The old ways never worked. The balance of the manufacturing world has caught up to General Motors' manufacturing practices and has painfully exposed them for what they are: uncompetitive.

In my humble analysis, the hourly employees are 5 percent responsible for the current state of General Motors. They have had little say in the running of the business. The culture on the plant floor has been in place since the inception of the company. This culture does not value hourly input. The hourly employees are almost victims of the success of corporate America in the 1940s and 1950s. But in today's competitive manufacturing environment, all human resources must be utilized in order to beat the competition. A company that is fighting for its competitive life on the outside while also fighting its internal employees on the inside cannot possibly win.

Lessons Learned: If Provided the Opportunity, What Would I Say to the Chairman of GM?

1. **Address quality and reliability issues with GM products.**

General Motors is still experiencing quality and reliability issues. In my little world, I have seen five major quality defects alone in 2009 that are becoming more unacceptable as GM strives to earn back its lost market share while fighting relentless global competition.

In 2006, a relative purchased a brand-new Pontiac G6 for his commuter drive to work. The car was three years old in 2009. It has been driven for seventy thousand miles. My relative likes the vehicle. However, he has had to replace both of the front wheel bearings twice for a cost close to sixteen hundred dollars. This is an unacceptable reliability rate. When I was assigned to a quality department in 2000, I viewed a quality immersion day event. This is where the vice presidents of the different manufacturing divisions got up on a stage and confessed all of their quality sins. They pledged from that day forward to do better. This vehicle doesn't display these efforts. This vehicle should go well over one hundred thousand miles before any of the wheel bearings should have to be replaced. I'm not sure if this customer will replace his G6 with a GM product when he goes to buy another vehicle.

The second mishap occurred this past summer (2009) to a golfing buddy. He owns a 2005 full-size GMC cargo van. He works in a local GM plant and also has a small business on the side. He uses the vehicle mainly for his business. He is very meticulous and takes good care of all of his equipment. His vehicle is always washed, cleaned, and the scheduled maintenance is up-to-date. One morning, on his way to the golf course, his vehicle experienced catastrophic electrical failure. The main wiring harness located under the passenger seat had melted down. The vehicle was rendered inoperable. He had the van towed to the dealership for repair. When the dealer discovered the faulty wiring harness, they attempted to have GM cover the cost of the meltdown. GM refused to pay, as the vehicle had seventy thousand miles on it and they stated it was normal wear and tear. It cost five thousand dollars to repair the vehicle. I question how electrical wiring can wear out? In my opinion, there was either an installation error or the wiring was sized too small for the job. Over time, the wiring may have weakened and then melted down.

This customer has purchased eleven GMC vehicles in a row between him and his wife. GM is lucky that he is an employee of the company, because they know he'll continue to purchase their products. But can you imagine all of the other owners of these commercial vehicles? Who, upon experiencing this costly failure so early into vehicle ownership, would remain loyal to the company?

A friend who is also a recently retired GM executive was in need of a new vehicle. He had driven a company car for just about thirty years. Now, riding off into the sunset, he retired to the good life. He purchased a brand-new 2009 Buick Lucerne with the idea that it would serve him well for a long time into retirement. As he became accustomed to the vehicle, he began to notice a vibration through the gas pedal as the vehicle was accelerating. My friend is an engineer and began his career in a power train facility. He knew that vibration such as this could cause premature mechanical failure if not corrected. He took his vehicle to the dealer a couple of times, and they tried to resolve the issue. I am not sure what all they tried, but the vibration stubbornly remained. Then, one time, at the dealer, my friend came in contact with a visiting GM power train engineer. They talked about his Lucerne. Come to find out the vibration turned out to be an inherent design flaw. The company knew about it but still chose to build the vehicle in this fashion. So my friend was told there was nothing further the company could do for him or his brand-new car.

Needless to say, this didn't settle right with my friend. It just wasn't right. He thought of ways he could seek to mitigate his unacceptable situation. He ended up in a meeting with a GM executive of sales and a couple of other people. After a little verbal wrestling, he got them to buy the vehicle back from him. Problem solved, case closed. Or was it? How many more of these vibration problems are out in the field waiting to rear their ugly heads?

Another golfing buddy just retired in April 2009. His facility in Drayton Plains, Michigan, closed, and he had nowhere to go. As part of his buyout package, he received a voucher to purchase a new vehicle. He replaced his older Montana minivan with a brand-new Pontiac Torrent. This vehicle was in its last year of production as GM phased Pontiac out into oblivion. My buddy is a smart car owner, and he purchased a lifetime extended warranty for his Torrent. I believe it cost him around two thousand dollars. He had had some warranty issues in the past with his Montana but was able to get GM to pick up the tab. He drove the car without incident throughout the summer of 2009. Into the early fall, he began to experience a quality issue with his vehicle. Sometimes, when he would go to start it, the entire dash panel wouldn't come up electrically. The electrical system for the dash would be blank, and he would have a message telling him to get his vehicle to the dealership for servicing. The first time this occurred, he drove the vehicle back to the dealer only to find that upon arriving, the vehicle functioned normally again. The dealer had no way of troubleshooting the problem while the vehicle was operating normally. So feeling a little perplexed, he left the dealer and didn't think too much of it until it happened a second time. Back to the dealer he went only to have a repeat of the first occurrence. Once again, upon arrival at the dealership, the vehicle began functioning normally. Without witnessing the problem, the dealer didn't have the capability of determining the source and fixing it.

Now I didn't think too much of this, didn't even know actually until I saw him pull up to the golf course in a loaner car that he was having problems with his new car. After the second occurrence, the dealer kept the vehicle overnight to try to simulate the problem. I asked him how he rated a loaner vehicle, and that was when he told me he always purchased the lifetime extended warranty on his vehicles. One of the bonuses of the warranty is the dealer will always provide you with a loaner. For the rest of us cheapies, we just had to make do without our cars for the time they were at the dealership getting repaired. The dealer could not find the problem the second time, and he got his car back.

Shortly thereafter, he and I went down to Toledo, Ohio, to play a round of golf. Toledo is about one hour's drive from our golf course. He drove. Now I was beginning to think I should have driven because I hadn't been experiencing any problems with my vehicle. He wanted to drive to see if the car was all right. He was leaving for an extended stay in Florida soon, and he was planning on driving his vehicle down there. He wanted to be confident with the performance of the Torrent. He told me not to worry though, because he was still able to drive the vehicle if the electrical system in the dash failed—although he had a hard time telling how fast he was going. That put a damper on things as we drove down to Toledo. I am happy to announce that we made it there and back without incident that day. But that was when these quality issues hit me. GM was still having too many quality failures for today's competitive marketplace. If I'm seeing these quality issues at random in my little world, what else is happening out there in the larger arena? I also thought what a terrible commercial this could make for our GM competitors. They could say, "Oh sure, go ahead and buy the GM vehicle, you'll only have to purchase the extended lifetime warranty to ensure you'll always be taken care of. That's an additional two grand!"

This was a very uncomfortable thought I was having. I was happy to find out that he successfully made it down to Florida for his vacation. Hopefully, he'll make it back so we can play some golf this coming spring.

I still didn't think too much of GM's state of quality until the final event happened. I was talking to another relative at Christmas time. He also experienced a quality issue. He had just purchased a brand-new Chevrolet Tahoe in June of 2009. This was his company vehicle; they had purchased the Tahoe in case they needed the extra heavy-duty towing capacity that it is rated for.

He took his staff out for their annual Christmas luncheon. They work for a financial institution located in Southeast Michigan. On the way back to the office, his Tahoe experienced a complete electrical failure. It shut the vehicle down and left a message that it must be immediately driven to the nearest GM dealer for service. Now this was no easy task as they found themselves on Woodard Avenue in the middle of heavy lunchtime traffic. They almost didn't make it across Woodard in the time frame of one complete full green light. The vehicle disabled itself and would only get up to a top speed of five miles per hour. He did get it to a GM dealer, and they looked at it to determine the problem. When he saw his car again, it had yellow caution tape wrapped around the steering, and he was told that no one could drive the vehicle. Some type of electrical board had malfunctioned in the steering column, and the vehicle was unsafe to drive until it was fixed. Now herein lies the problem. Apparently, the supplier of the module was either out of business or was soon to be out of business. They told my relative that it would be either February or March before they could get the replacement for the faulty part. That was a whopping eight to ten weeks. Now I have to tell you, that that didn't go over very big with the customer. Although in this case, they did provide a loaner vehicle, there were additional problems associated with this. The main one being that in late February, this guy and his wife were supposed to drive down to Alabama to spend the entire month of March. They had been doing this for years. My relative told the dealer that he had to have a vehicle that he could drive down to Alabama for his vacation.

I see two major problems here. Upon purchasing brand-new vehicles, these customers are experiencing quality failures. While these problems are being taken care of for the most part, they are without their vehicles. Most people purchase their vehicles because they need them for transportation. When they are at the dealer's for warranty work, they are not available for transportation. The second issue is all of the personal time involved with these problems. Who in the hell wants to continually sit at the dealership getting warranty work done? Who needs the hassle? So my first thought to Chairman Ed or whoever is running the company is you had better get a handle on quality fast. These problems I've written about didn't come by me by a fancy survey or a documented report, they just happened. It doesn't take a genius to figure out that if this is happening in my little world, then it is happening on a larger scale everywhere. The customer is very smart and will figure this out all by himself or herself.

The long-term reliability of GM vehicles still seems to be suspect. Looking at the first two quality issues I wrote about, if given the chance, those two owners would have purchased a lifetime warranty for two thousand dollars. It would have proven to be a wise investment. But GM shouldn't want this reputation. It should strive for no reliability issues until after at least the one-hundred-thousand-mile threshold has been reached. The perception is that other manufacturers are achieving this goal.

2. Are the right executives, the ones who are left, in place?

As I left the company in December 2008, I became disillusioned with it. I realized it was my time to go, but what I experienced shook me profoundly. I had worked for many years while I was on salary to bring about cultural change within the company. I first attempted this by establishing a maintenance improvement program in the mid 1980s. In the late 1990s, I co-led a quality improvement process in the stamping plant where I was assigned. After that, I was next assigned to co-lead a team concept process. We did this in an attempt to save the plant from closure. The leader who led this process knew he must have everyone working in small teams to improve our overall competitive position. Less than two short years after implementation, our leader was retired out of the company. I witnessed the proverbial waters falling back into the Red Sea, if you will. The overwhelming, long-standing, entrenched corporate culture crushed the attempt to change it with the loss of the catalyst and the leader. We went right back to our old ways and methods of doing things. This was mainly "I am the boss, the educated one, the anointed one who has been appointed to rule over this mess. Without me, you are nothing but disposable employees." Their thinking toward the hourly was akin to the "Let them eat cake" mentality. Shortly thereafter, the plant failed to meet its business objectives, and the closure of the plant was publicly announced. Production ceased in 2006.

However, a small department in the plant existed that built weld tools for the assembly plants in the corporation. With the local union contract in place, this department had several built-in advantages over its sister units that were located in other stamping plants. The decision was made to consolidate the three departments from the other locations in to one larger facility. My closed stamping plant was chosen as the home of the consolidated weld tooling centers.

Our plant took this assignment head-on and became quite good at its trade. Once again, the plant leader was instrumental in leading the forward charge. Then in the late fall of 2008, this leader too was retired out of the company. A dynamic four-headed monstrosity took his place. I refer to them as the Tequila Club. We reverted right back to the same old ways, the same old culture, and same old days. Now, these guys were new at leading, but it didn't take long before the "Do as I say, not as I do" mentality took over. These are the same types who treasure executive privilege and class over the hourly morons. The previous leader had come in and embraced the team concept and the value of the hourly involvement. In his earlier life, he had once been an hourly employee. He had the street smarts to navigate and lead the tooling center into a very competitive position when the company was plotting its death because of the uncompetitive cost of tool build. The four headless horsemen couldn't wait to show how smart and intelligent they were.

During the last month of my employment, all hell was breaking loose as General Motors publicly admitted it couldn't pay its bills and was heading into bankruptcy. The GM leadership was frantically trying to get the federal government to loan them money to see them through the difficult times they now faced. The financial leaders inside GM were in a panic and sent out strong demands for cost-cutting measures to help ease the cash-flow situation. They required each facility to develop cost-cutting measures, list them, and headquarters would then track their completion.

As good soldiers do, the anointed four called a meeting to develop a thorough list of cost-cutting measures. The thing was they were the only ones in attendance. I had been invited but declined to attend, as I was all set to take my early retirement in a few short days. I heard they created a lengthy list of cost-cutting items. This is where my disillusionment comes from. This is where the catalyst came for me to write this book.

While the new leadership was in this meeting where the best brains that money could buy were sure to find huge cost savings for the company, I walked the plant floor. This was close to my last walk as a GM employee. I couldn't help but notice the other four hundred employees scurrying about completing their job assignments. How ironic, I found this to be. There were four leaders locked in a conference room, slapping themselves on the back, telling themselves how smart they were, and frantically working to develop a list of genuine cost savings while four hundred other employees had no clue what was going on. They were literally walking around clueless as to the company's situation. This reminded me of my early days in the company, when I too was a "disposable hourly employee!" Here I was thirty-five years later, leaving the company, and my last days were no different than my first. What are the odds that four people can outthink four hundred? This doesn't make sense to me. I would think that the order of business would be to get ideas from the four hundred employees, which would also obtain their commitment to the cost savings. Not so! The sum of the four is seen to be greater than the sum of the four hundred and four. The big difference is that while only utilizing the ideas of the four, the other four hundred have no commitment whatsoever to the list. Good luck with your long-term cost savings initiative.

You see, the executives of GM still don't get it. They don't realize they are the reason the company failed, especially at the vice president and executive director levels. They're still doing what they've always done. Every time they get the chance, they fall back to the same old dominating culture that led GM into bankruptcy. They are all clones of each other. Certainly, you have thinned out their ranks and reduced their numbers, but these types of leaders are still leading in the same style that has gotten them into the executive ranks in the first place. The wannabe up-and-comings are doing exactly as they always have because that is the only route that gets them to executive compensation and privilege.

As the new chairman, you need to watch this. The old culture is alive and well. These executives have been trained in guerilla warfare. They know when to put on a happy face and wait in the weeds until you're gone. In GM, the leaders are never in position long, and the executives can and will wait you out. Somehow, you need to permanently change the top leadership of the company for its survival. The same old executives are all in the same old positions, and they haven't changed.

3. Do not attempt to implement the team concept on the plant floor.

I know the vaunted global manufacturing system (GMS) is based on utilizing the team concept down on the factory floor. As I wrote earlier, I co-led just such an effort for three years. In fact, my team won a coveted Chairman's Honor award for our efforts. At the time, this was a very prestigious award. This was also my third personal attempt at implementing cultural change within the company.

As part of our implementation plan, we created over forty-five production work teams of hourly workers. We had a mixed reaction to this concept within the teams. Some gelled quickly, accepted their changed responsibilities, and went about their work. Many teams did not gel or accept their new responsibilities under the teaming concept. A few were flat-out duds! I've concluded that neither the hourly employees nor plant management as a whole are ready for full teaming responsibilities. You'll always have a select few who are ready, but overall, the majority of folks are not ready to easily move into a successful teaming environment. The elected UAW representatives are not ready either. It is not yet politically safe for them to fully jump onboard. This is mainly due to the salary leadership in place in the plants.

The leaders in place right now may favor changing the work environment into a more favorable team concept, but in a relatively short time, all of them will probably change over to new positions within the company. The next group of leaders may not favor the use of teaming at all. They could favor the old ways. This constant shifting of leadership, especially among those who have different cultural beliefs, leads to everyone else on the staff being in fence-riding positions of "wait and see." The UAW politicians must do this as well for their long-term survival.

So, no matter how you look at it, neither side—salary or hourly—is ready for a full-blown teaming philosophy. Now, I truly believe that in order to survive, the company has to obtain a teaming methodology. That is, you have to arrive at a team concept where the company is utilizing 100 percent of its available human resources. But you have to prepare them for this, and executive management has to provide the leadership to safely get everyone there. Before all of the hourly can accept their full responsibilities in teaming, they first have to be moved toward involvement and participation. As a new hire in 1973 and as a retiree in 2008, I could see the hourly were still treated, managed, and led the same. They are still considered "disposable employees." You must first move the company toward a participative style of leadership before you can move into a team concept. You also have to educate, train, and maybe even coerce your entire salaried management workforce into understanding and embracing this concept. Otherwise, they'll wait you out and return to the good old ways just like they've always done in the past. Failing to ensure that salary is onboard ensures the failure of teaming. The failure of teaming means you'll have to continue to carry the hourly workforce on your back rather than making the journey together. If a large and old organization like the United States Marine Corps can do it, so can General Motors if its executive leadership demands it. Good luck to you, as I remain somewhat skeptical.

4. Adopt the leadership principles of the United States Marine Corps.

If it is good for a strict, disciplined outfit, such as the marines, then the principles are good for General Motors. I wouldn't hesitate to adopt these leadership principles. In fact, I would create a GM "boot camp" of leadership starting at the highest levels of the company and work my way down to the factory floor within one year's time. I wouldn't stop until I was sure everyone understood the marines' leadership principles, committed to using them, and demonstrated by their performance their acceptance. Only then can you begin to make full use of all of your human resources. By using all of your human resources, you can successfully compete in the global marketplace.

Author's Note

This is my first venture at writing a book. I have no idea if I have any talent to do so. I have written this book to show how I view my eleven years working as an hourly employee at General Motors. If this book has any merit, if it gains any kind of reception by its readers, I would desire to write about the rest of my time at General Motors. I still have twenty-four years of experience left to write about. This would take us right up to December 1, 2008, when I walked out of the factory for the last time. I took an early salaried retirement offer from the company, but I, in essence, jumped from a sinking ship. I grabbed what I think is a lifeline, and I hope it'll keep me afloat for a while.

www.ingramcontent.com/pod-product-compliance
Lightning Source LLC
Chambersburg PA
CBHW030004190526
45157CB00014B/414